Reading Genesis after Darwin

Reading Genesis after Darwin

Edited by

STEPHEN C. BARTON

DAVID WILKINSON

UNIVERSITY PRESS

2009

OXFORD
UNIVERSITY PRESS

Oxford University Press, Inc., publishes works that further
Oxford University's objective of excellence
in research, scholarship, and education.

Oxford   New York
Auckland   Cape Town   Dar es Salaam   Hong Kong   Karachi
Kuala Lumpur   Madrid   Melbourne   Mexico City   Nairobi
New Delhi   Shanghai   Taipei   Toronto

With offices in
Argentina   Austria   Brazil   Chile   Czech Republic   France   Greece
Guatemala   Hungary   Italy   Japan   Poland   Portugal   Singapore
South Korea   Switzerland   Thailand   Turkey   Ukraine   Vietnam

Library of Congress Cataloging-in-Publication Data

Reading Genesis after Darwin / [edited by] Stephen Barton and David Wilkinson.
    p. cm.
Includes index.
ISBN 978-0-19-538335-5; 978-0-19-538336-2 (pbk.)
   1. Bible and science. 2. Bible. O.T. Genesis I–III—Criticism, interpretation,
etc. 3. Bible and science—History. 4. Bible. O.T. Genesis I–III—Criticism,
interpretation, Etc.—History. 5. Darwin, Charles, 1809–1882. I. Barton, Stephen
C. II. Wilkinson, David
BS651.R37 2009
222'.110609—dc22   2009006235

9 8 7 6 5 4 3 2 1

Printed in the United States of America
on acid-free paper

Acknowledgments

The editors express their sincere thanks to all who made possible the successful series of public lectures on which these essays are based. Particular thanks go to Professor Ash Amin and the board of the Institute of Advanced Studies of Durham University for sponsoring the lecture series as part of the Institute's inaugural project in 2006–2007 on "The Legacy of Darwinism." For his editorial assistance, thanks are due also to one of our Durham doctoral graduates in New Testament studies, Dr. Michael Lakey.

Contents

Contributors

JEFF ASTLEY is Director of the North of England Institute of Christian Education and Honorary Professor in the Department of Theology and Religion, Durham University.

STEPHEN C. BARTON is Reader in New Testament, Department of Theology and Religion, Durham University.

RICHARD S. BRIGGS is Director of Biblical Studies and Hermeneutics, Cranmer Hall, St. John's College, Durham University.

JOHN HEDLEY BROOKE retired in 2006 from the Andreos Idreos Professorship of Science and Religion, Oxford University.

DAVID BROWN is Wardlaw Professor of Theology, Aesthetics and Culture at the University of St. Andrews.

DAVID CLOUGH is Senior Lecturer in Christian Ethics, Department of Theology and Religious Studies, University of Chester.

ELLEN F. DAVIS is Amos Ragan Kearns Professor of Bible and Practical Theology, Duke Divinity School, Durham, North Carolina.

MATHEW GUEST is Lecturer in Sociology of Religion, Department of Theology and Religion, Durham University.

ANDREW LOUTH is Professor of Patristic and Byzantine History, Department of Theology and Religion, Durham University.

WALTER MOBERLY is Professor of Biblical Theology, Department of Theology and Religion, Durham University.

John Rogerson is Emeritus Professor of Biblical Studies, Sheffield University.

Francis Watson holds the Chair of Biblical Interpretation, Department of Theology and Religion, Durham University.

David Wilkinson is Principal of St. John's College, Durham University.

Introduction

Stephen C. Barton and David Wilkinson

From six-day creationism to Richard Dawkins's *The God Delusion*,[1] the public dialogue on science and religion either uses the early chapters of Genesis in a naïve and simplistic way or rejects their relevance to contemporary questions. This is reinforced by the myth that Darwin undermined any possibility of an intelligent reading of Genesis 1, and, from that point on, most Christian theology lost confidence in these texts. Such a view can be seen not just in media presentations but also in the views of many students and teachers.

The truth is far more complex and far more engaging. Jewish and Christian interpretations of the early chapters of Genesis have had a long and fruitful history from the earliest of times. The nineteenth century had many more important issues at stake than biblical literalism and, indeed, many different interpretations of how the discoveries of Darwin helped or hindered the reading of the biblical text. In the twenty-first century, theologians are rediscovering the importance of Genesis 1–3 as a partner in dialogue with the natural and human sciences.

These questions engage not only the academic community but are highly popular also in the public arena. First, the questions of origins have been given fresh expression in Stephen Hawking's bestseller *A Brief History of Time*.[2] It can be argued that the big bang theory of the origin of the universe has made an impact of similar magnitude in the twentieth century to that made by Darwinian evolution in the nineteenth century. It has evoked great public interest and raised significant theological questions to do with the nature of creation and the Creator. Second, the success of the scientific method shown in evolutionary biology or, indeed, modern cosmology raises for many scientists questions of why scientific laws exist and why they are universal, intelligible, elegant, and awe inspiring. Third, one of the major contemporary questions of modern science is the question of what it means to be human. It is a question posed by evolution and is given current emphasis in the Human Genome Project, developments in artificial intelligence, and speculations about the existence of other intelligent life in the universe.[3] At the same time, theologians have been grappling with new developments in neuroscience and their implications for the question of whether humanity should be defined with reference to a soul.[4] Fourth, and also related to the question of what it means to be human, are fundamental questions about gender identity, along with their implications for roles, relations, and the exercise of power. Are the Genesis texts oppressive or redemptive for women and men? This is a subject which is the focus of ongoing and intensive investigation.[5] Fifth, the environmental crisis has posed questions both for science and religion. The historian Lynn White, in a now-famous paper presented at the American Association for the Advancement of Science in 1967, argued that our ability to harness natural resources was marred by the deep-rooted assumption that "we are superior to nature, contemptuous of it, willing to use it for our slightest whim" and proceeded to claim pointedly:

> We shall continue to have a worsening ecological crisis until we reject the Christian axiom that nature has no reason for existence but to serve man.... Both our present science and our present technology are so tinctured with orthodox Christian arrogance towards nature that no solution for our ecological crisis can be expected from them alone.[6]

Thus, Christianity, it is claimed, bears "a huge burden of guilt" for the environmental crisis. However, White then argued for a "refocused Christianity," which looks again at its theology of creation in order to make ecology an integrated concern.

In many of these issues, it is the interpretation of the Genesis texts that has led to problems, as well as possibilities, for Christian theologians. Six-day creationism, the oppression of women by men, and arrogance toward the natural world have each found a warrant in the Genesis texts. Yet White is correct in seeing that a fresh understanding of these passages can also lead to an affirmation of science, a challenging of social structures, and a theological foundation for environmental action. Arguably, then, far from burying these ancient texts, Darwin and his legacy may be seen to have liberated them to speak in new and different ways.

This is the conviction that led to a series of public lectures sponsored by the Institute of Advanced Studies of Durham University between November 2006 and May 2007. The sustained attendance at these lectures demonstrated a considerable hunger to explore the early chapters of Genesis within the legacy left by Darwin. The audience brought together professional theologians, academics, and students across a number of disciplines, as well as interested laypeople from Durham City and the region of the northeast of England. Lecturers were drawn not just from the Department of Theology and Religion at Durham, but also from other United Kingdom institutions and from the United States. The chapters in this volume are the happy outcome of those lectures. Taken as a whole, they explore three important dimensions of reading Genesis after Darwin.

First, a number of chapters explore both general questions of biblical hermeneutics and, more specifically, how the story of creation was interpreted in the time before Darwin. The fact that nonliteral interpretations were standard in early Christian thought is often overlooked or ignored. In fact, in their interaction with different cultural settings and epistemological frameworks, these insightful interpretations of the Genesis texts have much to teach as we engage questions of interpretation today.

A second dimension explored in the chapters is the history in their nineteenth-century context of the Darwinian controversies—controversies to which biblical scholars, scientists, philosophers, and artists all contributed. Exploding some of the myths surrounding this period, this fascinating history displays the various ways in which Darwin was received by many religious thinkers.

Third, there is the twenty-first-century application of the insights of Genesis "after Darwin" to contemporary issues: in particular, modern scientific questions about cosmology and evolution; questions about what it means to be human and what it means to be gendered; and questions about evil and environmental care. A final, sociological chapter discusses the rise of creationism in its current social and religious context.

John Durant has suggested that, in the history of the relationship of science and religion, it can be argued, along with Galileo, Darwin, and Freud, that human beings are "mere fragments in a world that appears to be neither about us nor for us."[7] The fresh engagements with the Genesis texts given in this book place that view in question and offer other ways of thinking, not only about ourselves, but also about God's ways with the world.

NOTES

1. R. Dawkins, *The God Delusion* (London: Bantam, 2006).

2. S. W. Hawking, *A Brief History of Time* (London: Bantam, 1988).

3. J. Zycinski, *God and Evolution: Fundamental Questions on Christian Evolutionism* (Washington, D.C.: Catholic University of America Press, 2006); B. Waters, *From Human to Posthuman: Christian Theology and Technology in a Postmodern World* (Aldershot, England: Ashgate, 2006); I. Barbour, *Nature, Human Nature and God* (London: SPCK, 2003); N. L. Herzfield, *In Our Image: Artificial Intelligence and the Human Spirit* (Minneapolis, Minn.: Fortress, 2002); E. McMullin, "Biology and the Theology of Human Nature," in *Controlling Our Destinies: Historical, Philosophical and Ethical Perspectives on the Human Genome Project*, ed. P. R. Sloan (Notre Dame, Ind.: University of Notre Dame Press, 2000), 367–393; S. J. Dick, ed., *Many Worlds: The New Universe, Extraterrestrial Life and the Theological Implications* (Philadelphia, Penn.: Templeton Foundation Press, 2000); D. Wilkinson, *Alone in the Universe? The X-Files, Aliens and God* (Crowborough, England: Monarch, 1997).

4. J. B. Green, ed., *What about the Soul? Neuroscience and Christian Anthropology* (Nashville, Tenn.: Abingdon, 2004).

5. Among a huge volume of scholarship, see Phyllis A. Bird, " 'Male and Female He Created Them': Genesis 1.27b in the Context of the Priestly Account of Creation," in *Missing Persons and Mistaken Identities: Women and Gender in Ancient Israel* (Minneapolis, Minn.: Fortress, 1997), 123–154; J. Richard Middleton, *The Liberating Image: The Imago Dei in Genesis 1* (Grand Rapids, Mich.: Brazos, 2005).

6. L. White, "The Historical Roots of Our Ecological Crisis," *Science* 155 (1967), 1203.

7. J. Durant, ed., *Darwinism and Divinity* (Oxford: Blackwell, 1985), 9.

Reading Genesis after Darwin

PART I

Engaging Again with the Scriptures

I

How Should One Read the Early Chapters of Genesis?

Walter Moberly

The question of how best to read the early chapters of Genesis seems to be something of a hardy perennial.[1] In one form or another, the question is rather regularly put to me in my capacity as a Christian scholar whose academic specialty is the Old Testament, with the expectation that I should be able to answer in just a few words.

Unfortunately, my answers tend not to be as succinct as my questioners hope for. On the one hand, I feel the need to say something about the genre of the material. You cannot put good questions and expect fruitful answers from a text apart from a grasp of the kind of material it is in the first place; misjudge the genre, and you may skew many of the things you try to do with the text. However, all of the common classificatory terms, most famously "myth," are used in a wide variety of ways, with something of a chasm between scholarly understandings and popular pejorative usages; so any such term on its own, without careful further definition, is of little or no use. On the other hand, people regularly combine the general question with interest in a point of detail. Not uncommonly, for example, I am asked about the Hebrew word used for "day" in Genesis 1. I duly point out that the Hebrew word *yom* has the same semantic range as the English *day*, and, depending on the context, it can mean daytime as opposed to nighttime or a period of twenty-four hours or an indefinite period of time.[2] However, this usually feels disappointing to my interlocutor. Since a specialist's knowledge of Hebrew does not here resolve the problem, we appear to be back to square one.

In addition to, or perhaps instead of, my rather unsatisfactory oral response, I am sometimes asked to recommend something good to read. Yet strangely, despite the voluminous literature of commentary on the early chapters of Genesis, I know of few good discussions of the basic question of how to read these texts. It is also difficult at the present time to discuss the early chapters of Genesis without being aware of the growth of creationism, which insists on a certain kind of "face-value" approach to the biblical text. I do not as such wish to discuss a creationist approach, which lies beyond my remit. Nonetheless, I hope that what I say will be helpful for, among others, creationists and those who cannot see a problem in a creationist approach to the biblical text.

This is all a way of saying that I am going to be strictly introductory in my remarks, and I make no claim to originality. In fact, I will be doing what I often complain that biblical scholars are unduly prepossessed with doing—that is, looking at questions about the text rather than at what the text itself is about.[3] Nonetheless, given the weight of contested interpretation that attaches to this material, the humble introductory question must surely have its place.

Learning from the History of Interpretation

At the outset, it is worth mentioning the value of the history of interpretation of these early chapters of Genesis. Among other things, this history can dispel facile assumptions—including the assumption that, prior to Darwin, there was a clear consensus among Christians about the reading of this material, and the assumption that it is only the issues raised by the natural sciences that have led to the predominant Christian assumption that the early chapters of Genesis do not constitute the kind of account of the world's early history that could appropriately be recognized as "historical" by contemporary criteria of knowledge.

Consider, for example, the first giant in the history of Christian biblical interpretation—Origen, in the third century. In the course of a general discussion of biblical interpretation, and in support of his thesis that a "spiritual" interpretation could be hidden in the text and might be indicated by a narrative of events that could not have happened, Origen uses, among other texts, the early chapters of Genesis:

> For who that has understanding will suppose that the first, and second, and third day, and the evening and the morning, existed without a sun, and moon, and stars? and that the first day was, as it were, also without a sky? And who is so foolish as to suppose that

God, after the manner of a husbandman, planted a paradise in Eden, towards the east, and placed in it a tree of life, visible and palpable, so that one tasting of the fruit by the bodily teeth obtained life? and again, that one was a partaker of good and evil by masticating what was taken from the tree? And if God is said to walk in the paradise in the evening, and Adam to hide himself under a tree, I do not suppose that any one doubts that these things figuratively indicate certain mysteries, the history having taken place in appearance, and not "literally."[4] Cain also, when going forth from the presence of God, certainly appears to thoughtful men as likely to lead the reader to inquire what is the presence of God, and what is the meaning of going out from Him. And what need is there to say more, since those who are not altogether blind can collect countless instances of a similar kind recorded as having occurred, but which did not "literally"[5] take place?[6]

One does not need to follow Origen's distinctive construal of the way in which surface difficulties in the biblical text give rise to a deeper spiritual reading to appreciate the basic force of his observations as to the difficulties in a certain kind of face-value reading of the text.[7]

Finding Our Bearings: The Story of Cain and Abel

For our present purposes, I suggest that the most fruitful starting point within the biblical text is the story of Cain and Abel in Genesis 4. This is not to deny that, in important respects, this narrative's characteristics may differ from those elsewhere in Genesis 1–11, such that one cannot simply generalize on the basis of what is discovered here. Nonetheless, its intrinsic suitability is suggested by numerous discussions down the ages, not least its key role in the beginnings of modern biblical criticism in the seventeenth century.

The problem posed by this narrative is simple. Its internal details are in significant ways at odds with its context at the outset of human life upon earth. The popular form of the problem has tended to be expressed as the question "Whence Cain's wife?" St. Augustine, for example, famously discussed this question, and his approach provided a conceptuality that was long influential; in essence, the problems of the text are to be explained in terms of omission because of selection and compression. Adam and Eve had many other children, the specifics about whom the biblical text, in its selectivity, omits even while it recognizes their existence (Gen. 5:4b).[8] So, Cain and Abel married their sisters, and the world's early population expanded rapidly even though few details are given in the biblical text.

One major drawback with focusing upon Cain's wife is that it can give the impression that the wife is the only detail of the narrative that is problematic within the wider context; but this is not the case.[9] For, although the story does not mention any specific human characters other than Cain and Abel, it nonetheless presupposes throughout that the earth is populated. First, at the outset (Gen. 4:2), Abel is said to be "a keeper of sheep" while Cain is "a tiller of the ground." Such divisions of labor with their particular categorizations would not be meaningful if there were only a handful of people upon the earth; rather, they presuppose a regular population with its familiar tasks. Second (4:8), it is when Cain and Abel are in the open countryside that Cain kills Abel. The point of being in the open countryside is that one is away from other people in their settlements[10]—which is why most manuscript traditions, though for some reason not the Masoretic text, have Cain make a specific proposal for going out to the countryside; murder is best committed without an audience (though Cain discovers that one cannot so easily escape the LORD as audience). Third (4:14), Cain complains to the LORD that if he has to become a "restless wanderer," then anyone who finds him may kill him. What is the problem here? If the world were populated by only a few offspring of Adam and Eve, they would naturally occupy a limited space,[11] and so the more Cain wandered, the farther away would he be from these other people. Rather, the implicit logic appears to be that someone constantly on the move, in the familiar populated world, lacks the protective support systems which go with belonging to a regular community; such an unprotected person is easily picked off by anyone in a merciless frame of mind.[12] Fourth, in the immediate aftermath of the main story, in the same context as the mention of Cain's wife, there is reference to the building of a "city" ('ir). This familiar translation of the most common Hebrew word for a human settlement is potentially misleading because it can encourage the contemporary reader to imagine far larger populations and settlements than were in fact characteristic of the ancient world; with a few exceptions, most "cities" in the Old Testament would be comparable in population size to hamlets and villages in the medieval and modern world. Nonetheless, this still presupposes the kind of population density and organization that are also presupposed at the outset by the roles of shepherd and farmer, and it is at odds with the story's own location at the very beginnings of human life on earth.

How is this mismatch between the story's own assumptions and its context best explained? The points I have raised (and many others also) were fascinatingly discussed by a now-obscure writer of the seventeenth century, who in his time had great influence, Isaac La Peyrère.[13] La Peyrère saw the

consistent intrinsic problems of the text much more clearly than did his predecessors (such as St. Augustine, who only discussed Cain's city and Cain's
wife). However, the concept of La Peyrère's resolution remained in principle
within Augustine's frame of reference, i.e., the difficulties within the text are
the result of selective omission. Nonetheless, although in principle La Peyrère
differed from St. Augustine in degree rather than in kind, he stretched the
concept of selective omission to the breaking point. His key move was to
argue that the Genesis text, in its selectivity, tells only the history of the Jews
and not of humanity as a whole—and thus, there were humans before Adam,
"pre-Adamites" (a proposal which generated a huge debate for the best part
of two centuries until a Darwinian frame of reference changed the shape
of the debate). The details of the Cain and Abel story show that the Bible is
aware of a larger human history, which it chooses not to tell. Thereby, La
Peyrère was able to accommodate the recent European discoveries of a geogra-
phy (supremely, the Americas) and a history (from the texts of the Chaldeans
and Egyptians) that apparently did not fit within a biblical view of the world.
According to La Peyrère's thesis, the apparent conflict between Genesis and
the new knowledge was thereby reconciled—a motivation which did not prevent his book from being burned in public and subjected to numerous rebut-
tals on the part of the affronted faithful, both in his own day and for many
years subsequently.[14]

On its own terms, the approach of St. Augustine or La Peyrère makes
reasonable sense and may still commend itself in one form or another to those
for whom it still appeals to engage in a certain kind of reconciling of conflicts between the Bible and other forms of knowledge. The phenomenon of
creationism attests, among other things, to the enduring attraction of such
an approach (however much creationists might dislike La Peyrère's particular proposals). However, the approach has been generally abandoned for the
reason that its narrowly conceived view of how to handle the problems does
justice neither to the Bible nor to other forms of knowledge. For the present, I
would simply note that, if the story in itself presupposes a regularly populated
earth, while its context requires an almost entirely unpopulated earth, there
is a hypothesis that readily commends itself. This is that the story itself has
a history, and in the course of that history, it has changed locations, moved
from an original context within the regular parameters of human history—
presumably, the world of ancient Israel, which would have been familiar to the
narrator[15]—to its present context at the very outset of human history.[16] Such a
movement of stories is a common phenomenon in the history of literature.

My basic point is simple. A story whose narrative assumptions apparently
originate from the world familiar at the time of the biblical narrator has been

set in a context long antecedent to that world—the very beginnings of life on earth. From this, it follows *not* that one should not take seriously the narrative sequence from Adam and Eve to Cain and Abel, but that this narrative sequence is, in an important sense, artificial. It should not be taken as ancient history in the kind of way that we understand ancient history today, but rather as a literary construction whose purpose appears to be to juxtapose certain archetypal portrayals of life under God so that an interpretive lens is provided for reading God's calling of Abraham and his descendants, which follows.

The Story of Noah and the Flood

My second case study is the story of Noah and the Flood. Again, I will look for indicators within the narrative as to the kind of material that it is.

Generally speaking, the story makes good sense on its own terms. It is a memorable account of human corruption of the world leading to a stark divine purging through unleashing the waters that were set aside at the outset to enable life on earth. Continuity with the past and hope for the future are made possible through divine grace to righteous Noah and his family, from whom the world is subsequently repopulated.

On internal grounds, however, the story poses particular problems for the reader. The root of most of these problems is that the narrative is clearly uninterested in many of the issues that have fascinated interpreters ancient and modern, who have tried to imagine and who have argued how the content of the story could have once taken place. To be sure, some of its details do indeed appear to be "realistic." If, for example, one takes the all-too-brief instructions in Genesis 6:14–16 to indicate that a transverse section of the ark would be virtually triangular—so that the ark should be envisaged "like a giant Toblerone bar"[17]—then such a vessel would apparently be stable in floating, which is all that it would be required to do.[18] Nonetheless, the way the story is told is suggestive of priorities other than those of interpreters concerned with historical realism.

Thus, the narrator reports the inner thoughts and words of God: divine soliloquies, which would by definition be without human audience, are narrated on a par with everything else in the story (Gen. 6:6–7, 8:21–22).[19] By contrast, the narrator reports nothing of Noah's thoughts or words—Noah utters not one word throughout.

On a different level, issues of practical feasibility are of no interest to the narrator. Numerous questions have indeed been raised by interpreters: Which animals were included (what about rattlesnakes, elephants, polar bears, kangaroos)? How did they get to the ark? What were their living conditions? What sorts of food did they have? How much was there, and how was it preserved as edible? The text offers no more than a summary statement about the provision of food (6:21–22). Attempts to answer the feasibility questions, though regularly ingenious and impressive in their own way,[20] add precisely nothing to a better understanding of the story's own concern—which has to do with the paradoxical mercy of God. And one might note that the narrator recounts in some detail the human and animal entries to and exits from the ark and the steady increase and decrease of the flood waters (7:6–16, 8:14–19)—matters which concern most readers rather little.

What about the ark itself? Despite the popularity of pictures of an attractive houseboat in countless children's books, the biblical text suggests something entirely different, along the lines of a punt with a superstructure—for the ark does not need to go anywhere, but only to float. Whatever its precise shape (Toblerone bar, or whatever), humans and animals appear to live in darkness within the ark, for, in terms of what we are told, the ark appears to have only one hatch that can be opened in addition to the door.[21] The "window" (hallon) out of which Noah sends the birds (8:6) is not a window in the sense that someone today might imagine,[22] because it does not allow Noah to see out—for if he could see, why would he need to dispatch the dove?[23] Most likely, it is a hatch in the roof, made of wood to keep the rain out, not with glass or air to let the light in. Noah reaches up his hand through this hatch to dispatch and receive the dove, who does the looking on Noah's behalf. Again, the narrative simply does not conform to the concerns of those who seek to imagine how such an ark could "really" have borne its load for over a year.

One final detail to note is the freshly plucked olive leaf, which shows that the waters had subsided (8:11). Within the general story line, this makes perfect sense, and it is memorable and moving. But the narrator appears to assume that, when the waters go down, growing things reappear in the same condition they were in before the waters came. The actual condition of any part of a tree after a year or so under the sea would presumably be indistinguishable from flotsam or seaweed; it would not show fresh life, nor would it offer a home for the dove just one week later (8:12). So, it would fail to make the point that the story needs. To try to deal with the difficulty by appealing in any way to the irregular or miraculous would undermine the point of the text, which is that the olive leaf shows the return of regular conditions upon earth. The point is that here, as elsewhere, the narrative's story line, while fully meaningful on its own terms, resists being rendered in categories of how what it relates could "really" have happened.[24]

In addition to these internal clues as to the nature of the text, the Flood story also raises problems in relation to its wider narrative context. These problems are not dissimilar to those raised by the Cain and Abel story, for again there is a tension between the internal logic of the story and its narrative setting.

First, we must note that the Flood is unambiguously envisaged as a universal flood, wiping out all life on earth other than that preserved with Noah in the ark. Although sometimes it has been argued, for apologetic reasons,[25] that the Flood was a local flood within the Middle East, that goes clearly contrary to both the specific detail and the general thrust of the biblical text. The universality of the perishing of animal and human life is explicit in Genesis 7:21–23. Nor would it be imaginable that the flood waters should cover the highest mountains, as is explicit in 7:19–20, if the Flood were local rather than universal. More generally, within the overall narrative sequence, the Flood represents a reversal of the initial creation. In Genesis 1, as the initially all-covering waters are restrained and removed, dry land appears, and life on earth is created. But in Genesis 7, all is undone, as the waters above and below are let out, land disappears, and life is extinguished by the again all-covering waters.[26] Thus, within the Flood narrative itself, the sole continuity of life between pre-Flood and post-Flood is represented by Noah and the others in the ark.

Beyond the Flood narrative proper, however, there are implicit pointers in a different direction. One issue is the presence of "the Nephilim" both before the Flood (Gen. 6:4) and subsequently in the land of Canaan as reported by Israel's spies (Num. 13:33). Indeed, there is a note in the text of Genesis 6:4 which explicitly points to the continuity of Nephilim pre- and post-Flood: "The Nephilim were on the earth in those days—*and also afterwards*" (my italics), a note which of course poses the problem rather than resolves it.[27] To be sure, the apparent problem can without undue difficulty be circumvented, as in this statement by the thoughtful commentator Nahum Sarna:

> It is contrary to the understanding of the biblical narrative that they [the Nephilim] should have survived the Flood. Hence, the reference in Numbers is not to the supposedly continued existence of Nephilim into Israelite times; rather, it is used simply for oratorical effect, much as "Huns" was used to designate Germans during the two world wars.[28]

Some rabbis, with rather less sophistication, sought to account for the continuity by the delightful (even if narratively implausible) expedient of having Og (the king of Bashan), who was one of the Nephilim, riding on the roof of the ark and so surviving the Flood![29] But whether the harmonizing instincts of the rabbis or of Sarna represent the best kind of explanation should not be decided in isolation from the wider narrative portrayal.

How should one understand the account of Cain's descendants in Genesis 4:17–24? Some of these descendants are said to be the ancestors of those engaged in certain well-known pursuits: Jabal is the ancestor of those who live in tents and have livestock (4:20); Jubal is the ancestor of those who play the lyre and pipe (4:21).[30] The natural implication of the text is that it refers to peoples known in the time of the narrator: the living in tents and the musical playing are depicted with present participles, and moreover, why bother to mention the ancestors here if the descendants are not familiar? In other words, this account of Cain's descendants seems entirely unaware of a Flood that wiped them all out.

Thus, we have another tension between the implication of a particular narrative in its own right—that Cain's descendants endure in the time of the narrator—and the wider narrative context in which that particular story is set: a subsequent Flood in which only Noah and his family, descendants of Seth and not Cain, survived. Again, a comparable solution suggests itself in terms of the individual narratives having histories of their own, in the course of which they have been transposed from their original context and relocated in their present context. In that way, one can both do justice to the implications of the particular units in their own right and still appreciate the use to which they have been put in their narrative context. But again, this indicates that the genre of the text needs careful handling.

An analogy may perhaps help. In certain ways, the early chapters of Genesis are rather like many churches and most cathedrals in the United Kingdom. Although each building is a unity as it now stands, careful inspection (and a helpful guidebook) reveals an internal history—differing kinds of stone and differing architectural styles from differing periods of history. Sometimes, the additions are obvious as additions—most obviously, graves in the floor and monuments on the walls; the narrative equivalent to these is the note or gloss which has been incorporated into the text.[31] However, one is sometimes confronted by marked differences within the fabric of a building. Almost always, the correct way of understanding a marked difference of architectural style is not to hypothesize one architect who changed his mind and his materials, but rather to recognize that the building is a composite and has a history. Thus, for example, the present east end of Durham Cathedral has displaced the original east end, which no longer remains as it fell down centuries ago; and even to the untrained eye, the style of the current east end, with its narrower multiple columns and greater height, differs from that of the nave, with the massive solidity of its shorter columns.

Once there was a time when biblical interpreters felt constrained to account for everything in the Genesis text in terms of the sole authorship of Moses as a kind of a priori. But one of the lasting benefits of modern biblical scholarship is the recognition that traditional ascriptions of authorship do not (and indeed probably were not originally intended to) function as guides to composition in the kind of way that has been of concern to historians of antiquity in the modern world. This frees one up to work inductively with the evidence that the text itself provides. In many contexts, the supposition that differences in content and style are best explained in terms of the construction of a whole out of originally diverse parts has widely commended itself. To be sure, such an approach does not solve all problems. But at least, with regard to the specific problems posed by the texts we have been considering, this approach does enable one to make sense of what otherwise is either inexplicable or can lead to rather forced harmonized readings of the text.

The Perspective and Convention Embodied in the
Use of Hebrew Language

The final issue I would like to consider is the use of the Hebrew language throughout the early chapters of Genesis—a feature so well known and often so taken for granted that one may not linger sufficiently to consider its possible implications.

The particular aspect on which I will focus is the use of Hebrew for speech by all of the speaking characters in the story. First and foremost, God, who is the prime speaker in this material, speaks in Hebrew. Hebrew is the language he uses, not only when in conversation with humans, such as Adam or Cain (Gen. 3:9–19, 4:6–15), but also when making pronouncements inaccessible to the human ear—such as the speaking into being of creation throughout Genesis 1 and the soliloquies that portray the divine will before and after the Flood (Gen. 6:6–7, 8:21–22). Correspondingly, all of the human characters speak in Hebrew. Indeed, the very first speech set on human lips not only is in Hebrew but also contains a Hebrew wordplay of a kind characteristic of the Old Testament generally—and which only works in Hebrew in its mature classical form. As he expresses his delight with Eve, Adam says: "This one shall be called Woman [ishshah], for out of Man [ish] this one was taken" (Gen. 2:23).

How should this phenomenon be understood? The time-honored premodern approach was to appeal to Genesis 11:1—"Now the whole earth had one language and the same words"—and to construe this in a historicizing way: all of the early inhabitants of earth, pre-Babel, spoke Hebrew, the language of God himself.[32] A historical claim, however, that Hebrew is the oldest—indeed, the original—language upon earth runs into a barrage of general historical and philological difficulties[33] and is incapable of giving a convincing explanation of the particular biblical texts in which Hebrew is used in contexts far removed from ancient Israel in both space and time.

The root of the problem is the assumption that the portrayal of speech in Hebrew should be historicized. There is an obvious alternative. What if, instead, one construes the biblical depiction in terms of the general convention of all storytellers, ancient and modern, which is to depict one's characters as speaking in the language of the storyteller and of the target audience? When Shakespeare depicts all of the characters in *Julius Caesar* or *Coriolanus* as speaking Tudor English in the context of ancient Rome, one would be unwise to assume that Shakespeare is making a historical claim about the language of ancient Rome rather than making the historical scenario accessible to his contemporaries. Or, to take a few other examples, when Mary Renault in her novels or Oliver Stone in his film *Alexander* depict the figures of ancient Greece speaking in English, or when James Michener in his novel *The Source* has inhabitants of the Holy Land from antiquity to the present speak in English, one would again be unwise to historicize the linguistic depiction, whatever the historical accuracy of other aspects of the general portrayal (where the writer or film producer has done historical homework to try to ensure some verisimilitude of the setting).[34] Similarly, when God soliloquizes in Hebrew or when Adam makes a wordplay in Hebrew, one can instantly make sense of the phenomenon in terms of the imaginative convention of the language being that of the narrator and the implied audience, but one can make no good sense at all if one is constrained to argue that these Hebrew words are what was "really" said in the frame of reference of ancient history rather than of dramatic narrative portrayal.

Thus, the portrayal of characters speaking in Hebrew poses an issue not dissimilar to our previous examples; the content of the text in an important respect stands in tension with the context at the beginnings of the world in which it is now set. Or, to put it differently, all of my examples underline the need to take seriously the biblical text as a literary phenomenon, whose conventions must be understood and respected on their own terms and not prejudged in terms of their conformity (or otherwise) to the interpreter's initial expectations. Biblical literature and life in the ancient world are indeed intimately and inseparably related, but the relationship, especially in the early chapters of Genesis, is complex.

Conclusions

First, I am conscious that I have said relatively little about Genesis 1–3, which are the chapters upon which the most interpretive weight has been laid. However, if the argument thus far be granted, one would not, I hope, be disposed to approach Genesis 1–3 in a way that differed significantly from one's approach to Genesis 4–9.

Second, the recognition that the narrative sequence in the early chapters of Genesis is "constructed" out of originally disparate material is, of course, open to be taken in more than one way. All too often, sadly, it has led to a reductive debunking: the material is, at best, a *merely* human construct, an eloquent example of the ancient Hebrew imagination but not of God nor the true nature of the world; at worst, it is a farrago of misguided stories about the world, "legends" in a popular pejorative sense whose only good location is in histories of human error. Polemical rhetoric along these lines featured, for example, in the influential late eighteenth-century writings of Tom Paine:

> Take away from Genesis the belief that Moses was the author, on which only the strange belief that it is the word of God has stood, and there remains nothing of Genesis, but an anonymous book of stories, fables and traditionary [*sic*] or invented absurdities or downright lies.[35]

More recently, one of Paine's intellectual descendants, Richard Dawkins, expressed himself in comparable terms:

> To be fair, much of the Bible is not systematically evil but just plain weird, as you would expect of a chaotically cobbled-together anthology of disjointed documents, composed, revised, translated, distorted and "improved" by hundreds of anonymous authors, editors and copyists, unknown to us and mostly unknown to each other.[36]

Such polemic has often produced defensive responses which have too readily accepted the questionable categories within which the critique is articulated. But none of this follows from the basic recognition of the text's constructed nature. For what comes into play at this point is one's understanding of revelation, that is, whether it is theologically responsible to recognize God's self-communication and enduring truth about humanity and the world in variegated texts that bear the hallmarks of regular literary conventions and historical processes. Suffice it to say that I can see no good reason to deny this further recognition, however contested it may be. Thus, for example, over against Tom Paine and Richard Dawkins, one might note the no less stringent tones of Karl Barth:

> We must dismiss and resist to the very last any idea of the inferior-
> ity or untrustworthiness or even worthlessness of a "non-historical"
> depiction and narration of history. This is in fact only a ridiculous
> and middle-class habit of the modern Western mind which is
> supremely phantastic in its chronic lack of imaginative phantasy, and
> hopes to rid itself of its complexes through suppression. This habit
> has really no claim to the dignity and validity which it pretends.[37]

Third, how does this chapter relate to the wider context of "reading Genesis after Darwin"? Specifically, does Darwin make any difference to one's reading of the early chapters of Genesis? In terms of perceiving the peculiarities of the genre of the text, I have argued that Darwin makes no real difference. Internal clues as to the genre of the text are there for any reader to see, and appropriate inferences can be drawn irrespective of one's views about the nature of creation and evolution. It is at the conceptual level, of course, in relation to understanding the content of the biblical text, that Darwinian and post-Darwinian biology have their impact; in what way, if any, can a creature that has evolved through processes of natural selection be seen as "created in the image of God"?

Here, I judge the key issue to be what a belief in creation does, and does not, entail; this is an issue where the adequacy of one's categories of thought is all-important. Belief in creation needs to be retrieved from its characteris-tic modern distortion in terms of "design"[38] and understood afresh in other, more biblical terms. These should include—at the least, in terms of Genesis 1–3—the wonder and delight of the world, creaturely contingency, creaturely responsibility, the gift of relationship between creature and Creator, and the difficulty that humans have in genuinely trusting God as a wise Creator and living accordingly.

NOTES

1. I use "early chapters of Genesis" to refer to Genesis 1–11, whose generally distinctive character, in relation to the rest of Genesis, is widely acknowledged, even though there is no clear cut-off, but rather various continuities, between Genesis 11 and Genesis 12.

2. "Day," as in "the day of the LORD," is a period of time as in, say, novel titles such as *The Day of the Triffids* or *The Day of the Jackal*.

3. For substantive interpretation, see R. W. L. Moberly, *The Theology of the Book of Genesis* (Cambridge: Cambridge University Press, 2009).

4. The Greek at this point—*dia dokousēs historias kai ou sōmatikōs gegenēmenēs*—needs careful rendering so as not to couch it in categories which are eloquent of subsequent debates but not of Origen's frame of reference. I think "not literally" is infelicitous in this regard, for Origen is indeed attentive to the letter of the text. It is the fact that the meaning of the words resists comprehension in terms of the familiar categories of action in space and time that moves him to read on a "spiritual" level.

5. The Greek here—*kata tēn lexin*—seems to signify something like "in the terms of the wording of the text."

6. *De Principiis* IV.1.16. The translation is by Frederick Crombie in *The Writings of Origen* (Edinburgh: Clark, 1869), 1:315–317.

7. There is a comparable contemporary example in the course of Brian McLaren's commending of a thoughtful Christian faith which, among other things, eschews creationism. In the course of clearing the ground for a positive account of creation and evolution, Neo says:

> Do they imagine God literally saying, "Let there be light"? In what language?...And where did the air come from to propagate the sound waves for God's literal words; and for that matter, where did the vocal cords come from for God to say those words? And as for the business of the six days, assuming that you're not a flat-earther, you have to acknowledge that when it's day on one side of the globe, it's night on the other. So when Genesis says that the first day begins and ends, from whose vantage point does it mean— Sydney, Australia, or Greenwich, England? (Brian D. McLaren, *The Story We Find Ourselves In* [San Francisco: Jossey-Bass, 2003], 32)

8. See *Questions on the Heptateuch* I:1. The more general issue of the necessary marriage of brothers and sisters in early times is discussed in *City of God* XV.16.

9. As Augustine recognized. He clearly saw that the reference to a "city" was the substantive problem needing discussion (*Questions on the Heptateuch* I.1; *City of God* XV.8).

10. The Hebrew term for open territory, *sadeh*, can be a kind of opposite to ʿir, settled space (e.g., Lev. 14:53).

11. Peoples are scattered far and wide only after Babel (Gen. 11:9).

12. One may compare the regular legal injunctions to care for the *ger*, the "resident alien," i.e., someone on foreign territory away from their own clan or tribe, who, like the orphan and widow, was a particularly vulnerable person because lacking in regular support and protection (e.g., Lev. 19:33; Deut. 10:17–19).

13. A convenient introduction to La Peyrère is Heikki Räisänen, "The Bible and the Traditions of the Nations: Isaac La Peyrère as a Precursor of Biblical Criticism," in Räisänen, *Marcion, Muhammad and the Mahatma* (London: SCM, 1997), 137–152. A full account, which sets La Peyrère in his intellectual context and helps with a recognition of his importance, is R. H. Popkin, *Isaac La Peyrère (1596–1676): His Life, Work and Influence* (Leiden: Brill, 1987).

14. There was, however, much else in La Peyrère which was provocative.

15. For the purposes of the argument, it makes no difference whether the story is ascribed to Moses in the fifteenth or thirteenth century BC, the Yahwist in the tenth or sixth century BC, or anyone else within the general historical context of ancient Israel.

16. It might also perhaps be possible to attribute the problems to a certain imaginative failure on the part of the narrator, who could not sufficiently envisage the conditions of life upon an unpopulated earth.

17. For this nice formulation, I am indebted to Lizzie Hartley, in the context of a Hebrew prose texts class in 2004–2005.

18. E. D. Morgan, "Noah's Ark Was a Masterpiece: A Mystery of Correct Engineering Design before the Flood," *Meccano Magazine* (December 1926): 767. The contention that the design of the ark would give it stability is an ancient one (cf. M. Zlotowitz and N. Scherman, *Bereishis/Genesis*, vol. 1 (New York: Mesorah, 1986), 231). However, the instructions in 6:14–16 are open to widely differing construals of the shape and seaworthiness of the ark.

19. It should be noted, however, that each soliloquy is followed by an address to Noah in which the divine resolve is made known, albeit in words other than those of the soliloquies.

20. See, for example, John Woodmorappe, *Noah's Ark: A Feasibility Study* (San Diego, CA: Institute for Creation Research, 1996).

21. The meaning of *tsohar*, the first word in 6:16, is unclear. The NRSV renders it "roof," with a marginal alternative of "window." Given the word's position in the instructions, which are still dealing with the overall structure of the ark, and given that it is "for" (*le*) the ark and not "in its side" (*betsiddah*) as is that opening which is the door, the sense of "window" would be inappropriate; "roof" is a less unlikely guess at its meaning.

22. Nor, for example, as was imagined by the artist responsible for the famous twelfth-century mosaic in Venice at San Marco. One can see this and a good selection of other historic artistic depictions of the ark in Norman Cohn, *Noah's Flood: The Genesis Story in Western Thought* (New Haven, Conn.: Yale University Press, 1996).

23. Of course, this could be rationalized in terms of a need to see beyond the horizon, even though the text does not mention this.

24. It is not possible in this chapter to discuss the well-known existence of numerous flood narratives from other cultures (stories, no doubt, rooted in lingering ancient memories of calamitous flooding conditions in various regions of the world). The best-known version from the wider world of ancient Israel is Tablet XI of the Epic of Gilgamesh, which tells of Utnapishtim and a flood (see, e.g., James B. Pritchard, ed., *Ancient Near Eastern Texts Relating to the Old Testament*, 3rd ed. [Princeton, N.J.: Princeton University Press, 1969], 93–97), a version which has sufficient commonality with the Genesis account to make direct comparison illuminating. The relationship between the biblical and the Babylonian account can be, and has been, argued every which way, for we lack evidence and must make intelligent inferences. I would simply suggest that at least one reasonably uncontroversial dimension of the biblical story is that it is a Hebrew retelling of a common story, whose details are to some

extent shaped by the concern to set the well-known story in a particular light: think about it *this* way, and one will understand more truly the situation of the world under God.

25. See, for example, Bernard Ramm, *The Christian View of Science and Scripture* (London: Paternoster, 1955), of which there is a sharp discussion by James Barr, *Fundamentalism* (London: SCM, 1977), 94–96.

26. To be sure, sea life would not be adversely affected by the Flood's waters, but this is of no interest to the narrator. In a later context, certain rabbis, in an attempt to rationalize this apparent inconsistency within the logic of the narrative, argued that the fish must have been sinless! (cf. Zlotowitz and Scherman, *Bereishis*, 257).

27. Since the wording "and also afterwards" is intrusive in the Hebrew between the preceding "in those days" and the following "when," for which "those days" and not "and also afterwards" is clearly the antecedent, most modern scholars have judged "and also afterwards" to be an early marginal gloss added in recognition of the Nephilim in a post-Flood context.

28. Nahum M. Sarna, *The JPS Torah Commentary: Genesis* (Philadelphia: Jewish Publication Society, 1989), 46.

29. See Zlotowitz and Scherman, *Bereishis*, 187.

30. Perhaps also Tubal-Cain is the ancestor of those who make bronze and iron tools (4:22), though there is a text-critical problem, since the Masoretic text and versions lack the expected "father of."

31. Apart from "and also afterwards" in 6:4, there are many notes which give currently familiar place names to clarify the older place names contained in the narrative; thus, for example, the place named in the story as Luz is subsequently known as Bethel (Gen. 35:6); cf. Gen. 14:2, 3, 7, 17.

32. So, for example, Rashi (eleventh century) glosses "one language" in Genesis 11:1 with "the holy tongue," i.e., Hebrew. M. Rosenbaum and A. M. Silbermann, eds., *The Pentateuch with the Commentary of Rashi: Genesis* (Jerusalem: Silbermann, 1972), 44.

33. This issue was debated extensively in the seventeenth and eighteenth centuries in the context of the emergence of a more sharply focused sense of the nature of ancient history and of appropriate scholarly approaches to such history.

34. So prevalent and recognized is the convention that an attempt at linguistic "realism," such as the characters speaking ancient languages in Mel Gibson's *The Passion of the Christ*, does not, I think, succeed in its purpose; realism is attained by (a) a quality of acting and filming that so engages the imagination that any kind of self-distancing or suspension of disbelief becomes impossible for the duration of the film, and (b) the ability of the film creatively to inform thought and practice subsequent to its viewing.

35. Thomas Paine, *The Age of Reason, Part the Second, Being an Investigation of True and Fabulous Theology* (London, 1795), 4.

36. Richard Dawkins, *The God Delusion* (London: Bantam, 2006), 237.

37. Karl Barth, *Church Dogmatics*, vol. 3, pt. 1, ed. G. W. Bromiley and T. F. Torrance, trans. J. W. Edwards, O. Bussey, and Harold Knight (Edinburgh: Clark,

1958), 81. Karl Barth is the most notable proponent in recent times of an under-standing of biblical revelation in terms of ordinary and fallible human language as the vehicle for God's self-communication. The passage cited is taken from a larger discussion of the genre and significance of the creation narratives; *Church Dogmatics*, vol. 3, pt. 1:61–94.

38. Paley's initially widely persuasive apologetic construal of creation in terms of an argument from design was one of the cultural factors that contributed to the strongly negative psychological and imaginative impact of Darwin's demonstration that apparent design in nature is explicable without recourse to a designer.

2

Genesis before Darwin
Why Scripture Needed
Liberating from Science

Francis Watson

In treating the first chapter of the book of Genesis, interpreters have always had to reckon with alternative accounts of the world's origin and constitution. Sometimes, this reckoning takes polemical form. The commentator may point out that the words "[i]n the beginning God created the heavens and the earth" exclude the theory that the world originated in random atomic interactions, or that it is eternal.[1] Where philosophy and scripture conflict over matters of fundamental concern, theologians have sought to uphold the scriptural teaching. Yet it has also been recognized that truths about the constitution of the world may be found outside the scriptural text and that, in interpreting the text, space must be conceded to these nonscriptural truths. Here and elsewhere, scripture purports to tell us only what we most need to know; it does not tell us everything that we might wish to know or that we are capable of knowing even without it. In speaking of the constitution of heaven and earth, it speaks of everything that is, yet it does so by way of a brief and simplified outline concerned almost exclusively with the relation of heaven and earth to their transcendent origin, "God." This outline occupies only a small part even of the book of Genesis itself. There is no lack of space here for additional truths about the world, even where these represent a different perspective from the narrator's. Truths are not necessarily of a piece. They function within particular contexts, outside which they cannot straightforwardly be coordinated with one another. The Genesis text claims no monopoly on truth about the world.

Yet there is a received view of this text which sees in it only a discredited monopolistic claim. In secularizing Western contexts, this received view has become synonymous with the name of its supposed progenitor: thus, "Darwin" represents not only the great theorist of evolution but also the intellectual over-throw of Genesis and of biblical religion more generally. Until the nineteenth century, it is said, Genesis or its advocates *did* claim a monopoly on truth about the world's origin. In consequence, the scriptural text entered into competition with modern science—and lost, conclusively and irrevocably. Genesis taught that the world was created recently and in six days and that plants and animals are now as they were at the dawn of creation. Darwin taught that plant and animal life had evolved over countless millennia through mechanisms such as "natural selection." The vast preponderance of informed opinion followed Darwin and rejected the Bible. In the received view, "Darwin" signifies the moment when the forces of secularization won the intellectual argument. In his person, science comes of age and throws off the shackles of outmoded world views. The memory of this perceived triumph of scientific enlighten-ment over ancient superstition is kept alive by the ongoing combat with an intellectually negligible but politically powerful "creationism," still committed to a so-called literal truth of Genesis.

So, scientific secularity triumphs over the Bible and one monopolistic truth claim overcomes another. It is assumed that truth is of a piece, that its various components can be marshaled into a single comprehensive structure, and that whatever refuses integration is of doubtful legitimacy. In this ideology, the natural sciences no longer represent localized though interrelated perspectives on the world, organized and developed along mainly pragmatic lines; rather, they are supposed to coalesce into a generalized "scientific outlook" or world view. The strange question whether science "can explain everything" begins to be debated—as though total explanation were a coherent and meaningful concept, as though there actually existed a science that aspired to such a thing, whose cause must be either furthered or thwarted. On the nonmonopolistic assumption that truth is context- or discourse-specific, such a debate becomes impossible. And the story it presupposes, which tells of the triumph of sci-ence over religion, "Darwin" over "Genesis," is revealed precisely as a *story*—one possible and partial account of a certain complex development alongside others.[2]

In this chapter, I shall attempt to tell the story differently. In this retelling, "Darwin" will represent *the liberation of the biblical text from its captivity to the natural sciences*—from its annexation by geology and biology, which Darwin brought to an end. The retold story begins not with nineteenth-century geol-ogy or biology but with sixteenth-century astronomy.

On the Size of the Moon

In Genesis 1:16, God makes "two great lights, the greater light to rule the day and the lesser light to rule the night." The sun and moon are here distinguished from the stars, whose creation is described so succinctly that even the distinction between fixed stars and planets passes without mention. According to John Calvin, it is crucially important to recognize that Moses does not speak here as a philosopher. Moses appears to suggest that the two great lights are both independent light sources, without reference to the fact that "the moon would not have sufficient brightness to illumine the earth unless it borrowed from the sun."[3] He also passes over the fact that "the star of Saturn, which owing to its great distance appears the least of all, is greater than the moon."[4] It is astronomy and not scripture that brings to light these truths about the universe, and this science is to be commended for doing so:

> For astronomy is not only pleasant but also very useful to know. It cannot be denied that this art discloses the wonderful wisdom of God. Therefore, just as able people who have usefully devoted their attention to this subject are to be honoured, so those with leisure and ability should not neglect this form of study.[5]

Why then does Genesis 1 speak of the moon as a luminary second only to the sun? The answer is that

> Moses here addresses himself to our senses, so that the knowledge of the divine gifts we enjoy may not vanish away. Therefore, in order to grasp his meaning, it is to no purpose to soar above the heavens. Rather, let us open our eyes to behold this light which God enkindles for us in the earth.... For as it became a theologian, [Moses] had respect to *us* rather than to the stars.[6]

Scripture says one thing, science another. Calvin's deceptively simple resolution of this issue is highly suggestive and offers a model that might usefully have been applied to later, related issues. In the following paragraphs, I shall offer an interpretive paraphrase of his statements.

We are to study astronomy to gain one kind of truth and scripture to gain another. The two truths both derive from God and may both be acquired by the same person; and yet they are incommensurable, since they presuppose the perspectives of heavenly and earthly observers, respectively. Human reason is capable of attaining the heavenly perspective in which it becomes evident that, contrary to appearances, Saturn is actually larger than the moon; but it cannot ultimately escape the primary earthly perspective within which the moon illumines the earth with its own light. Owing to this incommensurability of perspective, Calvin does *not* propose to harmonize the scriptural and the astronomical accounts along the following lines:

> And God made two great lights (lights, that is, that appear great
> to us); the greater light to rule the day, the lesser to rule the night
> (lesser in that it borrows light from the greater). He made the stars
> also (including planets which may actually exceed the lesser of the
> two great lights in greatness).

A harmony along these lines would not be a harmony at all but an unnatural conflation of scriptural and scientific truths whose significance only comes to light if they are kept distinct.

The scriptural account describes the appearance, which is that there are just two large heavenly bodies alongside the many that are so small as to be mere points of light. The scientific account begins to disclose a reality quite different from the appearance. If we enter into this field of investigation as Calvin exhorts us to do, we may well find that this gulf between appearance and reality is broader and deeper than we could have imagined. And so a problem comes to light: if appearance is the realm of scripture and reality that of science, we may be forced to conclude that scientific truth takes precedence over scriptural. The person who has understood that Saturn is "really" larger than the moon may seem to dwell on a higher epistemic plane than the person misled by sensory experience—unchallenged by scripture—into thinking that the moon is larger than Saturn.

While Calvin might seem to have correlated scripture with appearance and astronomical science with reality, it is crucially important to note the anti-Platonic moves that preclude the downgrading of appearance. As we have seen, Calvin argues that "Moses here addresses himself to the senses." The senses cannot be said to mislead us, since it is through our senses—specifically, our power of vision—that we truly "behold this light which God enkindles for us in the earth," that is, the lesser light of the moon. Our eyes tell us that moonlight is second only to sunlight in brightness and that no other heavenly body can compare with it. This is no mere appearance; it belongs to the God-given reality of life on earth. For the Genesis narrator, as Calvin understands him, our experience of life on earth is both *given,* in the sense that it does not rest on any allegedly more basic reality, and *given by God.* In that sense, appearance and reality coincide, for the appearance in question is that of reality in the particular configuration bestowed on us by God. That is why, in "address[ing] himself to our senses," Moses wrote "as it became a theologian": for the senses are our means of participation in a reality constituted by its God-givenness. This God-givenness guarantees not only the practical reliability of the knowledge derived from the senses but also its epistemological and ontological status.[7]

For Calvin, our capacity for reason enables us both to operate within our own given and immediate perspective and to transcend it. We transcend it in the context of a scientific investigation in which a perspective on reality comes to light that is quite other than the one from which Genesis speaks. Here, we learn (among other things) that the least conspicuous of all the visible planets is actually much larger than the moon—in spite of appearances to the contrary. Our discovery of the scientific truth is all to the good: for astronomy "discloses the wonderful wisdom of God," and this branch of science should be diligently pursued by "those with leisure and ability" to do so. And yet, if we pursue this heavenly perspective to the detriment of our primary God-given and earthly one, there is a danger that "the knowledge of the divine gifts we enjoy" may "vanish away." That is to say, we may acquire a knowledge of abstracted natural phenomena at the cost of a knowledge of our own giftedness. If so, the idea that a scientifically explicable phenomenon such as moonlight is a gift of God will imperceptibly lose its persuasiveness, as we understand ourselves no longer as participants in a God-given order but as observers of a reality become neutral and indifferent.

Calvin merely hints at this danger, however, and is more concerned to demarcate two modes of knowing, which are both to be evaluated positively. His treatment of this single, small-scale interpretive issue suggests the following hermeneutical rules:

1. Where scripture and science differ, we are not to assume that the scientific finding or hypothesis should give way to the plain sense of the scriptural text. Each case must be considered on its merits, for a scientific finding or hypothesis may simply represent a different perspective from that of the scriptural text rather than the assertion of one truth claim in opposition to another.

2. Since the scriptural perspective is that of our own life-world understood as the gift of God, this perspective is primary and foundational to the additional perspectives on reality that come to light in the practice of the sciences. In that sense, the scriptural account should have precedence over the scientific one at points where the two come into contact.

3. Yet the scientific account is not to be neglected, as though the theologian had no stake in it. For one thing, it is speaking of a reality that (precisely for the theologian) is God's own creation—however clearly or otherwise it may seem to show itself to be such. For another thing,

it provokes a more insightful reading of the scriptural text that is not content merely to note and paraphrase its fact-like assertions, but seeks to uncover their significance and rationale.

4. Since the scientific account operates within a different frame of reference from the scriptural one, the interpreter should seek to *explain* the difference rather than *deny* it. Where one attempts to show that scripture is confirmed by science or science by scripture, the integrity of both discourses may be compromised.

Calvin analyzes a point of contact between Genesis and science that relates to the work of the fourth day of creation. Yet astronomy was not the most important terrain for later debates about this relationship. The great astronomical advances of the seventeenth century had to do with the solar system in its present form, not with its origins. In the geological and biological sciences, too, empirical investigation of natural phenomena took precedence over speculations about their origins. Where consideration of origins did occur, however, a relationship to the Genesis account had to be negotiated. In the ensuing debates, the possibility of incommensurability—so strikingly articulated by Calvin—was overlooked. Either science confirmed scripture, or it refuted scripture. Skeptics and atheists advocated the second conclusion, Christian believers the first. The shared assumption was that scripture is in principle *falsifiable* by science: if well-grounded scientific findings turn out to be incompatible with scripture, scripture will be fatally undermined. Some work to bring that result about, others to prevent it, but both parties are committed to the assumption that all truth claims occur within a single semantic domain that prescribes neutral criteria for assessing them.

One reason why this assumption remained unchallenged was that it seemed to produce just the results the Christian majority wanted. Until well into the nineteenth century, it could plausibly be argued that geology offered positive support to Genesis, God, and religion. Geology served as a valuable adjunct to the project of "natural theology," which drew especially on the biological sciences.[8] Indeed, unlike natural theology, geology came into direct contact with scripture itself, appearing to confirm key elements in the scriptural account of the origins of things.

Geology Reads Genesis

According to Genesis, dry land emerged out of the primeval ocean on the third day of creation, which also saw the beginnings of plant life. Having devoted the fourth day to the heavens, the Deity comes back down to earth on the fifth and sixth days, populating the sea, the air, and the land with various kinds of living creature. This sequence of events was temporarily reversed at the time of the Deluge, when the earth reverted to its original form as a watery chaos. But life was preserved, and the original order was restored. Initially, informed readers of Genesis thought they had good grounds for holding that geological science confirmed the scriptural account. Only gradually did it become clear that the rocks told a different story.

To begin with, it was noticed that the remains of marine creatures lay embedded in rock. Various explanations were proposed, of which the only rational one was that there was once sea where there is now dry land. As Leonardo da Vinci already noted, "The peaks of the Apennines once stood up in a sea, in the form of islands surrounded by salt water; and above the plains of Italy where flocks of birds are flying today, fishes were once moving in large shoals."[9]

In Genesis too, dry land emerges out of the sea. Here, however, the rocks of day three precede the marine life of day five, whereas the fossils attested a marine life that preceded the rocks in which it became embedded. A possible solution lay ready to hand. These fossil-bearing rocks were *secondary* formations. They came into being through the sedimentation caused by the universal Flood, and they therefore preserved vestiges of the antediluvian world. If fossilized sea creatures were to be found on high mountainsides, this strikingly confirmed the truth of the biblical story, which told how "the waters prevailed exceedingly upon the earth," so that "all the high hills that were under the whole heaven were covered" (Gen. 7:19 KJV).

Furthermore, these sedimentary, fossil-bearing formations were superimposed on primary rocks such as granite and basalt, which lacked organic traces. Perhaps these, too, were formed by processes of sedimentation? If so, then geology also confirmed the Genesis picture of an original universal ocean out of which dry land appeared. In that case, the geological distinction between primary and secondary formations would correspond closely to the scriptural distinction between the original watery chaos and the temporary reversion to it in the great Flood. If, as the Bible taught, there was indeed a universal Flood, then evidence of sedimentation and of organic remains was exactly what one would expect to find. In their absence from one set of rocks and their presence in another, the fossils were the key to this harmony between the sacred text and modern science. In this context, the skeptical claim that the sea may have "covered all parts of the earth one after the other," but "only by slow stages in a prodigious multitude of centuries," could seem like a desperate attempt to avoid the obvious.[10]

This sequence of rock formations seemed to many eighteenth-century readers to correspond broadly to the more precise scriptural chronology. Unusually, the pre- and postdiluvian genealogies of Genesis 5 and 11, respectively, specify the father's age at the time of his son's birth. As a result, it is possible to calculate that the Flood occurred in the year 1656 *anno mundi* and the birth of Abraham 292 years later, in 1948 AM.[11] Subsequent scriptural material makes an *anno mundi* dating possible up to around the end of the exile,[12] but thereafter extrabiblical information is required in order to assimilate the AM figures to the BC / AD system. Thus, in the influential scheme of Archbishop James Ussher (1650), year zero corresponded to 4004 BC, 1656 AM to 2348 BC, and so on.[13] A single timeline connected the creation of the world, the Flood, the life of Abraham, the fall of Jerusalem, and the birth of Christ with the Norman conquest, the Protestant Reformation, and the modern era. 4004 BC is a scholarly construct that represents the incorporation of scriptural chronology into world history; no such date can be derived from scripture alone. From around the beginning of the eighteenth century, such dates were incorporated into the margins of the Old Testament text and became an inseparable element of its claim to tell the truth about the world and its origin. The best of modern historical and geological science seemed to give the book of Genesis a secure foothold in reality—a reality construed as simple and singular, like the absolute space of Newtonian physics.

In all this, what took shape was an *interpretation* of Genesis. It was an interpretation that made reasonable if not compelling sense in view of the current state of geological and historical knowledge. As geological and historical knowledge continued to progress, this interpretation gradually ceased to make sense—and was succeeded by different attempts to show that the geological and scriptural narratives complement one another, before these too lost credibility. These developments are often recounted as the story of science's slow but inexorable self-liberation from the control of the sacred text. But that is to overlook the fact that, here as always, the text in question is an *interpreted* text. The interpretation in question is not simply arbitrary: Genesis does indeed provide chronological information that can be used to provide relative datings of the events it narrates. But it remains an interpretive *choice* to focus on this chronology and to coordinate it with other chronologies, including the geological one. Most readers have not taken up this interpretive option and have chosen to focus their attention elsewhere. Perhaps because they are preoccupied with genuinely theological concerns, it does not occur to them to add up the ages at which antediluvian patriarchs achieved paternity, with a view to a dating of the Flood in relation to the creation. Nor does it occur to them to seek vestiges of the Flood in local rock formations. Where such interpretive moves are made, the Genesis text is uprooted from its natural habitat within the scriptural narrative of salvation and assimilated to concerns of early modern science and historical scholarship. If it eventually becomes evident that science needs to be liberated from scriptural control, the problem has been caused not by scripture per se, in uninterpreted form, but by a scripture itself annexed by extraneous scientific and scholarly developments. What takes place in the mid-nineteenth century is best understood as an amicable divorce, in which it is finally acknowledged that the relationship is entangled in intractable difficulties because it has all along been based on the false premise of compatibility.

If two stories are to be compatible, they must occupy the same time frame. By the end of the eighteenth century, it became increasingly clear that the story told by the rocks could *not* be contained within a chronology derived from or imposed on scripture. As we shall see, however, this problem initially led not to divorce but to renewed attempts at conciliation.

In the beginning, primary rocks such as granite and basalt were supposedly formed by sedimentation within the universal primal ocean. For the so-called Neptunists, this claim fitted the geological evidence while remaining tolerably close to the Genesis text. It was opposed by "Plutonists" (or "Vulcanists"), for whom these rocks were of igneous rather than sedimentary origin. The world arose out of fire, not water. But perhaps the rocks tell us nothing at all about an absolute beginning? According to the uniformitarian position of James Hutton and Charles Lyell, they speak instead of an eternal recurrence of natural processes that continue to this day: erosion, sedimentation, earthquakes, volcanic activity, the alternation of sea and land. The world as we know it has been shaped not by sudden, quasi-miraculous interventions or catastrophes but by the inexorable cyclical operation of familiar natural causes. These processes take time. If the uniformitarian theory were correct, the earth would have to be almost unimaginably old. Six days or 6,000 years would no longer be adequate to shape a planet. Previously blended together, the scriptural and the geological narratives began to separate out. And it was the fossils that provided the crucial supporting evidence, as they were read more carefully.

The fossils had previously been interpreted in the light of the Genesis Flood narrative; consequently, the Genesis Flood narrative had been interpreted in the light of the fossils. Well into the nineteenth century, fossils could still be understood as *reliquiae diluvianae,* as "organic remains attesting the action of a universal deluge."[14] Yet it was no longer possible to explain the whole fossil record in this manner, for the rocks had been found to preserve a history of life on earth rather than a synopsis of organisms coexisting at a single time. The history of life corresponded to the history of the rocks. Within the rocks, strata could be distinguished and the sequence of their formation could be determined. The more recent strata contained a higher proportion of organisms similar or identical to those still extant, whereas lower strata contained a higher proportion of unfamiliar and extinct organisms. A stratum in one location could be correlated with a stratum in another on the basis of similarities between the organisms preserved in each, which were found to differ markedly from those preserved in adjacent higher or lower strata. In consequence, it became possible to piece together the outline of a history: "natural history" became genuinely historical. The stratified diversity of species (the majority now extinct) confirmed that life had developed over an unimaginably long time period, and not between the Tuesday and the Friday of the first week. The Genesis Flood could at best account only for the most recent fossil evidence.

In this way, a second account of the world's origin came into being alongside the first. Both stories still had to be regarded as true stories, proceeding from the same divine author, yet the extraordinary discrepancy between their respective time frames could not be ignored. The solution lay ready to hand in a time-honored though problematic exegetical tradition. According to this tradition, where two sacred texts diverge, they must be harmonized with one another. It must be shown that their "apparent discrepancies" are just that, only apparent and not real. One biblical narrative tells how event A was followed by events B and C; another tells how event A was followed by events D, E, and C. Given the agreement on A and C, D and E must be accommodated between A and B or B and C. By this technique of conflation, two narratives are blended into one. Alternatively, harmonization can be achieved by reinterpretation. One narrative asserts a at a point where the other asserts b, and the difficulty may be overcome if it can be shown that a possesses an extended semantic range ($a^{1,2,3,4...}$) within which is a possibility that approximates to b. Within Western Christianity, these two harmonizing techniques—conflation and reinterpretation—were applied especially to the Gospels. Here, Augustine's harmonizing program prevailed over Origen's rejection of this interpretive practice.[15] Thus, harmonizing techniques could also be extended to the discrepancies between the biblical and the natural histories, since (like the Gospels) these too proceeded from one and the same divine author. One might seek to accommodate the long-drawn-out natural account within the impossibly brief scriptural one (conflation); or one might find means to extend the scriptural chronology so that it coincided with the geological time scale (reinterpretation).

One traditional rule of conflation proved particularly useful—the rule that the harmonizer is not obliged to maintain a scriptural connection between one event and another. Augustine had taught that individual scriptural statements were all true but that their sequence sometimes passes over and conceals events narrated in another sacred text. Thus, Luke's infancy narrative tells us that, on completing the prescribed rituals in Jerusalem, the holy family returned to Nazareth (Luke 2:39). There is no indication here of anything other than a straightforward chronological sequence. And yet we read in Matthew of an extended train of events, passed over by Luke, that must be inserted prior to the return to Nazareth: the flight to Egypt, the massacre of the innocents, the death of Herod, and so on. Scriptural sequences can open up to accommodate new material, as required, with the result that distinct narratives are blended into one. Precisely this technique comes into play where a break is proposed between the first verse of Genesis 1 ("In the beginning God created the heaven and the earth") and the second ("And the earth was without form and void, and darkness was upon the face of the deep"). Into this newly created gap, the entire geological narrative can be inserted.

In preparing his readers to accept this harmonization, William Buckland acknowledges that "[m]inds which have long been accustomed to date the origin of the universe, as well as that of the human race, from an era of about six thousand years ago, receive reluctantly any information which, if true, demands some new modification of their present ideas of cosmogony."[16] Far from contradicting the sacred text, however, the geological narrative can help us to make better sense of it. In particular, we should carefully note what the opening of Genesis does and does not say:

> The Mosaic narrative commences with a declaration that "in the beginning God created the heaven and the earth." These first few words of Genesis may be fairly appealed to by the geologist as containing a brief statement of the creation of the material elements, at a time distinctly preceding the operations of the first day; it is nowhere affirmed that God created the heaven and the earth in the *first day*, but in the *beginning*; this beginning may have been an epoch at an unmeasured distance, followed by periods of undefined duration during which all the physical operations disclosed by geology were going on.[17]

Thus, the first verse of Genesis is genuinely speaking of the creation of all things. The second verse appears to follow directly from it, but in reality it does not. The developments of unimaginably long geological eras are passed over, and we find ourselves viewing the aftermath of a relatively recent catastrophe which left the whole world plunged into darkness, "without form and void"—an expression "which may be geologically considered as designating the wreck and ruins of a former world."[18] Thus, "the work of the first morning of this new creation was the calling forth of light, from a temporary darkness which had overspread the ruins of the ancient earth."[19]

On this basis, Buckland is able to offer a new solution to an old interpretive problem, the fact that light is said to have originated before the creation of
sun, moon, and stars. These heavenly bodies have in fact shone upon the earth
since its original creation, but they were momentarily obscured by the "temporary darkness produced by an accumulation of dense vapours 'upon the face
of the deep' "—that is, by the after-effects of the catastrophe that brought the
previous geological era to a close. But now the gloom begins to lift:

> [A]n incipient dispersion of these vapours may have readmitted light
> to the earth, upon the first day, whilst the exciting cause of light was
> still obscured; and the further purification of the atmosphere upon
> the fourth day may have caused the sun and moon and stars to reap-
> pear in the firmament of heaven, to assume their new relations to
> the newly modified earth, and to the human race.[20]

Buckland is aware that this interpretation is only an approximation to what
Genesis actually says, requiring some concessions from those who maintain
the literal sense of the text. According to Genesis 1:16, "God *made* two great
lights," together with the stars; it is not said that God restored them to their former brightness after a period of temporary invisibility. With a few such adjust-
ments, however, the geological and the scriptural narratives may be blended
together into a harmonious whole.

There is an alternative possibility, which is to *reinterpret* the discrepant
features of the scriptural text in order to bring it into line with geology. As
Buckland notes, many theologians and geologists independently agree that
"the Days of the Mosaic Creation need not be understood to imply the same
length of time that is now occupied by a single revolution of the globe, but
successive periods, each of great extent."[21] Reinterpreted along these lines,
the scriptural text refers directly to the epochs of geological time. The problem is that, according to the geological record, the animal life of the fifth day
goes back just as far as the plant life of the third. For Buckland, the conflation
approach seems the better of the two options.

Whether by way of conflation or reinterpretation, harmonization invariably creates new problems even as it purports to resolve existing ones. Seeking
to accommodate the requirements of both natural scientists and exegetes, such
solutions fail to satisfy either party. From the standpoint of the natural scientist, Buckland's combined narrative assumes that the earth's history has been
punctuated by a series of universal catastrophes and that the present order
has come into being through discrete acts of creation—assumptions that were
already vulnerable within their mid-nineteenth-century context.[22] From the
standpoint of the exegete, it is implausible to differentiate the initial reference

to a creation of "heaven and earth" from the references to particular acts of creation that follow, which include the creation of "heaven" (the firmament, vv. 6–8), "earth" (the dry land, vv. 9–10), and the varied inhabitants of both spheres (vv. 11–28). The situation is no better if the "days" are understood as geological eras. The natural scientist will be puzzled not only by the late creation of animals in relation to plants, but also by the late creation of sun, moon, and stars. No lengthening of the days can make it plausible that fruit trees existed before the sun did. The exegete will wonder how the geological eras can still be said to have had an evening and a morning.[23]

Harmonization merely produces a new, artificial narrative that fails to respect the integrity of the discrete narratives and forces them into unnatural union. Rather than blending the narratives together, they should have been allowed to go their separate ways. Just as science needed to be liberated from scripture, so scripture needed to be liberated from science. Or rather, each party needed to be liberated not from the other per se but from the unnatural union that had been imposed upon them, in the mistaken belief that truth claims are all essentially homogeneous and subject to assessment by the same neutral criteria.

Conclusion: Darwin as Negative Theologian

From this perspective, it is possible to see Darwin's significance in a new light. Darwin's primary significance for theology is precisely that, unlike so many of his predecessors, he does *not* interpret Genesis. He is concerned only to interpret the complex text of the natural world and makes no attempt to read the natural world into Genesis or Genesis into the natural world. Genesis is left to theologians, who will perhaps succeed in restoring it to its natural habitat within the Christian narrative of "salvation" or final human well-being—incidentally learning from Darwin to avoid some of the serious interpretive errors that have clustered around this text in the past.

Admittedly, it is easy to mistake Darwin's significance. The reason is that he was almost immediately converted into an ideology (an -*ism* and, indeed, an -*isme* and an -*ismus*).[24] "Darwin" or "Darwinism" have come to symbolize an alleged triumph of modern science over ancient superstition, progress over reaction, rationality over religion. Within this totalitarian ideology, "Darwin" represents the *elimination* of "Genesis," himself embodying the doctrine of the survival of the fittest and the corresponding demise of the unfit. So far as possible, Darwin must be detached from his own problematic ideological legacy. In liberating science from scripture, he also liberates scripture from science—bringing to an end an unhappy union that prevented each party from articulating its own truth in its own way.

NOTES

1. Basil, *Hexaemeron*, I.2–3 (English trans., *The Nicene and Post-Nicene Fathers*, vol. 8 [repr., Grand Rapids, Mich.: Eerdmans, 1989], 51–107).

2. Trenchant, not to say blustering, renditions of the standard story are to be found in the work of Richard Dawkins, e.g., *The Blind Watchmaker* (London: Penguin, 1991). For Dawkins, there is a "Darwinian *world-view*," according to which a "slow, gradual, cumulative natural selection is the *ultimate* explanation for our existence" (318; italics added). The Genesis story is just the creation myth "that happened to have been adopted by one particular tribe of Middle Eastern herders" and "has no more special status than the belief of a particular West African tribe that the world was created from the excrement of ants" (315). Belief in the racial superiority of Europeans over Jews and Africans has a long history within Darwinism.

3. John Calvin, *Genesis* (1554; English trans., Edinburgh: Banner of Truth Trust, 1975), 86.

4. Calvin, *Genesis*, 86.

5. Calvin, *Genesis*, 86–87.

6. Calvin, *Genesis*, 85–86.

7. As in Descartes, it is God here who guarantees the reliability of the senses. Traditional philosophical skepticism is refuted theistically.

8. Biology provides most of the material for William Paley's *Natural Theology; or, Evidences of the Existence and Attributes of the Deity, Collected from the Appearances of Nature*, ed. Matthew D. Eddy and David Knight (1802; Oxford: Oxford University Press, 2006). Paley's famous "watch" analogy relates to the human body rather than to a "clockwork" universe (7–31).

9. *The Notebooks of Leonardo da Vinci*, 2 vols., ed. Edward MacCurdy (London: Jonathan Cape, 1938); excerpted in John Carey, ed., *The Faber Book of Science* (London: Faber, 1995), 3.

10. Voltaire, *Philosophical Dictionary* (1764; English trans., London: Penguin, 1972), 251 ("Inondation"). Voltaire also claims that a universal flood is demonstrably impossible "by the laws of gravitation, by the laws of fluids, by the insufficient quantity of water," and concludes ironically that, at every point, the narrative seems to require a miracle (251–252).

11. These figures derive from the Hebrew text. The Septuagint has figures a century higher for most of the ante- and postdiluvian patriarchs, with the result that patristic estimates date the creation earlier than Ussher does (5199 BC in Eusebius's view, accepted by Jerome).

12. See Gen.16:15, 17:24, 25:26, 47:9; Exod. 12:40; 1 Kings 6:1; and the chronological information about the kings of Israel and Judah in the books of Kings.

13. Ussher's scheme is developed in his *Annales veteris testamenti a prima mundi origine deducti* (1650), translated as *Annals of the Old Testament Deduced from the First*

Origins of the World (1658). On this, see especially Stephen Jay Gould's sympathetic account, *Eight Little Piggies: Reflections in Natural History* (London: Jonathan Cape, 1993), 181–193; and James Barr, "Why the World Was Created in 4004 BC: Archbishop Ussher and Biblical Chronology," *Bulletin of the John Rylands Library* 67 (1984–1985): 575–608.

14. The allusion is to the title and subtitle of a work published in 1823 by William Buckland (1784–1856), variously Reader in Mineralogy and Geology at the University of Oxford, Canon of Christ Church, Dean of Westminster, and Vicar of Islip. Other major works by Buckland have equally revealing titles: *Vindiciae Geologiae; or, The Connexion of Geology with Religion Explained* (1820, an inaugural lecture); *Geology and Mineralogy Considered with Reference to Natural Theology* (1836, the sixth of the *Bridgewater Treatises,* on which see further below). Most nineteenth-century "natural theology" is actually popular science. Darwin's work represents a shift in the way science is presented to the wider public.

15. See Augustine's *De Consensu Evangelistarum* (English trans. in *The Nicene and Post-Nicene Fathers: St. Augustine,* vol. 6 [repr., Grand Rapids, Mich.: Eerdmans, 1991], 65–236). This work established the methods followed by most subsequent harmonies of the Gospels.

16. *The Bridgewater Treatises on the Power, Wisdom and Goodness of God, as Manifested in the Creation. Treatise VI: Geology and Mineralogy Considered with Reference to Natural Theology,* 2 vols. (Philadelphia: Lea and Blanchard, 1841), I:18.

17. *Geology and Mineralogy,* I:26. Buckland acknowledges that the same position has recently been taken by Thomas Chalmers, but points out that he himself had first developed it in his inaugural lecture of 1820 (25–26).

18. *Geology and Mineralogy,* I:30.

19. *Geology and Mineralogy,* I:30.

20. *Geology and Mineralogy,* I:34.

21. *Geology and Mineralogy,* I:24.

22. Admittedly, speculations about sudden catastrophes have continued (did an asteroid impact wipe out the dinosaurs?).

23. For a contemporary critique of these theories from both scientific and exegetical perspectives, see C. W. Goodwin, "On the Mosaic Cosmogony," in *Essays and Reviews* (London: Parker & Son, 1860), 207–253. Goodwin's solution is to incorporate the Genesis narrative into the Lessing-derived "education of the human race" model, which underlies the whole of this celebrated work of mid-Victorian liberal theology. See, especially, Frederick Temple, "The Education of the World," with which the volume opens (1–49).

24. In *The Descent of Man* (1879), Darwin's footnotes are already littered with references to works on "Schopenhauer and Darwinism," "Darwinism and Divinity," "Philology and Darwinism," "Darwinism in Morals," "Darwinism and National Life," "La Théorie Darwinienne," "Le Darwinisme et l'Origine de l'Homme," "Der Mensch im Lichte der Darwin'sche Lehre," "Religion, Moral, &c., der Darwin'schen Art-Lehre," "Die Fortschritte des Darwinismus," and so on.

3

The Six Days of Creation According to the Greek Fathers

Andrew Louth

The title of this volume is *Reading Genesis after Darwin*. However, this chapter at least is rather about reading Genesis *before* Darwin, indeed long before Darwin, for I shall be looking at the ways in which Genesis was read in the first Christian millennium—by Greek Christians and by Jews. Why? you might ask. Has not Darwin made all the difference? Maybe. But there is a danger when we say that Darwin—or something else—has made *all the difference*, and that is the danger of imagining that those who want to ignore Darwin are simply continuing the traditional account of what Christians have always believed. In reality, interpreters of Genesis who ignore what Darwin has taught us are *reacting against* Darwin, and their reading of Genesis is as much affected by that reaction as is the reading of Genesis by those who are willing, or eager, to learn from Darwin. I want to suggest that it is indeed a foreign country that we enter when we read the fathers; they do things differently there—and think things differently there. It is, however, not a *completely* foreign country. For many of us, and certainly for those in the Eastern Orthodox tradition to which I belong, it is more like our homeland, of which the fathers speak as "of a country they have been to," as "eyewitnesses," as the Slavophile Ivan Kireevsky put it.[1] We may learn a lot by trying to accustom ourselves to their ways of thought—without denying the different world that we now inhabit.

The Tradition of Reflection on the Six Days of Creation

It is striking how frequently Christians in the early centuries reflected on the six days of creation—the *Hexaemeron*, as it appears in Greek.[2] It was a tradition inherited from the Jews: Philo's treatise *On the Making of the World* had a great influence on subsequent Christian exegesis. Eusebius, a fourth-century church historian, refers to eight commentaries on the creation narrative in Genesis, most now lost, which date mainly from the end of the second century of the Christian era. Origen, the great third-century theologian, perhaps the greatest of all Christian exegetes, wrote a commentary and homilies on Genesis; of the commentary, only fragments survive, and in his homilies he moves through Genesis pretty quickly, only in the first homily discussing the six days. The later Greek tradition is dominated by Basil's *Homilies on the Hexaemeron*, which will be our main concern in this chapter; Gregory of Nyssa's *On the Making of Human Kind* is explicitly supplementary. There are many discussions of the Genesis account of creation by other Greek thinkers, though Basil's tends to cast a shadow over his successors. This reflection on the Genesis creation account is not at all confined to the Greek tradition. One of the longest and most comprehensive commentaries on Genesis, including the *Hexaemeron*, was composed by St. Ephrem, Basil's contemporary, who wrote in Syriac, the form of Aramaic spoken in Syria, and there are several later Syriac theologians who discuss the six days. The fifth-century Armenian writer Eznik of Kolb has a good deal of discussion of the creation account in his treatise *On God*. Exposition of Genesis was especially rich in the Latin tradition. The fourth-century Ambrose of Milan was not the first, and Augustine, on whom Ambrose made such an impression while he was still a rhetor, five times made an attempt at an exposition of the Genesis creation account. Whereas Basil's single account seems to have hampered later Greek reflection, Augustine's five different accounts only stimulated further reflection; in an article surveying the tradition of hexaemeral commentary, the late Père Yves Congar listed nearly forty Latin commentators between Augustine and the end of the Middle Ages (including the Venerable Bede and the twelfth-century Laurence of Durham), and that list is certainly not exhaustive.[3]

Theophilos of Antioch

The earliest Christian account of the six days of creation is found in the defence of Christianity written by a second-century bishop of Antioch, Theophilos.

The time and context give us some clues as to why reflection on Genesis seems to have been so urgent. Theophilos was one of the second-century "apologists," that is, defenders of Christianity, who were concerned about the threat of persecution the Christians faced from the Roman authorities. Most of these defences, or apologies, were addressed directly to the emperor; Theophilos's *Apology*, unusually, is addressed to some presumably high-ranking Roman official called Autolycus. Theophilos begins by meeting the challenge "Show me your God" with the forthright response "Show me your man, and I will show you my God." He goes on to affirm that only the eyes of the soul can see God and only the ears of the heart can hear him, but these eyes and ears are clouded by sin, and so, as he puts it, "O man, your ungodliness brings darkness upon you and you cannot see God." The sins that Theophilos lists are mostly moral failings, but as his account develops, it becomes plain that there are also intellectual failings that darken the eyes of the soul, ways of understanding the human situation and the nature of the world that cut one off from God. Such ideas include that the universe's existence is simply a matter of chance and that human beings can therefore find no meaning in this life. Or—the apparent opposite—that what happens in the world is not at all a matter of chance but is ruled by an iron necessity, fate, εἱμαρμένη, which some Christians liked to think derived from the word for a chain, εἱρμός, suggesting that humans were inexorably bound to their fate. The second century, too, was the period of what scholars have for a couple of centuries called gnosticism, with its ideas that the universe was the product of a god either incompetent or malevolent, and thus flawed or actually evil, with salvation being seen as escape from the evil meshes of the world and the clutches of an ill-disposed god. Such ideas, too, would, for Theophilos, blind the soul and prevent it from seeing God. This is the context in which Theophilos's account of the six days of creation in the second book of his *Apology* fits—and I expect the same is true of the lost second-century accounts of the *Hexaemeron*: it was reflection on Genesis that provided an accurate account of the nature of the universe, an account that disclosed, rather than obscured or occluded altogether, the nature of God.

But what God is revealed in Theophilos's reading of the Genesis account of creation? The answer is less obvious than we might suppose, for what Theophilos found in Genesis was an account of creation by God, who created out of nothing. We are so accustomed to thinking that creation means creation out of nothing that we perhaps find this obvious, our only doubts being whether Genesis, derived from a genre of Near Eastern creation myths that presuppose no such thing, has such a radical notion of creation. That Theophilos reads Genesis like that seems unsurprising; one cannot expect him to have known about ancient myths of creation. But, in the second century, when Christians and Jews were a small countercultural minority, most people thought very differently. The idea of God as Creator, fashioning the universe ex nihilo, was a new and revolutionary idea, perhaps just as striking as the Gospel of Jesus Christ and, indeed, an integral part of it, for if one did not grasp that the Father of the Lord Jesus Christ was the Creator of the universe, who had indeed created the universe through his Son, Jesus Christ, then one could never grasp the universal significance of Christ's death and resurrection. A little more than a century after Theophilos, St. Athanasios, the great bishop of Alexandria, twice at the beginning of his treatise *On the Incarnation* asserts that, if we are to discuss the doctrine of the incarnation, "it is necessary first to speak about the creation of the universe and its creator, God, so that in this way it may be seen to be fitting that its renewal was effected by the Word who created it in the beginning."[4] And along with the idea of God as Creator went the conviction that God created everything *out of nothing, ex nihilo,* a concept of which Theophilos is one of the earliest witnesses. It is this conviction—that God created the universe out of nothing—that these early Christians found expressed in the Genesis account of creation, and that was why it was so important to them.

Such is the importance of this notion of creation that we need to dwell on it for a bit. Though Christians and Jews read in Genesis an account of creation out of nothing, they recognized that it was no more than implicit in that text and knew that there is very little explicit support for the doctrine of creation ex nihilo in the scriptures. This is clear in the evident embarrassment of the early Christian thinkers who, searching for biblical texts to support creation ex nihilo, find themselves reduced to only two scriptural texts to support the idea. The first is 2 Maccabees 7:28, where the mother of the Maccabean martyrs, by tradition Solomonia, encourages her youngest son to accept martyrdom bravely, by asserting that "it was not out of what already existed [ἐξ οὐκ ὄντων] that God made" the "heaven and the earth," so in dying her son is entrusting his life to the one who gave him it and who "will in his mercy give life and breath back to you again" in the resurrection (2 Macc. 7:23). The second is a passage from the Shepherd of Hermas, Mandates 1, where we read: "first of all believe that God is one . . . who brought everything into being from what does not exist [ἐκ τοῦ μὴ ὄντος]." Such a slender scriptural basis for such an important doctrine suggests that we are looking for the wrong thing, looking for a clearly defined concept, rather than an overwhelming conviction of the reality of God. It is striking that the first explicit assertion of creation out of nothing in the Judeo-Christian tradition—in the passage from 2 Maccabees just quoted—occurs in the context of martyrdom and resurrection: the doctrine is presented as something entailed by belief and trust in God, to whom one can commit one's life to the point of dying. Solomonia's youngest son did not accept martyrdom because he believed in creation out of nothing, though he did, but because he believed in God, the source of life. Strictly speaking, the doctrine of creation out of nothing is not a cosmological doctrine, but a consequence—or, really, a part—of Jewish and Christian belief in God, so fundamental that in the scriptures it is mostly taken for granted or expressed almost parenthetically, as when the apostle Paul confesses his faith in "one God, the Father, from whom are all things and for whom we exist, and one Lord, Jesus Christ, through whom are all things and through whom we exist" (1 Cor. 8:6). But in the second century, Christians found themselves in a religious milieu in which could be taken for granted neither the notion of a transcendent, all-caring God nor the idea of creation as owing its existence solely to him. It was this they found in Genesis, and for this reason they so readily reflected on the account there of creation. We might reflect, too, that we now find ourselves once again in such a world, where the idea of creation, with its message that existence is a gift, is barely recognized.

Theophilos begins his exposition of Genesis thus:

> In the first place, in complete harmony they [that is, the prophets, the scriptural writers] taught us that he made everything out of nothing [ἐξ οὐκ ὄντων]. For there was nothing coeval with God; he was his own place; he lacked nothing; he "existed before the ages" (Ps. 54:20). He wished to make man so that he might be known by him; for him, then, he prepared the world. For he who is created has needs, but he who is uncreated lacks nothing.[5]

Along with the idea that God created the world out of nothing, Theophilos emphasizes that God made the world as a preparation for making humankind, and the purpose of creation is that God might be known by the human creation. The centrality of the human to the Christian notion of creation is something we shall encounter further on. These ideas are held together by Theophilos through his conviction that the universe was made by wisdom, which is expressed in the order and beauty of the cosmos and which inspires humans to seek the Creator through the creation—wisdom under its aspect of teeming variety, ἡ πολυποίκιλος σοφία τοῦ Θεοῦ (Eph. 3:10). For Theophilos, this point is made in two complementary ways: first, his constant sense of the wonder of the cosmos, and then second, the way in which he sees significance in the ordering of the cosmos. So he exclaims at the beginning of his account:

> No one can adequately set forth the whole exegesis and plan of the six days' creation, even if he were to have ten thousand mouths

and ten thousand tongues. Not even if he were to live ten thousand years, continuing in this life, would he be competent to say anything adequately in regard to these matters, because of the "surpassing greatness" (Eph. 1:19) and the "riches of the Wisdom of God" (Rom. 11:33) to be found in this account of the six days just quoted.[6]

It is perhaps worth noting, parenthetically, that, despite the way in which Theophilos lards his account of creation with disparaging references to the Greek poets and philosophers, he can't prevent himself from alluding to Homer's account of the massed Achaean army, which Homer says he could not recount "had he even ten tongues, or ten mouths."[7] In the account of Genesis itself, Theophilos draws attention to the significance of numbers, to the way the world is described in the likeness of the sea, the way in which the two great luminaries symbolize God and humankind, and how the three days prior to the creation of the luminaries contain an allusion to the Christian τριάς, or Trinity. Theophilos is also the first to refer to God in this way. He sees other analogies in the accounts of the creation of the fish and animals. Creation is, for Theophilos, a great code, which, if we interpret it properly, discloses the nature and ways of God; it contains, as he says repeatedly, a "great mystery."

Basil on the *Hexaemeron*

The finest account of the *Hexaemeron*, the six days, in the Greek tradition—so great that it eclipsed most of the earlier accounts and encouraged later Greek expositors simply to repeat what he had said—is that composed by St. Basil the Great toward the end of his life (he died on 1 January 379). There are nine homilies which end with a promise to account for the creation of human kind on the sixth day. His brother Gregory of Nyssa clearly thought that Basil had never got round to fulfilling that promise, as he provided an account of the creation of human kind to supplement his brother's homilies, though there survive a couple of sermons—quite separate from the nine of the *Hexaemeron* in the manuscript tradition—often attributed to Basil.

From Basil's references in the homilies themselves, it would appear that the first four and the last four were delivered on two pairs of days—two homilies, one in the morning and one in the evening, each day—while the remaining homily was delivered separately on some day in between. All the sermons were delivered during Lent, and presumably at the beginning of the season, as it seems to have been an ancient tradition to read the whole of Genesis during Lent. So, on the first day, Basil discussed the events of "day one" (he specifically makes the point that Genesis says not the "first day," ἡμέρα πρώτη, but "day one," ἡμέρα μία), expounding the creation of heaven and earth in the morning and of light in the evening. On the next day, he discussed the events of the second day, the morning sermon concerning the creation of the firmament and the evening sermon the gathering together of the waters. The fifth sermon discussed the third day of creation: the creation of the plants. Then there followed another two-day set, discussing the fourth day, the creation of the luminaries of heaven, in the morning, and the events of the fifth day, the creation of the reptiles and fish, in the evening. The following day, Basil returned to the reptiles in the morning and went on to discuss the birds, also a work of the fifth day, and then in the evening, he turned to the events of the sixth day, the creation of the earthly animals, culminating in the creation of humankind, about which he makes some preliminary remarks, promising to treat the subject fully on another day. As mentioned above, it is unclear whether he ever got around to fulfilling that promise. I've spelled out the liturgical setting of the homilies because it seems to me significant, as we shall see.

Basil's starting point and emphasis is much the same as that of Theophilos. The account is about creation, and creation by God. Basil brings this out by repeating the first words of Genesis and developing them in different ways—a rhetorical figure known as anaphora.

> "In the beginning God created ['Εν ἀρχῇ ἐποίησεν ὁ Θεός] heaven and earth." The wonder of the notion brings my discourse to a standstill! What shall I say first? How shall I begin my discourse?...[This is another rhetorical figure known as adynaton, but I won't continue with the rhetorical analysis; just remember that we are reading one of the best rhetoricians of his day.]
>
> "In the beginning God created heaven and earth." Therefore those who think that all that exists is without government or direction, but borne about by chance, are revealed as infected by the deceit of atheism....
>
> "In the beginning God created." What an excellent order of words! He puts "beginning" [ἀρχή] first, lest anyone think that [the cosmos] is without beginning. Then he adds "he created," to show that what has been made is only the tiniest part of the divine power....
>
> "In the beginning God created"—the blessed nature, goodness without envy, beloved by everyone that partakes of reason, the much-longed-for beauty, the beginning of beings, the source of life, the intellectual light, the unapproachable wisdom: this it is that "in the beginning created heaven and earth."[8]

All through his homilies, Basil conveys his sense of the majesty and glory of God, revealed in the wonder and beauty of the cosmos. When, at the beginning of his discussion of the fourth day of creation, he considers the two great luminaries created on that day, he exclaims:

> If sometimes on a clear night you look up at the inexpressible beauties of the stars, you get an idea of the maker of the universe, of who it is who has adorned the heavens with the variety of these flowers, and how in these visible bodies the serene necessity of their movements surpasses what is merely pleasant. And again if in the day you consider with sober thought the wonders of the day, and through what is seen make an analogy with what is unseen, you will be ready as a hearer, fit to join the august and blessed assembly.[9]

The "blessed assembly" means the church in Caesarea, where Basil was preaching, and also, I believe, the assembly of the saints. Commentators often remark on what they feel are the liturgical cadences of Basil's language. There is another striking liturgical passage a few lines later, following further reflection on the wonder of creation:

> If we have learnt these things, we shall come to understand ourselves, to know God, to worship the creator, to serve the Master, to glorify the Father, to love what he gives for our nourishment, to reverence our benefactor, and we shall not cease to worship the one who provides for our present life and that which is to come, who through the wealth already procured for us can be trusted in what has been promised, and through experience of what is present assures us of what is longed for.[10]

Compare that with this:

> Master, the One who Is, Lord God, Father Almighty, who are to be worshipped, it is truly right and fitting, and becomes the majesty of your holiness to praise you, to hymn you, to bless you, to worship you, to thank you, to glorify you, who alone are true God; to offer you with a broken heart and a spirit of humility this our reasonable worship. For it is you who have granted us the knowledge of your truth. And who is able to tell of all your acts of power? To make all your praises heard or to recount all your wonders at every moment?[11]

This passage comes from the beginning of the eucharistic prayer, the Anaphora, ascribed, probably correctly, to St. Basil himself.[12] If we recognize the liturgical cadences in Basil's glorying in creation, we see more deeply how, in this hymn of glory, Basil is seeking to inculcate in his congregation a spirit of thanks-giving as the fundamental disposition of the creatures to their Creator and, indeed, to all life.

But what kind of an account of creation do we find in Basil's hexaemeral homilies? This is a question Basil himself addresses explicitly several times. Twice, he insists that the Genesis account must be interpreted literally, not allegorically. First, when he comes to discuss the waters separated by the fir-mament in verse 6, he objects to those who, contrary to the mind of the church, resort to allegory and see in the reference to "waters" some figurative language for "spiritual and incorporeal powers."[13] And again, at the beginning of the ninth homily, he returns to his attack on allegory and remarks that "when I hear 'green herb,' I understand green herb, and so with plant, fish, wild animal and domestic animal: I take all these as they are said."[14] Allegorical interpreta-tion of these terms he dismisses as the "fancy of dreams and old wives' tales."[15] What he has in mind, doubtless, is the way Origen is said to have interpreted Genesis in terms of an initial creation of spiritual beings which turned away from God, leading to the Fall—into bodies in the material cosmos. Origen's surviving homily on the six days—the first in the Genesis series—is not so explicit but does interpret the waters as spiritual beings and finds in the animal creation allegories of human behaviour, as indeed Theophilos had.[16] Basil's point is that the account of the six days of creation is about the origin of the created order: it gives an account of the created cosmos. Allegorizing the account draws attention away from the repeated insistence that this cosmos was created by God in all its order and variety and that it was created good. To find here allegories of spiritual beings or of the way in which fallen human behaviour can be regarded as bestial or reptilian—even if all of this is true and edifying—draws attention away from the point of the creation narrative: to proclaim the Creator and the goodness of his creation.

But it would be unwise to claim Basil as an advocate of something like what we think of as the historical critical method. Basil is not averse to allegory; it is just that here, with the example of Origen to warn us, allegory may well miss the real point of the creation narrative. Nor does it mean that Basil regards the Genesis account as telling us all we need to know about creation. This point can be illustrated in two ways. First of all, one motive that Origen and others had for allegorizing aspects of the Genesis story was in order to get it to tell a fuller story. What about the creation of the angelic beings, for instance? There is nothing explicit in the Genesis account, and yet they appear in the rest of the scriptures, and no one, Jew or Christian, in Basil's time thought that they were uncreated. Origen finds them referred to in the waters above the firmament and supports this interpretation by referring to Psalm 148:4, which calls on the "water above the firmament" to praise God. Ordinary water cannot praise God, Origen and others reasoned; this must be a figurative way of referring to the angelic hosts above the heavenly firmament. Basil will not admit this interpretation, but that does not mean that he did not believe in an angelic creation. He is quite clear that there was a creation of the angels, but the angelic world is "beyond time, eternal and everlasting"; the formation of the angelic realm is "not related" (ἀνιστόρητον) in Genesis because it is unsuitable for those only just initiated in the faith; it belongs instead to the unwritten tradition of the church.[17] Whatever Basil means by avoiding allegory, he is no advocate of any biblical literalism.

Second, how then does Basil expound the very spare account of the creation that we find in Genesis? What he does is appeal to what, for him, was contemporary science. He explains in the first homily that when it says that God created heaven and earth, by "earth" we are to understand all four elements of the cosmos (earth, fire, air, and water), and he explains the order, harmony, balance, and beauty of the cosmos by showing how the opposites represented by the elements—earth being cold and dry, fire hot and dry, air hot and wet, and water cold and wet—are held in tension by God's wisdom.[18] An even more striking example of the way in which Basil and his brother Gregory read the Genesis account in terms of contemporary Greek science occurs in the very first chapter of Gregory's *On the Making of Human Kind*, which begins by quoting Genesis 2:4—"This is the book of the coming into being of heaven and earth"—and then goes on to describe what we would call the Ptolemaic system of the cosmos, with the earth at the centre surrounded by celestial spheres rotating at fearsome speeds.[19] In the homily on the creation of the great heavenly luminaries, Basil discusses astronomical and calendrical matters and takes the opportunity to make clear the church's opposition to astrology.[20] When he discusses the creation of plants, reptiles, fish, birds, and animals, he produces lots of information about their different kinds and habits drawn from some contemporary natural history, and he occasionally draws moral lessons.[21] The notes in the critical edition are full of references to classical parallels—to the elder Pliny, for instance, not that Basil could have used Pliny's *Natural History*, but because it is the most extensive to survive from antiquity, and also to Aristotle and, interestingly, to the great medical doctor Galen, both of whose works Basil may well have known and used. When he comes to discuss human beings, his picture, as we shall see, draws heavily on Plato's *Timaeus*. For Basil, there was no opposition between scripture and science; he used contemporary science to fill in the bare outline of the cosmos found in Genesis. He can do this because he is quite clear that the scriptural account is not a scientific account. It is no criticism of Moses, he remarks, that he did not clarify whether the earth is a sphere, a cylinder, a disc, or like a great basket, hollowed out in the middle, or that he did not give the measurement of the circumference of the earth. All these things, interesting though they might be, are irrelevant to Moses's purpose: to proclaim God as Creator, the cosmos as his good creation, and the place of the human in all of this.[22]

Let us look now at three points on which Basil lays some stress: first, his understanding of the "beginning," the ἀρχή, of creation; second, how he conceives the cosmos as a whole; and third, his insistence on the goodness of creation.

Basil on the "Beginning" (ἀρχή)

Basil devotes a good deal of the first homily to discussing the beginning of creation, the moment of creation. The words "in the beginning" mean "in this temporal beginning" or "in the beginning of time"—which is why Genesis does not tell us about the creation of the angelic realm, which is outside time. But Basil faces a philosophical puzzle here, with which others—St. Augustine, John Philoponos, St. Thomas Aquinas—also wrestled. How does the eternal God, who is beyond time, create in time? Or, to quote a poet, where is "The point of intersection of the timeless / with time"? T. S. Eliot was concerned in *Four Quartets* with how time-bound beings discern this point. Basil is rather looking at it from the other side. He is clearly anxious to avoid the kind of anthropomorphism that would effectively make God a temporal being, intervening in the temporal sequence from alongside, as it were. To solve this, Basil draws on contemporary mathematical thought, the kind of speculation that goes back to Pythagoras, but which had experienced a revival among the Neoplatonists such as Plotinos. He suggests that "the beginning" refers to "something momentary and timeless belonging to creation";[23] it is worth noting that Basil's phrase includes no noun—it is something that escapes ostensive definition—and he goes on to suggest that this beginning is "indivisible and without extension," initiating what follows, but not part of it. "For, just as the beginning of a road is not yet a road, nor the beginning of a house a house, so the beginning of time is not yet time, not even the smallest part of it."[24] The analogy that lies behind his illustrations is the idea of a mathematical series, the same analogy the Neoplatonists used to illustrate procession from the One. This beginning, not itself part of the series, is, in this context, "the point of intersection of the timeless / with time." Basil treats this question very briefly—he is preaching, not giving a lecture—but he points the way that other Christian thinkers would follow.

The Nature of the Cosmos

When Basil thinks of the cosmos as a whole, he is struck especially by the way it all hangs together, by its harmony, its interconnectedness. In this, he is picking up a theme from the wisdom literature of the Greek Bible, where we read, "Wisdom is more mobile than any motion; because of her pureness she pervades and penetrates all things.... She reaches mightily from one end of the earth to the other, and she orders all things sweetly" (Wisd. 7:24, 8:1). The way Basil puts this perception, however, recalls the language of Plato's *Timaeus* and the Stoics, for he speaks of the parts of the cosmos being "bound together by a certain unbreakable ordinance of love in one communion and harmony, so that the most distant parts are united by sympathy."[25]

The Harmony and Goodness of the Cosmos

It is this harmony that manifests the goodness of creation. At the end of the account of each day (even the second day in the Septuagint), the Genesis account remarks that God saw that it was good—ὅτι καλόν—good, not in the moral sense, but fine, beautiful. Basil often comments on this, and he always remarks that this does not mean that it is pleasing to the eyes or adorned with some human beauty, "for beauty is that which according to the principles of art realizes the end intended."[26] It is an austere, not a comforting beauty that Basil sees in God's creation. This austerity manifests itself in another way. Basil will not have it that the darkness and the abyss spoken of in Genesis are substantial realities made by God, for that would make God the author of evil and let humans off the hook, for they could lay the blame on God for the evil in their lives. For Basil, as with Plato, "the blame is with the one who chooses, God is blameless."[27] The darkness spoken of in Genesis is not substantial; it is a matter of shadows that cut off the light—similarly with the abyss. Basil begins his discussion of all this with a very direct address to his congregation: "Don't search for evil outside, nor imagine that the origin of evil is some nature, but let each of us recognize that we are ourselves the source of the evil we find in ourselves." And after saying that, we can choose "whether to master our passions and give in to the appeals of pleasure, to contain our anger or to raise our hand against the one who irritates us, to tell the truth or to lie, to have an equable and moderate character or be overcome by pride and pretence." He tells his congregation: "for of all these you are the master, do not seek their origin in another, but recognize that what is properly evil has its origins in misfortunes to which we have freely assented."[28] "The fault, dear Brutus, lies in ourselves..." It is not surprising that Basil actually names the Manichees in these homilies, though with reference to their belief that everything has a soul, for he saw in dualism, not least theirs, a fundamental slur against the Creator, with the most insidious consequences for human moral endeavour.

The Place of the Human in the Cosmos

Everyone knows that in Genesis we have two creation accounts: one in chapter 1, which tells the story of the six days of creation, and another in chapter 2, which focuses on the human creation and tells the story of the creation of Adam and Eve, their being placed in paradise and their disobedience and exclusion from paradise, then continuing with a history of the human race. Nowadays, scholars tend to see two different accounts that have been laid side by side—though that still leaves the question as to why they were placed together: it was surely not oversight. The fathers read the two accounts as a single literary whole, indeed, as the composition of Moses, to whom the law had been revealed. Read like that, the creation of human kind seems pivotal: the six days lead up to the creation of human kind, which chapter 2 then develops. In the homilies on the six days, Basil did not get to treat the creation of human kind properly; in the last homily, as we have already seen, he sketched out what he promised to treat in more detail later on. But the outline of his account is clear, and I shall close by briefly considering it.

He first mentions humankind at the very beginning of his exposition of the sixth day, which begins with God saying, "Let the earth bring forth a living soul," and goes on to contrast human beings, who stand upright, with the animals, which are bent down to the ground:

> The earthly animals are bowed down towards the ground, but
> the heavenly plant, the human being, is different, as much by the
> form of his bodily fashioning as by the dignity of his soul. What
> is the attitude of the four-footed animals? Their head is bent down
> to the earth, they look at their bellies, and they seek what pleases
> it in any way. Your head [Basil says, addressing his congregation]
> is lifted up to heaven. Your eyes look on high, as if you would be
> dishonouring yourself with the passions of the flesh, if you served
> the belly and what is beneath it, "being compared to the beasts
> without understanding and becoming like them" (Ps. 48:13 LXX).
> But your care should be "to seek what is on high, where Christ is"

(cf. Col. 3:1), be in your mind above earthly things. As your body
has been fashioned, so should you order your way of life: "let your
citizenship be in the heavens!" (Phil. 3:20). Your true fatherland
is Jerusalem on high, your fellow-citizens and compatriots are
"the first-born, whose names are written in the heavens" (Heb.
12:23).[29]

Despite all the allusions to the New Testament, the basis of Basil's comparison here—the human as a heavenly plant, with its roots in the heavens—is
Plato, at the end of the *Timaeus*.[30] Indeed, Basil's understanding of what it is
to be human, like his understanding of the cosmos, is a blending of Genesis
and the *Timaeus*, or even a reading of Genesis within a universe of discourse
derived from the *Timaeus*. He combines, as do most of the Greek fathers, the
biblical idea of the human as created in the image of God with the idea from
the *Timaeus* that the human is a little cosmos, μικρὸς κόσμος, so that the structure of the cosmos is reflected in miniature in the human, while humans find
their own structure writ large in the cosmos. Basil does not accept the idea of
Plato's that the cosmos is a living being, nor the implication drawn by many
interpreters of Plato's *Timaeus* that this correspondence provides a justification for astrology, but the idea that the fate of the cosmos is implicated in the
human, that the human is the bond of the cosmos, σύνδεσμος τοῦ κόσμου,
is an idea that Basil shares with most of the Greek fathers. Humans fulfil
this role because they are in the image of God, and so fulfil a role in the cosmos analogous to that of God—they are not the Creator himself, but those
through whom the cosmos is bound together in that communion and harmony, in that συμπάθεια, that we remarked on earlier. For this reason, Basil
lays stress on the significant role that human kind has been given in relation
to the cosmos—to care for it, to be a veritable shepherd of being—and what
this entails for humans themselves: fundamentally, the requirement to "know
themselves," which, Basil says, is "in reality the most difficult thing of all."
This privileged—and demanding—role for human kind is signalled in the
Genesis account by the fact that God is presented as *considering* the creation of
humans. Instead of simply saying "Let there be..." light, a firmament, or saying "Let the waters bring forth creeping things and birds," or "Let the earth
bring forth a living soul," God says, "Let us make human kind in accordance
with our image and our likeness" (Gen. 1:26), and only then does the account
go on to say that "God made human kind in accordance with his image" (Gen.
1:27). The fact of God's considering, the allusion to the persons of the Trinity
that Basil detects in the use of the plural—all of this invests the creation of
the human with a solemnity that is not found in the making of the rest of

creation. Furthermore, *what* God considers is to make in the human an image of himself: that, again, draws attention to something special in the creation of human kind.

To go on to consider that in any detail would be another chapter—or several! And it would take us beyond the account of the six days, since what is meant by the human is unfolded in a more discursive way in the second chapter of Genesis. Let me conclude by indicating a few ways in which the fathers' consideration of the six days of creation—and especially in St. Basil's account, although a pre-Darwinian account—might still have something from which we may learn. First and most obviously, Basil is not afraid of what was, for him, contemporary science. It does not occur to him to oppose the Genesis account to that commonly accepted by the science of his day, though he is not afraid to argue against philosophical positions that then, as now, scientists thought were entailed by their discoveries and convictions. Curiously, one of the places where Basil draws the line is over the tendency of a complete scientific account to advance a deterministic view of the cosmos. For him, on the contrary, the cosmos is the result of God's free creation, and within that creation, there are beings created to be free, in the image of their Creator. Second, and consequent on that fundamental intuition, is his constant awareness of the wonder of creation. Out of that sense of wonder there grows a sense of creation as gift and life as gift, so that life in God's creation is always informed by a sense of thanksgiving, εὐχαριστία. Third, we find in Basil's exposition of the created order a sense of humility. Basil knows a lot, and rejoices in that knowledge, but he is still tentative, open to correction, aware that there are problems to which he has, as yet, no convincing answer. Finally, despite the limited nature of his knowledge, St. Basil has a conviction of the connectedness of everything created, a connectedness rooted in the creative energies of God, in the one word, or logos, of God, in whom all the diverse meanings, or logoi, of creation find unity and harmony (an idea that would be later developed by one of the greatest of the Greek fathers, St. Maximus the Confessor). That sense of wholeness has been fragmented by the dramatic advances of the sciences. Yet there still remains a widespread nostalgia for wholeness and interconnectedness, a nostalgia that finds many unhealthy outlets in the modern world in cults and philosophies that repudiate the advance of science and seek a sense of wholeness in various esoteric practices and beliefs. We need some way of recapturing that sense of wholeness, and the Fathers and St. Basil, unafraid and unembarrassed in their acknowledgment of any true knowledge and also unshakably confident in God's creative word, may still perhaps help us to recover some sense of the wholeness of God's manifold creation.

NOTES

1. I. V. Kireevsky, *Otryvki*, in *Polnoe Sobranie Sochineniy*, vol. 2 (Moscow, 1861; repr., Ann Arbor, Mich.: 1983), 340, 334 (English trans., *On Spiritual Unity: A Slavophile Reader*, trans. and ed. Boris Jakim and Robert Bird [Hudson, N.Y.: Lindisfarne, 1998], 288, 283).

2. There is relatively little secondary literature on the subject. Apart from the article by Congar, cited in the next note, see *In Principio: Interprétations des premiers versets de la Genèse* (Paris: Études Augustiniennes, 1973); J. Zahlten, *Creatio mundi: Darstellungen des sechs Schöpfungstage und naturwissenschaftliches Welt im Mittelalter*, Stuttgarter Beiträge zur Geschichte und Politik 13 (1979); D. S. Wallace-Hadrill, *The Greek Patristic View of Nature* (Manchester, England: Manchester University Press, 1968).

3. See Yves-M. J. Congar, O.P., "Le thème de *Dieu-créateur* et les explications de l'Hexaméron dans la tradition chrétienne," in *L'Homme devant Dieu: Mélanges offerts au père Henri de Lubac*, 3 vols. (Paris: Aubier, 1964), 1:189–222 ("inventaire litéraire" on 215–222).

4. Athanasios, *De Incarnatione* 1, in Athanasius, *Contra Gentes and De Incarnatione*, ed. and trans. Robert W. Thomson (Oxford: Clarendon, 1971), 136f. (trans. slightly modified).

5. Theophilos, *Ad Autolycum* II.10, in Theophilus of Antioch, *Ad Autolycum*, ed. and trans. Robert M. Grant (Oxford: Clarendon, 1970), 38–41 (trans. somewhat modified).

6. Theophilos, *Ad Autolycum* II.12 (Grant, 44f.).

7. Homer, *Iliad* II.489.

8. Basil, *Hom. in Hexaemeron* I.2, in Basile de Césarée, *Homélies sur l'Hexaéméron*, ed. with French trans. by Stanislas Giet (Paris: Cerf, 1968), 92–96.

9. *Hexam.* VI.1 (Giet, 326).

10. *Hexam.* VI.1 (Giet, 328).

11. *The Divine Liturgy of Our Father among the Saints: Basil the Great*, trans. Archimandrite Ephrem (Manchester, England: St Andrew's Press, 2001), 27.

12. Or perhaps not. Since writing that, I have met and discovered the work of the liturgical scholar Gabriela Winkler. Her doubts seem convincing; see Winkler, *Die Basilius-Anaphora: Edition der beiden armenischen Redaktionen und der relevanten Fragmente, Übersetzung und Zusammenschau aller Versionen im Licht der orientalischen Überlieferungen* (Rome: Edizioni Orientalia Christiana, 2005). It remains that the Vulgate text of the Anaphora has been influenced by St. Basil's language.

13. *Hexam.* III.9 (Giet, 236).

14. *Hexam.* IX.1 (Giet, 480).

15. *Hexam.* III.9 (Giet, 236).

16. Origen, *Hom. in Genesim* 1.2, 9–11, in *Origenis Omnia Opera*, ed. Lommatsch (Berlin, 1837), VII:108, 116–119; and cf. Theophilos, *Ad Autolycum* 16f. (Grant, 52–54).

17. *Hexam.* I.5 (Giet, 104). For Basil's notion of unwritten tradition, see *On the Holy Spirit* 27.66, in Basile de Césarée, *Sur le Saint-Esprit*, ed. with French trans. by Benoît Pruche, O.P. (Paris: Cerf, 1968), 478–486.

18. *Hexam.* I.7, 10 (Giet, 116–118, 126–130).
19. Gregory of Nyssa, *De opificio hominis* 1 (PG 44.128C–132C).
20. *Hexam.* VI.4–8 (Giet, 342–370).
21. *Hexam.* VII, VIII, IX.1–5 (Giet, 390–510).
22. *Hexam.* IX.1 (Giet, 480–482).
23. *Hexam.* I.6 (Giet, 110).
24. *Hexam.* I.6 (Giet, 112).
25. *Hexam.* II.2 (Giet, 148); cf. Plato, *Tim.* 32BC.
26. *Hexam.* III.10 (Giet, 240).
27. Plato, *Republic* X.617E.
28. *Hexam.* II.5 (Giet, 160).
29. *Hexam.* IX.2 (Giet, 486–488).
30. Plato, *Tim.* 90AB.

4

The Hermeneutics of Reading
Genesis after Darwin

Richard S. Briggs

In David Lodge's *Small World*, Persse McGarrigle, a young lecturer in "Modern English," finds himself in an awkward position at an academic conference and decides to annoy a morose senior scholar by pretending that his M.A. thesis, which was on Shakespeare's influence on T. S. Eliot, was actually about the influence of T. S. Eliot on Shakespeare. "Well, what I try to show," says Persse, "is that we can't avoid reading Shakespeare through the lens of T. S. Eliot's poetry. I mean, who can read *Hamlet* today without thinking of 'Prufrock'?"[1] This is immediately greeted as a more interesting idea, and a publisher snaps him up, leaving Persse with the task of having to write a nonexistent thesis.

In this whimsical way, Lodge, whose novels in general offer narrative accounts of his own commanding work in literary theory, sets up a dynamic which matches quite closely the hermeneutical task of reading Genesis after Darwin. One can imagine Persse as a theologian, asking: "I mean, who can read Genesis today without thinking of *The Descent of Man*?"

Nevertheless, this is a hermeneutical task which does require careful attention to the issue of how to pose proper and productive questions to texts in contexts other than their own. The goal of this chapter is to analyze this hermeneutical issue and to map out what is at stake in the reading of a text (Genesis) in a context (after Darwin) which is not integrally related to it in terms of the text's own original production. We shall suggest that this is not a new dynamic for biblical scholars, who have a great deal of experience in dealing with a strikingly similar question, namely: what are the issues raised by reading the early chapters of Genesis in the context of other ancient Near Eastern accounts of creation, origins, and flood?

This is not the place for an analysis of the difference between "hermeneutics" and "interpretation," but perhaps we can proceed on the working understanding that hermeneutics consists not least in the negotiation of agendas—typically, competing agendas—held by different stakeholders in the text. The question "what does it mean to read text A in context B?" is thus its home territory. In the process, we will of course suggest interpretive moves with regard to (the early chapters of) Genesis, but the focus is on the interdisciplinary question of "what does it mean to read Genesis after Darwin?"

Genesis at the Time of Darwin

It is important to recognize that reading "after Darwin," to be specific, does not equate to a full-scale discussion of the long-running interaction between scientific theories of origins and the creation accounts of Genesis. This is not the place to attempt a historical analysis of what impact Darwin did in fact have on biblical studies. John Rogerson addresses this elsewhere in this volume, and he earlier noted that "Darwin's *Origins of Species* (1859) seems to have made little impression on Old Testament circles," suggesting that "the major battles were fought in the 1820's" regarding the great age of the earth.[2] Thus, in his fascinating study of the history of the garden of Eden in the interpretive tradition, Jean Delumeau is able to offer without undue difficulty a chart of nineteen different proposals for the date of the creation of the universe (ranging from 3928 BC to 4051 BC), all drawn from sixteenth- and seventeenth-century authors.[3] Nevertheless, writes Delumeau, "an entire line of critics, English in particular and active especially from 1640 to 1660, had anticipated Voltaire's abrasive sarcasm in regard to the opening chapters of Genesis,"[4] such that, by the mid-eighteenth century, it is basically impossible to speak of a consensus, let alone a "prescientific consensus" regarding how to read Genesis.

Significantly, the kinds of issues which provoked dissatisfaction with the reading of Genesis as a historical account of what happened were drawn from a range of concerns: from the implausibility of Eve talking to a snake, to the worry that if Eden had existed then it would still be there somewhere (guarded by cherubim and a fiery sword), to moral and theological worries regarding the extraordinary scale of the punishment inflicted over the breaking of a law about fruit eating, and what we might term hermeneutical concerns about whether Genesis served some function, such as justifying subsequent Jewish claims to land.[5] Indeed, upon turning to the interpretive tradition of the early church regarding these chapters, it is not difficult to discover a wide range of frameworks, proposals, and understandings regarding Genesis 1–3 already.[6]

There is, however, one interesting feature of the historical context of Darwin's writings which impinges rather more acutely on the interpretation of Genesis, even though it is usually considered entirely separately. It is a feature more or less coincidentally linked by historical accident: the observation that Darwin's writings coincided with the discovery of alternative ancient Near Eastern accounts of creation and flood. There is, doubtless, scope to explore the nature of the Victorian mindset which encouraged the exploratory spirit which underlay both the voyage of the HMS *Beagle* and the archaeological work at the sites of ancient Near Eastern texts, but for our purposes a single point may be made. The result of two fresh interpretive frameworks coming into focus at the same time was in the main that Old Testament scholarship, arguably battered by the long-running debate about the age of the earth, found a way to effectively change the subject at the point when Darwin's work arrived.

Darwin published *The Descent of Man* in early 1871. On 3 December 1872, George Smith addressed the Society of Biblical Archaeology in London with news that he had discovered an account of the Flood among some Assyrian tablets at the British Museum. By 1875, he was able to add to this a record of a Babylonian creation account.[7] These two texts, eventually known as the *Gilgamesh* epic and *enuma elish*, respectively, now constitute some of the core resources of any attempt to read Genesis 1–11 "in historical context." *Enuma elish* was first discovered in 1849, though it took a while for its relevance to come to the attention of biblical scholars. The paradigm for biblical scholarship working with Genesis had well and truly shifted by the time of Gunkel's classic 1895 study, *Schöpfung und Chaos*, which read Genesis 1 (as well as Revelation 12) against the background of Babylonian categories and concepts.[8] The influence of Gunkel's line of thinking in biblical studies has been immense: his is a thesis belonging to the category of ideas which retain their influence long after being considerably disproved. One example must suffice: the Hebrew $t^e h\hat{o}m$ (deep; Gen. 1:2) almost certainly has nothing to do with the primeval Babylonian goddess Tiamat, but whether the link will ever disappear from commentaries on Genesis appears rather more doubtful.[9]

Hermeneutical Frameworks and Historical Frameworks

Readers of Genesis in the late nineteenth century thus found themselves pressed on two fronts—by Darwin et al., on the one hand, and *Gilgamesh* et al., on the other—and it is important to look carefully at how one might distinguish the nature of these two issues. In one significant sense, they are the same: they are both hermeneutical challenges to how to read Genesis because they both offer a reference point exterior to the dialogue of text and reader(s), which makes up the basic Christian engagement with the biblical text. One might almost say that they offer a triangulation of the text: between the reader and Genesis comes a third framework, which changes the nature of the questions we want to put to Genesis. Rather than a triangle, hermeneutical theory usually talks of a circle or a spiral of engagement, whereby the reader always comes to the text with a set of questions or perspectives informed and reshaped by previous engagements with it (or with any aspect of human existence).[10] The triangle image simply suggests that, in these two cases, there is a fixed point on the circle which fundamentally reorients the interpretive framework at hand.

However, in another sense, there seems to be a key difference between the two cases, a difference of historical relevance to the conditions of production of Genesis. This last phrase, with its Marxist overtones, reminds us that Genesis had its own battles to fight in its own original context(s), and, simply put, Darwin was not among them. This point does, of course, sound like a statement of the blindingly obvious, but nevertheless I want to argue that the interplay between the hermeneutical and the historical framework is more complicated than this. My thesis is that historically relevant frameworks function hermeneutically in comparable ways to historically irrelevant ones, and on closer inspection, the case of the ancient Near Eastern texts and their relevance to Genesis is primarily hermeneutical rather than historical.

One can always ask the historically oriented question of whether there was, in fact, any link between the Genesis narrative and some other text or context which formed a part of the background agenda to Genesis. Was Genesis 1, to take Gunkel's example, written in interaction with Babylonian creation myths? John Day has argued that the more likely echoes are of Canaanite, not Babylonian, myths—a view which has only been possible since the discovery of Ugaritic Baal texts from 1929 onward.[11] However, Genesis 1 may still be read in contrast to the Babylonian myths even if there is not a historical link between their originating contexts. The question is now more of a literary or hermeneutical one: what happens if one reads the text against, or in the light of, the proposed alternative framework? This is, of course, possible and arguably illuminating, regardless of any historical (causal) link. It also, evidently, has considerable points of overlap with the situation implied in the question of "reading Genesis after Darwin." Obviously, no one proposes that a post-Darwinian perspective was germane to the production of the text of Genesis on a historical level. If one grants, then, that Genesis was not written to engage with views of evolution and natural selection, it is still nevertheless the case that reading Genesis in the light of such views puts an interpretive agenda to the text, which in turn generates readings of Genesis not previously available.

In theory, and not just in the wilder reaches of postmodern theory either, hermeneutical frameworks generate readings—readings which are "after their own kinds," we might say. This is true of many so-called newer approaches, for example, the Earth Bible project's *Readings from the Perspective of Earth* and such notable ecologically inclined readings of Genesis 1–3 as Ellen van Wolde's account of humanity and the earth: the *'ādām* and the *'adāmâ*, as the Hebrew wordplay has it.[12] But it is also true of such traditionally oriented frameworks as readings which presuppose that the text possesses a "literary unity," or "theological coherence," or "historical accuracy." The hermeneutical (as against the interpretive) project comes sharply into focus when we begin to ask how to evaluate such frameworks, in all of their massive diversity, both technical and ideological.

Hermeneutics insists that such evaluation is multifaceted. At the simplest level, the task is not to measure the text against a Procrustean bed devised of an interpretive framework drawn from elsewhere. Such projects nevertheless remain common: the world is not short of voices arguing that Darwin must be wrong because Genesis disagrees and, of course, vice versa. But at a more complex level, even quite sophisticated interpreters run into problems with the hermeneutical task. The difficulty comes in discerning how to adjudicate the significance of a detail in one frame of reference with respect to some comparable element of a different frame of reference. More simply: how do we know that when X says one thing and Y says the opposite, that this is a relevant factor in evaluating X? In due course, this will allow us to reflect on the Genesis-Darwin question, but first we will take a detour through the ancient Near East.

Light from the Ancient Near East—but What Sort of Light?

The history of how Genesis has been interpreted against the comparisons provided by the ancient Near Eastern texts of origins and flood provides an illuminating series of case studies. We shall consider three variations on this theme, which will indicate that there is a range of cases to consider regarding agendas which overlap either substantially, in part, or not at all.[13]

Creation as Monotheistic?

It is often noted that when a reader familiar with Genesis turns to such accounts as *Atrahasis* or *enuma elish*, one of the most striking things about these accounts is their unabashed polytheism. In *Atrahasis*, the divine assembly commissions Enki and Nintu to do the work of creation on behalf of the beleaguered gods.[14] In *enuma elish*, Ea creates humans at Marduk's instruction.[15] In the delightful phrase of Norman Whybray, the great Babylonian god Marduk was "appointed as king by a 'committee' of gods."[16] Genesis 1 seems suddenly and irrevocably cast into a fresh focus: biblical creation is monotheistic, thus the bracing opening: "In the beginning God created." This is often given as the textbook example of the value of reading the Old Testament in the light of its ancient Near Eastern context(s). It is, we might say, a case of reading Genesis after *enuma elish*.

Nevertheless, there are several potential pitfalls in this argument. First, which "God" is in view? Doubtless, the God of Genesis 1 (Elohim) is intended to be one and the same as Israel's own God, YHWH, introduced in an unusual double-naming in chapter 2, but the question of the identity of this God is at least partly at stake in the opening chapters of the biblical narrative, rather than being presupposed as an uncontested God. Linked to this, the very category of "monotheism," as is increasingly recognized, seems at best a rough-and-ready category for reading these ancient texts. These texts, Genesis included, operate with a concept altogether more complicated than that of one uncontested God.[17] Second, even if one allows the category, one could not make the case that monotheism is a surface-level agenda of the text in anything like the way that one could argue that Genesis 1 is concerned with issues such as order, structure, progression, symmetry (between days 1–3 and 4–6), and the location and significance of lights, water, and so forth. All of these are foregrounded in the text, so the best one could argue with regard to monotheism is that it is an assumption of the text, which becomes interesting once the text is read in dialogue with some other possibility, such as *Atrahasis*. But third, the concept presupposed by the Genesis text stretches explicitly to the famous "Let us make…" of 1:26, and this is most likely an assumption of God enthroned in his divine council, the heavenly court, presiding over a world ordered after the pattern of celestial government.[18]

For the sake of our argument, it is important to separate historical plausibility and hermeneutical function here. If Genesis 1 were to be read today by a devoted polytheist for whom polytheism was part of his agenda, it seems entirely likely that he would immediately perceive the import of the Genesis text as cutting across such an agenda, although perhaps the points noted above would constitute cause for further exploration. But in the main, the hermeneu-tical framework of such a reader at least in part generates the salient features of such a reading, regardless of whether there is any historical link. It would take us too far afield to enter here into a discussion of the dating of Genesis 1, although it is relevant to point out that Richard Middleton has reviewed this issue in a refreshingly thoughtful analysis precisely because he wants to argue that Genesis 1–11 serves as an "ideology critique" against Mesopotamian sacral kingship, and historical plausibility is one part of his thesis. His conclusion will suffice: "the evidence for dating is fundamentally ambiguous," though he correctly notes that Jeremiah 4:19–27 most likely presupposes Genesis 1, plac-ing the latter in the seventh century (or earlier) rather than during the exile.[19] So much for the historical argument, but we should note that the historical point is not the issue with regard to how Genesis 1 might strike our hypoth-esized twenty-first-century polytheist.

The Creation of Humans

A second example concerns the creation of humanity. In Genesis 2:7, YHWH-Elohim forms a man from the dust of the ground and breathes into him the breath of life. In *Atrahasis*, Nintu, the creating goddess, mixes clay with the blood of the slain god Geshtu-e, adds the spittle of the Igigi, the great gods, and under the supervision of the womb goddesses makes fourteen bricks, which in turn become seven men and seven women.[20] Genesis 2, meanwhile, has not succeeded in providing any woman for its solitary man, and after the provision of various forms of livestock has failed to relieve the man's loneliness (v. 18), God makes a woman out of one of the man's ribs.

What do we observe this time from the comparison? Dust and breath con-trast with clay, blood, and spittle. Yet, in each case, we have a physical sub-stance and a life-giving divine element (or elements). However, in *enuma elish*, the sole named creation material is the blood of the slain god Qingu, who is chosen because he started the war which brought Marduk to prominence.[21] Perhaps Genesis is then validating the physical-divine mixture over against the idea of the essentially divine nature of humanity? Or is breath rather than blood the key image? Since a case might be made that we do not return to clay when we die, but rather to dust (Gen. 3:19), perhaps it is the dust which car-ries significance.[22] Or are we looking in the wrong place, and the key is simply that biblical woman is one step removed from the whole process, being made out of man's rib—a rejoinder to the more evident equality between the sexes in *Atrahasis*? It is hard to imagine that equality between the sexes was on the agenda of either *Atrahasis* or Genesis.[23] Even if it were, some scholars see the biblical text as the pro-equality one: "Against the background of these common motifs, the particular way in which Gen[esis] 2 describes the position of the woman and the importance of sexuality is evident."[24] Whether or not we know enough to resolve such an issue, some aspect of the question of how human creation is or is not continuous with divine nature over against the rest of the animals does seem to be at stake.

Lifespans before the Flood

Our third example is removed from the interpretive turmoil of the creation accounts but relates quite directly to the context of reading after Darwin. It concerns the ages of Adam's descendants in Genesis 5. These prediluvian figures attain ages ranging from 777 to 969 years, except Enoch, who is taken by God (rather than dying) at a mere 365. The import of the claim that Genesis would have us believe that Methuselah lived to 969 is radically recast by comparing it with a reading of the Sumerian king list, which originated in about 2000 BC.[25] This text opens with the words "When kingship was lowered from heaven..." and goes on to offer lengths of reign ranging from around 21,000 years up to 72,000 years.[26] Two points of theological substance emerge immediately: first, Genesis 5 does not concern kings, but ordinary "sons of Adam" (man); and second, they were mortal humans like "us," though the mathematics of Genesis 5 and 11 do seem to allow that it took a while for lifespans to settle to later norms. In the words of Umberto Cassuto:

> The Babylonian tradition was essentially... of a mythological epic character.... The Torah sets itself in opposition to all this.... It is correct—the Bible comes to tell us—that there lived before the Flood ten generations of notable personages; but they were only ordinary mortals, not gods, or demi-gods, or even men transformed into divinities, and they had no mythological associations whatsoever.[27]

The precise mathematical schema in view (probably relying on sexagesimal, or base 60, symbolism) may be left for another day, but here the text of Genesis, so strikingly odd from a standard modern scientific view, becomes strikingly different in the diametrically opposed direction when read against relevant ancient texts. It also, one might note, attains immediately a coherence and relevance which even the most optimistic readers today must struggle to find otherwise. Such is the hermeneutical relevance of the comparison that it does tend to suggest that there must be a historically plausible link in this case too, which does indeed turn out to be the case. The details of Genesis 5 indicate the strong likelihood that it was written with an awareness of the Sumerian text or something very like it; Genesis 5 is an even more sure candidate for its status as a late priestly (P) text than Genesis 1 turned out to be when we raised that question earlier.[28]

The three examples discussed have sought to demonstrate that there are a variety of cases to consider when seeking a hermeneutical evaluation of the reading of Genesis in contexts other than those which generated it. Only in the third case can we be clear that the Genesis text is historically in the business of countering a tradition known to it, though it remains entirely plausible that Genesis 1 and 2 were both written in an environment not unaware of alternative tales told in other cultures. However, the third case is different. Genesis 5 is a focused polemic against a specific tradition. There seems to be little chance that comparing it to the Sumerian king lists has *generated* a reading of Genesis 5 unrelated to its own concerns. It operates within the categories of another frame of reference, and within those categories it flatly contradicts the fundamental points being made. Our readings of Genesis 1 and 2, on the other hand, indicate a more complex relationship between the categories at work and the content with which they are filled. Genesis 2 alongside *Atrahasis* and *enuma elish* suggests that certain types of questions are common to stories of origins—the triangular relationship among humans, god(s), and work, for example, or the question of a divine element in the constitution of humans— but it is harder to evaluate the points at which Genesis may or may not be seeking to contest the other accounts.

With Genesis 1, the textbook case, it is particularly intriguing to recognize that scholarly disagreement over the polemical background to the Genesis text may have inadvertently demonstrated our thesis that the key results of comparison are hermeneutical rather than historical. For all those who have followed Gunkel in reading Genesis 1 "against Babylon" (to simplify the labeling for the sake of argument) and have found this to shed a great light in the interpretive firmament, it has to be noted that this light may have been *generated* by the comparison rather than discovered in it.

In his helpful survey of comparative approaches to Genesis 1–11, Richard Hess offers, by way of brisk conclusion, the thesis that "[i]f we are to understand the biblical text in terms of its own message, the comparative approach is necessary to show parallels and points of incongruence."[29] What I have tried to demonstrate is that this is not quite right. It does not help us to evaluate the points of incongruence and may not even enable us to identify them properly.

The conclusion, however, is not that it should be abandoned nor that we have wasted our time with it. Rather, there is a significant hermeneutical achievement at stake; it is just that it is not (in general) the achievement of telling us what the historical agenda of Genesis was. What the comparative approach has highlighted is the ways in which Genesis, to some extent regardless of what its intentions were historically, speaks in response to issues put to it from other perspectives.[30] It is this light (a hermeneutical light?) which we may now bring to bear on the task of reading Genesis after Darwin.

Reading Genesis *Differently*: Before and After Darwin

The first thing to say is that, as was widely perceived in the late nineteenth century, there is a conflict. But this is too easily said by some, and perhaps too easily denied by others, for want of carefully specifying what exactly the conflict is. In his detailed analysis of the science-religion controversies of the era, Peter Addinall demonstrates with ease that much that was said by scientists cut directly across the claims of those who thought they were simply being faithful to their reading of Genesis. He writes: "Religious belief put into propositions about nature, man and God was somehow incompatible with propositions about nature and man, along with the deliberate exclusion of propositions about God, made by science."[31] He even suggests that alternative (conciliatory or harmonistic) accounts give "the impression of whistling in the dark to keep up courage."[32] Nevertheless, he is right to say that this does not close down the discussion: "It was relatively easy to show that the Bible and geology made irreconcilable assertions...but for the serious religious believer this was not so much the conclusion of the argument as the beginning."[33]

The hermeneutical effect of reading Darwin (and the whole nineteenth-century investigation of origins) has certain fundamental similarities to the effect of reading the ancient Near Eastern accounts. It challenges categories, reorganizes perceptions of what may or may not be at stake, and in the process refines our estimates of the various agendas at work in the Genesis text. It is true, as we noted earlier, that church traditions recognized long before Darwin the flexible possibilities for chronology on the evidence of Genesis 1 itself. Nevertheless, it is also true that, in the light of Darwin, one reads Genesis differently and is predisposed to seek out ways in which the text is not committed to making historical claims. This is perhaps hermeneutically comparable to seeking out ways in which the text is not committed to polytheism; neither approach is reading Genesis on its own terms so much as probing it with questions it could not have anticipated. As Mark Brett has put it in responding to a claim that we might regard Genesis 1 in and of itself as "proto-historical": "It seems much more likely that with respect to the author's intention, we are dealing here with ancient standards of historiography."[34] At the risk of oversimplification, Augustine and others recognized the flexibility within those standards, while post-Darwin readings recognize that the standards themselves are relative and replace them with standards derived from a different set of criteria. Such a move is certainly facilitated by having recourse to ancient Near Eastern texts which highlight the kinds of historiographical standards in view, and it is thus a much easier move to make now, with the benefit of long reflection on the king lists from Sumer, than it was in the midst of debates about the age of the earth in the nineteenth century.

Two further points by way of conclusion, the first of which is a question about the relative significance of recognizing the polemical dimension of a text. We have seen enough examples from Genesis to appreciate that we are certainly missing something without such knowledge. Of course, we have not dwelt on the equal and opposite point, a kind of third law of hermeneutical motion, that all that we have said of Genesis and its agendas could, *mutatis mutandis*, be said of *enuma elish* and the rest. These also were polemical texts, concerned to represent their own cases against (or, at least, in awareness of) other views. But more simply: what do biblical interpreters talk about when they are not triangulating a biblical text against some third-party view? The traditional answer is the plain sense of the text, a notion frequently confused in the late twentieth and early twenty-first centuries with some philosophically defined idea of the meaning of the text. John Barton offers a clarifying definition of what biblical scholars are after: "biblical criticism, in its quest for this plain sense, is a semantic or linguistic and a literary operation first and foremost, only indirectly concerned with the original, the intended, the historical, or the literal meaning."[35] In these terms, then, the plain sense of Genesis will long outrun Darwin and the ancient Near East, but perhaps the hermeneutical question is whether one can access the plain sense in isolation from considering these other perspectives. One study of Barth's work on Genesis 1–3 suggests, "His refusal to judge the texts by external standards (such as those of the Ancient Near Eastern creation myths) allows him to read the biblical texts according to their plain sense as he sees it." One wonders how much hangs on the "as he sees it," and whether Barth has used precisely a knowledge of these external standards in order to avoid judging by them.[36] I suspect that most abiding plain-sense readings of Genesis may give the impression of serenely navigating the text on its own terms but are actually informed at quite a deep level by a profound knowledge of all kinds of polemical rocks which lie below the surface and which are to be avoided. Plain-sense readings work best, in other words, when part of what guides them is a knowledge of what not to say.

Second, I will offer a comment on the appropriate hermeneutical frame-work for thinking about competing agendas in general. This is an issue which has frequently exercised hermeneutical theorists, especially in the course of the drive toward ever more expansive theories of the "universality of hermeneu-tics" through the twentieth century.[37] Paul Ricoeur has articulated one com-pelling way of conceptualizing the issue. Given two competing frameworks, which each offer accounts of a certain situation, and assuming that each is tried and tested to the point where there are fair reasons to subscribe to such a view, then the hermeneutical task cannot be to explain which one is right, but rather to show how each framework's theory can accommodate the insights of the other.[38] In our case, readers can accommodate the perspective of Genesis to incorporate the insights of Darwin within the framework offered by Genesis (such as by way of mapping the concepts of evolution into the logic of creation in Genesis 1), and equally vice versa: the insights of Darwin can accommodate the perspectives offered by Genesis (such as by interpreting Genesis in ways which downplay any historical claim of the text), but in neither situation will such a move do justice to the opposite framework *on its own terms*. A simple example of the kinds of issues at stake here might be the significance of the order in which one takes up particular topics, their relative significance, or the ways in which they are introduced into the discussion in mutual interrela-tionship. Genesis and Darwin could perhaps be read as discussing the same topics, even in commensurable ways, while at the same time the framework of discussion in one effectively precludes the point or purpose of the other from being taken seriously. It is not, in the first instance, a matter of whether they agree or not, but rather, the adjudication between the frameworks cannot be made on neutral ground: that is precisely the point about the two frameworks being competing ones in the first place.

Ricoeur offers two scenarios for what might happen. In one, the discus-sion is foreclosed: each framework asserts its totalizing right to pronounce upon the way it is, and, in Ricoeur's terms, each is thereby reduced to simply an ideology. In the other, he holds out an eschatological hope that continued dialogue between the frameworks will facilitate further understanding and the bringing back of better interpretive questions.

Hermeneutics helps us to map out such a scenario, but it does not enable us to make the substantive judgments necessary to make progress with either exegesis or scientific understanding. Likewise, our analysis of the hermeneu-tics of reading Genesis after Darwin has not been primarily concerned with the actual interpretation of either Genesis or Darwin, although some pointers have been given along the way. The more modest goal has been to attempt to map out the issues raised by reading Genesis in the light of interpretive frameworks brought from elsewhere, in which sense, I have argued, Darwin was not the first such challenge and, doubtless, will not be the last.

NOTES

1. David Lodge, *Small World* (London: Penguin, 1984), 52.

2. John Rogerson, "The Old Testament," in *The Study and Use of the Bible*, ed. John Rogerson, Christopher Rowland, and Barnabas Lindars (Basingstoke, England: Marshall Pickering, 1988), 1–150, here 126–127.

3. Jean Delumeau, *History of Paradise: The Garden of Eden in Myth and Tradition* (New York: Continuum, 1995), 185–186. His main source is the study of C. A. Patrides, "Renaissance Estimates of the Year of Creation," *Huntington Library Quarterly* 26, no. 4 (1963): 315–322.

4. Delumeau, *History of Paradise*, 218.

5. Delumeau surveys some of these in *History of Paradise*, 218–220, and more generally in his ch. 11, "The Disappearance of the Enchanted Garden," 211–228.

6. See the chapter in this volume by Andrew Louth, as well as the resources he gathered in Andrew Louth, ed., *Genesis 1–11* (Downers Grove, Ill.: InterVarsity, 2001).

7. This tale is told in Richard S. Hess, "One Hundred Fifty Years of Comparative Studies on Genesis 1–11: An Overview," in *I Studied Inscriptions from Before the Flood: Ancient Near Eastern, Literary, and Linguistic Approaches to Genesis 1–11*, ed. Richard S. Hess and David Toshio Tsumura (Winona Lake, Ind.: Eisenbrauns, 1994), 3–26, here 4–6. On Smith, see P. L. Trudinger, "Smith, George (1840–76)," in *Dictionary of Biblical Interpretation*, ed. John H. Hayes (Nashville, Tenn.: Abingdon, 1999), 2:472–473.

8. Now available as Hermann Gunkel, *Creation and Chaos in the Primeval Era and the Eschaton: A Religio-Historical Study of Genesis 1 and Revelation 12*, trans. K. William Whitney Jr. (Grand Rapids, Mich.: Eerdmans, 2006).

9. On this issue, see David Tsumura, *Creation and Destruction: A Reappraisal of the* Chaoskampf *Theory in the Old Testament* (Winona Lake, Ind.: Eisenbrauns, 2005), 36–57.

10. A good account which emphasizes the central importance of the "hermeneutic circle" to the whole nature of hermeneutics is Lawrence K. Schmidt, *Understanding Hermeneutics* (Stocksfield, England: Acumen, 2006).

11. John Day, *Yahweh and the Gods and Goddesses of Canaan* (Sheffield, England: Sheffield Academic Press, 2000), 98–99.

12. For the five-volume Earth Bible project, see especially Norman C. Habel, ed., *Readings from the Perspective of Earth* (Sheffield, England: Sheffield Academic Press, 2000). Van Wolde's work is most usefully summarized in her "Facing the Earth: Primaeval History in a New Perspective," in *The World of Genesis: Persons, Places, Perspectives*, ed. Philip R. Davies and David J. A. Clines (Sheffield, England: Sheffield Academic Press, 1998), 22–47.

13. Aspects of the first two examples which follow borrow from my reader-response analysis of this issue: Richard S. Briggs, "The Implied Author and the

Creation of the World: A Test Case in Reader-Response Criticism," *Expository Times* 113, no. 8 (2002): 264–270.

14. One of the most convenient presentations is in Stephanie Dalley, *Myths from Mesopotamia* (Oxford: Oxford University Press, 1989), 14–17.

15. Dalley, *Myths*, 261.

16. R. N. Whybray, *The Second Isaiah* (Sheffield, England: Journal for the Study of the Old Testament Press, 1983), 54.

17. I have explored these issues further in Richard Briggs, *One God among Many?* (Cambridge: Grove, 2006).

18. See, e.g., Patrick D. Miller, "Cosmology and World Order in the Old Testament: The Divine Council as Cosmic-Political Symbol," in his *Israelite Religion and Biblical Theology: Collected Essays* (Sheffield, England: Sheffield Academic Press, 2000), 422–444.

19. J. Richard Middleton, *The Liberating Image: The* Imago Dei *in Genesis 1* (Grand Rapids, Mich.: Brazos, 2005), 136–145.

20. Dalley, *Myths*, 15–16.

21. Dalley, *Myths*, 261.

22. One might mention here the different suggestion of Walter Brueggemann that the creation of Adam from the dust is designed to call to mind no less than a formula of royal enthronement, in his "From Dust to Kingship," *Zeitschrift für die alttestamentliche Wissenschaft* 84 (1972): 1–18. Is it just the hermeneutical framework that fashions something from the dust here, perhaps?

23. The monumental effort of Phyllis Trible, *God and the Rhetoric of Sexuality* (Philadelphia: Fortress, 1978), 72–143, notwithstanding. On the beginnings of gender sensitivity with regard to ancient Near Eastern texts, note the striking survey of Julia M. Asher-Greve, "Feminist Research and Ancient Mesopotamia: Problems and Prospects," in *A Feminist Companion to Reading the Bible: Approaches, Methods and Strategies*, ed. Athalya Brenner and Carole Fontaine (Sheffield, England: Sheffield Academic Press, 1997), 218–237.

24. Ed Noort, "The Creation of Man and Woman in Biblical and Ancient Near Eastern Traditions," in *The Creation of Man and Woman: Interpretations of the Biblical Narratives in Jewish and Christian Traditions*, ed. Gerard P. Luttikhuizen (Leiden: Brill: 2000), 1–18, here 18.

25. A translation may be found in *Ancient Near Eastern Texts Relating to the Old Testament*, ed. J.B. Pritchard (3rd edition, Princeton, N.J.: Princeton University Press, 1969), 265–266.

26. I am taking the data for this example from the fascinating study of Lloyd R. Bailey, "Biblical Math as Heilsgeschichte?" in *A Gift of God in Due Season: Essays on Scripture and Community in Honor of James A. Sanders*, ed. Richard D. Weis and David M. Carr (Sheffield, England: Sheffield Academic Press, 1996), 84–102. Bailey's longer work, *Genesis, Creation, and Creationism* (Mahwah, N.J.: Paulist, 1993), was unavailable to me.

27. Umberto Cassuto, *A Commentary on the Book of Genesis*, vol. 1, *From Adam to Noah* (Jerusalem: Magnes, 1961), 262–263; cited in Bailey, "Biblical Math," 99–100.

28. The case that Genesis 5 is a late priestly (P) text is admittedly not straightforward: the genealogy "was actually a preexisting document that the P author adapted," says Carr, but even so it was, he suggests, an Israelite parallel to the Sumerian list. See the discussion in David M. Carr, *Reading the Fractures of Genesis: Historical and Literary Approaches* (Louisville, Ky.: Westminster John Knox, 1996), 68–73, esp. 71.

29. Hess, "One Hundred Fifty Years," 24.

30. If space permitted, we could explore this idea with reference to yet further frameworks, such as the analysis of six twentieth-century novelists (including John Steinbeck and Thomas Mann) writing in dialogue with Genesis: Terry R. Wright, *The Genesis of Fiction: Modern Novelists as Biblical Interpreters* (Aldershot, England: Ashgate, 2007).

31. Peter Addinall, *Philosophy and Biblical Interpretation: A Study in Nineteenth-Century Conflict* (Cambridge: Cambridge University Press, 1991), 15.

32. Addinall, *Philosophy and Biblical Interpretation,* 9.

33. Addinall, *Philosophy and Biblical Interpretation,* 144–145. Addinall's own response is to utilize Kant's philosophy to articulate the limits of empiricism, thus requiring science to be controlled by moral responsibility, and he then argues that Genesis 1–2 operates with a perspective strikingly close to that of Kant. Thus, Kant's philosophy gives us the proper framework for biblical interpretation. It is interesting that Addinall does not consider perspectives arising from the ancient Near East.

34. Mark G. Brett, "Motives and Intentions in Genesis 1," *Journal of Theological Studies* 42 (1991): 1–16, here 15–16.

35. John Barton, *The Nature of Biblical Criticism* (Louisville, Ky.: Westminster John Knox, 2007), 101.

36. The quotation is from K. E. Greene-McCreight, *Ad Litteram: How Augustine, Calvin, and Barth Read the "Plain Sense" of Genesis 1–3* (New York: Peter Lang, 1999), 204. Her study is the key resource for pursuing this area.

37. See, most concisely, Hans-Georg Gadamer, "The Universality of the Hermeneutical Problem," in his *Philosophical Hermeneutics,* trans. and ed. David E. Linge (Berkeley: University of California Press, 1976), 3–17.

38. This is a somewhat brutal summary of the argument of Ricoeur's essay "Hermeneutics and the Critique of Ideology," in *From Text to Action: Essays in Hermeneutics II,* trans. Kathleen Blamey and John B. Thompson (Evanston, Ill.: Northwestern University Press, 1991), 270–307.

PART II

Understanding the History

5

What Difference Did Darwin Make?

The Interpretation of Genesis in the Nineteenth Century

John Rogerson

"Whatever faith we may settle down into, opinions can never go back exactly to what they were before Darwin came out."[1] Thus wrote the eminent geologist Charles Lyell to George Ricknor on 29 November 1860, a year after the publication of *On the Origin of Species*. No one was arguably better placed than Lyell to judge the impact of Darwin's book on the scientific community and on the intelligent public in general. Also, Lyell had close ties with liberal churchmen and would take a keen interest in the crises that were about to rock the established church in the form of *Essays and Reviews*[2] and the first volume of Bishop J. W. Colenso's work on the Pentateuch.

Yet, whatever impact that *On the Origin of Species* may have had on the scientific community and the general public, its effect on the interpretation of the opening chapters of Genesis was surprisingly minimal. One of the main reasons for this was that Lyell's own geological researches and those of other specialists had been affecting biblical scholarship profoundly for over thirty years before the publication of Darwin's book. Further, biblical scholarship in Britain was trying to come to terms with the implications of German biblical criticism, with its denial that Moses had written the Pentateuch. Finally, although some churchmen could see in Darwin's theory a direct challenge to the Christian belief based on Genesis 1:27 that humankind was made in the image and likeness of God, others could simply say that Darwin had described the mechanisms that God had used in order to bring humanity into existence. Of course, such a simple harmonization of Darwin with religious belief rested upon a profound misunderstanding both of Darwin's theory of natural selection and of the nature of scientific and religious language.

In what follows in this chapter, I shall try to illustrate the points made in these opening remarks and indicate some other aspects of the diversity of the interpretation of the early chapters of Genesis in the nineteenth century.

Horne's *Introduction*, 1825

I begin with Thomas Hartwell Horne's *An Introduction to the Critical Study and Knowledge of the Holy Scriptures*, whose fifth edition appeared in 1825. An impressively comprehensive four-volume work of impeccable orthodoxy, Horne's *Introduction* was the benchmark of English-speaking biblical scholarship in the first quarter of the nineteenth century. In defending the "Mosaic narrative" (as he called it) of the creation of the world in six days, Horne alluded to the distorted traditions (as he called them) found in the "Chaldean, Egyptian, Phoenician, Hindoo, Chinese, Etruscan, Gothic, Greek, and American Cosmogonies."[3] These he regarded as "collateral confirmations" of the Mosaic account, showing, in spite of the distortions, that there had been a remote tradition generally among the nations that had never been totally obliterated from human memory. The fact that the various cosmogonies cited came from nations that had had little or no contact with each other and were mostly unknown to the Hebrews was further evidence for the trustworthiness of the ancient traditions about the creation, whose most accurate version was found in the inspired biblical version.

Geology made an appearance in Horne's exposition in connection with the Genesis account of the Flood. Discoveries of the bones and fossils of extinct and still-existing animals in various unlikely parts of the world—in 1821, for example, the remains of hyenas, elephants, and rhinoceroses had been found in a cave at Kirkdale, two miles west of Kirkbymoorside in North Yorkshire—proved that a gigantic flood had swept animals far from their normal habitats to places where they never had existed.[4] However, not all geological evidence necessarily confirmed the Genesis narrative. Horne took particular exception to the view of a Count Borch that Mount Etna must be 8,000 years old and of a Canon Recupero that the lowest stratum of Etna must have flowed from the volcano 14,000 years ago—findings at odds with Archbishop Ussher's chronology based on the Bible, which made the earth less than 6,000 years old. Recupero's estimate was based on the assumption that each of the seven strata that he had observed would require a period of 2,000 years for the soil to accumulate on it. Horne could not conceal his contempt for such an argument.

> Who has kept a register of the eruptions of any burning mountain for one thousand years, to say nothing of four thousands years? Who can say that the strata of earth were formed in equal periods? The time for the formation of the uppermost and last is probably not known.... One might have been formed in a year, another in a century. The philosophers above mentioned are wholly ignorant of the cause of any one of these earthy strata.[5]

Having dismissed the objections that might be based upon geology, Horne was able to uphold the veracity of the Mosaic account of a universal deluge, first by drawing attention to other flood stories, such as those of the Babylonians as related by Berossus,[6] and second by dealing with particular difficulties arising from the story, such as the question of why there are differences among humans (e.g., blacks and whites) if they all descended from the family of Noah.

Delitzsch's *Commentary on Genesis*, 1853

It is interesting to compare this traditional and conservative defense of Genesis with an equally conservative German counterpart, in the form of Franz Delitzsch's *Commentary on Genesis*, of which the second edition appeared in 1853.[7] Delitzsch wrote in the shadow of great German expositors, such as Johann Gottfried Herder, and great poets and philosophers, such as Kant, Hegel, and Schelling, who had expressed opinions on the origin of the world and humankind. Also, the source criticism of Genesis and attempts to refute it had occupied many scholars from Wilhelm M.L. de Wette and Wilhelm Vatke, on the critical side, to Ernst W. Hengstenberg and Johann C.K. von Hofmann, on the conservative side. Delitzsch sought to take all of this into account in great detail, while advancing his own reasons for regarding the Pentateuch as essentially Mosaic, even if not every part of it was actually written by Moses.[8]

When it came to the interpretation of Genesis 1, Delitzsch had to take account of Herder's view that the chapter described not the way in which the world had been created, but the way in which God had communicated to the first humans the fact that he was the Creator. On this view, Genesis 1 described not objective facts but a subjective experience of the first humans.[9] Delitzsch rejected this idea on the ground that it did not explain the existence of the cosmologies of other ancient peoples that bore resemblances to the biblical account. But Herder had posed a question that needed to be answered, namely, that of the origin of the material in Genesis 1 and 2. Delitzsch answered the question by arguing that the creation account in Genesis was *Sage*, i.e. a tradition that was based upon facts that had been revealed to the first humans and that had been passed down orally for many generations. However, this process of oral transmission had led to reshapings of the biblical account. God did not speak Hebrew to the earliest humans but a language common to the human race before it was scattered into different nations with their own languages. This was why the *Sage* disclosed to the earliest humans could be found in various forms among the ancient nations. Further, the existence of these parallel accounts suggested that what was now found in Genesis was not the original revelation in its unadulterated purity. The versions found among other peoples indicated that Genesis omitted details from the primal story. Yet this had not been an arbitrary or fortuitous process. It had been a conscious shaping of the narrative to enable it to express the fundamental biblical themes of election and redemption and of the revealing of divine law—all of them matters that had been revealed to the Hebrews as part of their historical involvement with God as his people. This put the Genesis creation narrative into a dynamic form. Although rooted in God's revelation to the earliest humans, it had assumed a specific Israelite form during its transmission in the life of the people with whom God was dealing in its history. It *did* contain divinely revealed information about the origin of the world; but it also had a theological function, which was to introduce the great themes that would be brought to expression in the remainder of the Pentateuch. It is doubtful whether Horne and other traditionalists in Britain would have been at all happy with this account of the origin of Genesis 1–2, and it shows how perilous it is to suppose that all conservative or traditional treatments of Genesis adopted a uniform, literalist reading of the text.

Delitzsch also utilized geological findings in his discussion of the biblical account of the Flood, in a way that would not have pleased orthodox defenders of the narrative in Britain at that time. After stating boldly that the support of geology was not necessary in the matter of the Flood but that "unser Glaube ruht auf dem Zeugniss der Ueberlieferung und zwar auf dem Geschichszeugniss der heiligen Schrift,"[10] Delitzsch went on to mention Lyell's discoveries in the volcanic region of the Auvergne in southern France, which Lyell had visited in May 1828.[11] Lyell had discovered deposits of volcanic ash that he believed predated the creation of humanity and that could not possibly have withstood the violence of the Flood, from which it followed that there were parts of the earth that had not been affected by the Flood. Delitzsch concluded:

> Gesetzt dass die Geologie solche und andere Beweise gegen die
> schlechthinige Allgemeinheit der Fluth bis zu unwiderlegbarer
> Ueberzeugungskraft zu steigern vermöchte, so besteht für uns keine
> apologetische Verpflichtung, das Gegentheil wie einen Glaubenssatz
> zu bejahen. Die Aussage der Schrift fordert Allgemeinheit der Fluth
> in gewissem Sinne, aber nicht in jedem, Allgemeinheit der Fluth
> für die Erde als bewohnte, aber nicht für die Erde als solche. Denn
> die Schrift hat kein Interesse an der Allgemeinheit der Fluth an
> sich, sondern nur an der Allgemeinheit des durch sie vollzogenen
> Gerichts.[12]

F. D. Maurice, 1851

Horne and Delitzsch indicate differing ways in which conservative and traditional scholars were interpreting Genesis in the nineteenth century before the appearance of *On the Origin of Species*. A quite different approach was adopted by a man who was in theory open to the conclusions of biblical criticism but in practice appalled at their results: Frederick Denison Maurice. In a sermon preached at Lincoln's Inn on 16 February 1851, Maurice attacked those who sought to place any restriction upon the scientific investigation of the universe.[13] What such investigation discovered was "truths which God has revealed to those who have honestly studied His universe."[14] Maurice was similarly dismissive of those who sought to reconcile the biblical account of creation with the conclusions of physical science. He wished to dispense with such efforts "not in order to make peace with science, not even in order to assert the letter of Scripture... but because, as long as these conceptions last, we cannot enter into that idea of creation which the Scripture is in every page bringing out before us."[15] What Maurice's "idea of creation" was, I shall try to explain in a moment; but I want first to quote some words from Augustine that Maurice cited at this point, in order to reinforce his argument that Christians ought not to assert the letter of scripture against scientific discoveries. Augustine had written in *De Genesi ad Litteram*:

> It is a very disgraceful and pernicious thing, and one greatly to be
> watched against, that any infidel should hear a Christian talking
> wild nonsense about the earth and the heaven, about the motions
> and magnitude and intervals of the stars, the courses of years and

times, the natures of animals, stones, and other matters of the same
kind, pretending that he has the authority of the Scriptures on his
side. The other who understands these things from reason or experience, seeing that the Christian is utterly ignorant of the subject,
that he is wide of the mark by a whole heaven, cannot refrain from
laughter. What pain and sorrow these rash dogmatists cause to their
wiser brethren, can scarcely be told.[16]

I have quoted Augustine here as a reminder that the exegesis of Genesis
has taken many different forms in the history of interpretation and has never
exhibited a uniform literal understanding. But back to Maurice. How did he
understand the opening chapters of Genesis? He began from the view that
there were two separate accounts of creation, one in the first chapter of Genesis
and another in the second chapter. However, he did not assign these accounts
to two different sources, as German biblical criticism did, but saw them as
necessarily complementary. The first account, in stating that God created
male and female in the divine image, described the *ideal*. The second account,
about God breathing life into the creature formed from the dust of the earth,
described the creation of *actual* humanity. As Maurice stated:

If we had the first without the second, we should have the description of an ideal man, without being told that there was an actual
man. If we had merely the second, we should have the history of the
appearance of a solitary creature in the universe, without knowing
what he was, or why he was put there, or what relation he bore to all
the things about him.[17]

The distinction between the ideal in chapter 1 and the actual in chapter 2
became the basis for Maurice to claim that what Genesis 1 described was not
the creation of the actual world as it presented itself to human perception, but
the creation of the world as it was in the mind of God.[18] Maurice accepted that
this view was open to the criticism that the biblical text said of the creation of
the various parts of the earth, "and it was so" followed by a description of the
coming into being of the object or objects in question. Maurice's explanation
was that these passages described not what had happened at creation, in the
past, but what happened all the time, down to the present hour. Although
uttered once, the creative divine word "is never for a moment suspended; never
ceases to fulfil its own proclamation."[19] What, then, is the meaning or function
of the six days that serve as the framework of the creation story in Genesis 1?
Anyone who has studied Maurice's writings will know that he can be annoy-
ingly obscure precisely when clarity is demanded, and his treatment of the

six days is, I am afraid, shrouded in obfuscation. The following is what I can make of it.

Maurice began from the feature of the biblical text that had been observed by interpreters from at least the third Christian century: although the week is implicit in the narrative as soon as it mentions the first day in Genesis 1:5, the sun and the moon, with their function to determine day and night and times and seasons, are not created until day four. Maurice concluded from this that the purpose of the week, with its six days of work and one of rest, was to point to God. It was to teach humanity that the week was not something regulated by the sun and moon but "an order which the unseen God had created; which included Sun, Moon, Stars."[20] By living according to the week, and observing the sabbath rest, the Jew (Maurice's term) was able to relate to God in a way which helped him to feel at home in the universe. Part of this feeling of being at home in the universe was achieved by what Maurice called "the great Lawgiver" teaching the Jew to associate the different days of the week with different aspects of the coming-into-being of the world. However, it was never God's intention that people should think that the world was created in six days. The purpose of the narrative was not to describe origins but to deliver humanity from idolatry, from worshipping objects in the natural world or universe, by pointing humanity to the divine order that is at the heart of reality.

> The more he meditated on the clear simple view of the Order of the
> Universe, as it unfolded itself in the mind of the divine Artist, and as
> it was set forth to man in his week of seven days...the more certain
> would be his assurance that the glory of man consists in looking
> up direct to Him; in beholding Him in His own proper nature, not
> through dim reflections or earthly images.[21]

For Maurice, then, attempts to reconcile Genesis with science were mistaken because they diverted attention away from what the biblical text was actually saying. Of course, opinions about "what the text was saying" varied considerably, and Maurice's own interpretation, as far as I can judge, was highly individualistic; but his general point was surely sound.

Moses Kalisch, 1858

A similar approach, for very different reasons, was taken by the German Jewish émigré Moses Kalisch, whose commentary on Genesis appeared in 1858, a year before Darwin's seminal work. Kalisch devoted much space to the argument that it was impossible to reconcile Genesis with scientific findings, his motive being his desire to uphold a literal exposition of the Genesis account of creation as revealing the nature and will of God. His knowledge of contemporary science was encyclopedic, and he employed this knowledge with great skill and acumen. His general position, clearly rooted in the great Jewish medieval tradition of thinkers such as Maimonides, was summed up in the statement "The Bible was not…intended to supercede science, but only to control it; faith should not awe reason, but guide it, and protect its daring flight from degrading aberrations."[22] By this, he meant that science and religion each had their appropriate spheres and that religion should not hamper science, while science should not presume to pontificate on matters such as the nature and destiny of humankind and humankind's relationship to God. However, my main reason for mentioning Kalisch is in order to note that his scientific knowledge included the theory of the evolution of humanity from "lower" species *before* the publication of *On the Origin of Species*. This will surprise no one familiar with the history of science, who will know that while Darwin made the general public aware of the theory of evolution, he was not its inventor, but he was the originator of the theory of natural selection. Kalisch stated the theory of evolution, in order to refute it, in the following words:

> It was asserted, that all organic beings, with their various classes,
> orders and types, are literally the lineal descendants of each
> other…that, for instance, the fishes are the ancestors of the reptiles;
> which, in their turn, are the progenitors of the birds; and so on.…A
> Batrachian [a class of reptiles that includes frogs and toads] (or,
> according to older naturalists, a monkey) is the father of man.[23]

It is noteworthy that, prior to the publication of Darwin's book, Kalisch could observe that the evolutionary theory regarding the origin of humans was "unfortunately, making so rapid progress, that it is impossible to overlook it, and the spirit of our age is peculiarly favourable to its pernicious propagation."[24]

Christopher Wordsworth, 1865

Not everyone agreed that it was a mistake to try to reconcile Genesis and science. I want now to mention two attempts to defend the Bible against science that belong to the period after 1859. The first, in 1865, was the volume on Genesis in Christopher Wordsworth's *Notes and Introduction to the Holy Bible*. Wordsworth would later be bishop of Lincoln (1869–1885) in which office he tried to persuade Wesleyan Methodists to return to the Church of England, developed close relationships with the Old Catholic and Greek Orthodox churches, and founded the Scholae Cancelarii at Lincoln for the training of clergy. For Wordsworth, it was the authority of the New Testament that decided matters of controversy regarding the Old Testament. Thus, the authenticity of the incident of Balaam's talking ass in Numbers 22:28–30, a passage that had troubled scholars since at least the third century AD, was guaranteed by the fact that "the divinely-inspired Apostle St. Peter" referred to it in 2 Peter 2:16.[25] Similarly, the question of the origin of the human race was settled not only by the statement in Genesis 1:27 that God created male and female in his image, but by the place of this statement within the whole Christian understanding of the loss of the divine image at the Fall of mankind and its restoration in Jesus Christ. Also, the original human pair, Adam and Eve, prefigured Christ and the church.[26] Darwin's view, which was carefully examined, was rejected on the basis of its incompatibility with Christian doctrine. The one concession to scientific discovery that Wordsworth allowed was the acceptance that geology indicated that the earth was of great antiquity and inhabited by many species of animals, some now extinct. However, all this had been *before* the six days of creation described in Genesis 1. The statement in Genesis 1:2 that the earth was without form and void indicated that an agency hostile to God had somehow managed to distort God's original creation, which then necessitated a re-creation of the world in six days, as stated in Genesis. Wordsworth is said to have presented every licensed clergyman in his diocese with a copy of his commentary on the Bible. His stance indicates the attitude taken toward Darwin and nineteenth-century science by a highly intelligent and influential churchman who believed that the Bible had to be understood in accordance with traditional Christian doctrines and not in the light of the emerging biblical criticism or natural science.

The Pulpit Commentary, 1882

A work more representative of what might be called intelligent traditionalism was *The Pulpit Commentary*, which began to appear in 1882 under the general editorship of the dean of Gloucester, H. D. M. Spence. The volume on Genesis was reissued in a new edition in 1897, an indication that as late as the end of the nineteenth century, an intelligent, traditional interpretation of Genesis could still command attention from a broad spectrum of churchmen. The main work of the commentary on Genesis fell to Thomas Whitelaw, and the volume included homilies by various authors and a general introduction to the Old Testament by the dean of Canterbury and erstwhile Bampton lecturer F. W. Farrar. Intended to assist preachers, *The Pulpit Commentary* paid close and detailed attention to recent developments in biblical criticism and the natural sciences.

Whitelaw's introductory essay on the authorship of the Pentateuch offered a comprehensive survey of the arguments for dividing the Pentateuch into different sources and for denying that Moses was its author. These arguments were rejected, with much dependence upon German defenders of the traditional position, such as Hengstenberg and Carl Friedrich Keil. A survey of the arguments in favor of Mosaic authorship concluded that there was not sufficient ground for challenging the Pentateuch's substantial Mosaic authorship,[27] although it may have been subsequently revised by Ezra. Significantly, there was no reference to S. R. Driver's *Introduction to the Literature of the Old Testament* of 1891.

On Genesis 1, Whitelaw accepted the theory of the German Johann Heinrich Kurtz that the mode of the creation had been revealed to its author in the same way that Daniel and John the Divine had heard and received visions.

> [The recipient] may have beheld in sublime panorama the evolution of the light, the uplifting of the atmosphere, the parting of the waters, the placing of the orbs, the filling of the land, sea and sky with life, while he listened with awestruck silence to the voices of Elohim, as they were uttered at the opening of each creative day.[28]

But how did what had been revealed correspond with what had taken place? Whitelaw would have no truck with Kalisch's view that it was a mistake to harmonize "science and revelation." Noting that "the opinion of neither Jewish nor Christian antiquity was entirely on the side of the natural-day theory" (i.e., the view that the six days of creation were normal twenty-four-hour days), Whitelaw opted for the approach that took the six days to be indefinitely long epochs, which in turn could be compared with and be said to coincide with the findings of geology. A main argument in favor of each creation day as a long epoch was the fact that "God's sabbatic rest is understood by the best interpreters of Scripture to have continued from creation's close until the present hour; so that consistency demands the previous six days to be considered as not of short, but of indefinite, duration."[29]

A crucial passage was, of course, Genesis 1:27 with its assertion that God created male and female in his image and likeness. A section of homiletics was quoted from naturalists such as T. H. Huxley and John Tyndall to the effect that science was currently unable to bridge the gap between the living and the nonliving, leaving Whitelaw to conclude that God was the originator of life. But how had it evolved? Another quotation from Huxley summed up Darwin's fundamental contribution:

> Mr. Darwin has shown good reason for believing that the interaction between living matter and surrounding conditions, which results

in the survival of the fittest, is sufficient to account for the gradual evolution of plants and animals from their simplest to their most complex form.[30]

For Whitelaw, it was sufficient to reject this by saying, "Moses accounts for the origination of living creatures by a Divine creation, and for their continuance by the Divine benediction which made it the law of their being to propagate their kind and to multiply in masses."[31]

Geology played an important part in Whitelaw's treatment of the Flood, but with some differences as compared with earlier commentators. Horne, it will be remembered, had seen in the violent force of the inundation a reason for the existence of the remains of elephants and rhinoceroses in North Yorkshire, while Delitzsch had accepted Lyell's discovery of undisturbed volcanic ash in the Auvergne as evidence that the Flood had not affected the whole earth. Whitelaw rejected both views on the ground that the Bible did not speak of a *violent* flood. The waters had risen and subsided slowly and had "effected comparatively little change upon the face of nature."[32] At the same time, he accepted the view that the Flood had not covered the whole earth but only the inhabited earth, a view that, he claimed, had been rejected by the great Jewish commentator Ibn Ezra (and thus had been current in the twelfth century) and considered by the Puritan commentator Matthew Poole at the end of the seventeenth century.[33] A section on "The Antiquity of Man" shows how reluctant churchmen were at the end of the nineteenth century to give up the biblical chronology in favor of the findings of natural science. Humans, according to the biblical account (Whitelaw recognized that Archbishop James Ussher was not the only scholar who had worked out a biblical chronology), had appeared on the earth not less than 5,652 and not more than 7,536 years ago. It was noted that geology suggested a thousand centuries and probably ten times that. Also, reference was made to Lyell's book *The Geological Evidence of the Antiquity of Man* (1863). But after reviewing the geological evidence, Whitelaw concluded, "the Bible student will do well to pause before displacing the currently-received [i.e., biblical] age of man by the fabulous duration claimed for him by the first-named writers [Alfred Russell Wallace and Lyell]."[34]

S. R. Driver, 1883

The Pulpit Commentary volume on Genesis had appeared in 1882, with apparently no revisions for the new edition of 1897, from which I have quoted. The lack of revision explains the omission of any reference to the scholar in Britain who made the most important and influential efforts to come to terms with the findings of both natural science and biblical criticism, Samuel Rolles Driver. On 21 October 1883, Driver preached a university sermon in St. Mary's, Oxford, on the subject "Evolution Compatible with Faith," and he followed this up with an article in the January number of the *Expositor* for 1886 on "The Cosmogony of Genesis." In 1891, there appeared his classic work *An Introduction to the Literature of the Old Testament*, which contains what I think is still the best examination and exposition in English of the so-called Graf-Wellhausen hypothesis.[35]

Driver's sermon, published together with other sermons in 1892, offered the clearest possible discussion of the relation between science and theology and faced head on the implications of Darwin's theory of the origin of species by natural selection. Beginning from the text in Genesis 2:7—"And the Lord God formed man of the dust of the ground, and breathed into his nostrils the breath of life"—Driver considered, first, the nature of the narrative in which it occurred, and second, what it meant to say that the narrative was inspired. The fact that the Bible contains many genres of writing, including poetry, parable, and allegory, was a warning against the idea that the only way to treat biblical material is by assuming that it is *literally* true. The *inspiration* of biblical texts was not a direct process of divine communication to biblical authors, but by way of what Driver called a "Divine intuition" whereby biblical writers, dependent upon materials from ordinary human sources, infused them with insights drawn from their religious life and traditions. In the case of the Genesis narratives, this could be demonstrated from both the similarities between the opening chapters of Genesis and the recently discovered Assyrian and Babylonian accounts and the profound differences that they displayed.

Driver next turned to the claim in Genesis 2:7 that "a spirit sent from God . . . is both the source of life, and creates the human personality" and the apparent problem caused to this by modern science. According to this, "[man] arose in accordance with well-defined laws of natural development out of anthropoid ancestors, and his pedigree is even carried further back, till its primitive source is discovered in a humble organism inhabiting the deep."[36] For Driver, it was important to accept that "the theory has . . . an intrinsic plausibility and reasonableness sufficient to compensate for some admitted deficiencies in its proof."[37] Theologians had no contribution to make to this scientific discussion; the questions at issue would be decided on scientific grounds alone.

This acceptance raised the question of the relation between final causes (i.e., a belief in God as the originator of life) and sufficient causes (i.e., a purely naturalistic explanation of the origin of life), and here Driver contended strongly for the separation of scientific and theological claims.

> Men of science are jealous of the introduction of the idea of the final cause at particular points in the organic series. They think, and justly, that to admit it is to abnegate one of their most valued rights; but to those who, for reasons not within the cognisance of science, choose to view the entire series as the manifestation of a purpose, they have nothing to oppose. As before, they may personally disbe- lieve it, but all that they can logically object is, that the subject lies beyond their province, and, that, as students of science, they profess no opinion upon it.[38]

The proper sphere of theology lay elsewhere.

> If we think to expel the super-sensual from nature, we embark upon a hopeless task. There are phenomena which *will* not be explained by the premises of materialism. There are facts which cannot by any intelligible process of thought be connected with the data of sense. There is, within each one of us a permanent and undying witness to the reality of the super-sensual—the fact of consciousness. While human consciousness survives, philosophy has an unassailable basis on which to assert for mind, whencesoever derived, its indepen- dence and supremacy. Here is a fact which no theory of the origin of human consciousness can get rid of, and which any theory having a claim to validity must preserve intact.[39]

Consistent with this view, Driver made no attempt to harmonize Genesis with the findings of natural science, and in his commentary on Genesis pub- lished in 1904, he powerfully argued the case for the impossibility of harmoniz- ing Genesis with science. Although the commentary sometimes frustratingly told readers much that they did not want to know and little about what they did want to know, it was said to have saved the faith of a generation.

J. W. Colenso, 1865

It would be tempting to end the chapter at this point, but I must succumb to another temptation, to give the last word to a man who was hated by the church establishment of his day and much admired by scientists such as Huxley, Lyell, Tyndall, and even Darwin: Bishop J. W. Colenso.[40] In a public lecture to the Marylebone Literary Institute on 23 May 1865, in which he spoke about his missionary work among the Zulus and described modern science as a means by which God continued to reveal himself to the human race, Colenso sharply attacked those who believed that to give up belief in the literal truth of the Bible was to give up the Bible itself. He attacked those who maintained—as Christopher Wordsworth did—that "to give up the date of the creation, the account of the rib turned into a woman, the stories of the fall and the deluge, of the speaking ass, of the sun and moon standing still—to give up any one of these as an historical fact, is to give up the Bible."[41] Colenso was adamant that what he was doing by embracing biblical criticism and the findings of science was seeking to establish faith

> not, indeed in the mere Book, but in that Living Word which speaks
> in the Book, and speaks also by the lips of apostles and prophets
> in all ages, of all good men and true, whose heart God's Spirit has
> quickened to be the bearers of His message of truth to their fellow
> men.[42]

I do not know what Darwin would have made of this, but if he had felt that his work had made a difference at least to this one brave missionary, I hope that he would have felt that it had not been in vain.

Conclusion

The twenty-first-century debate in Britain and the United States about whether children should be taught a theory of "creative design" instead of, or in addition to, the theory of evolution has revived some of the debates of the nineteenth century about the interpretation of the opening chapters of Genesis. However, as this chapter has shown, there was no unanimity, especially among traditionalists (i.e., those whose work predated that of Darwin or who rejected his theories about the origins of the human race), as to the meaning of these chapters. F. D. Maurice was clear that the Bible did *not* teach that the world was created in six days and that to suppose it did was to miss the point of what it was saying about creation. Other traditionalists insisted that the "days" were in fact epochs of long duration, while Wordsworth claimed that it was the *re*-creation of an invaded and disfigured universe that was accomplished in six days. Another view was that the six days referred to the subjective process of how the fact of divine creation was communicated to humankind, not to the objective fact of how the universe was brought into being. Many of these differing views predated the publication of Darwin's seminal work, which in itself did not radically affect the interpretation of Genesis. Another point on which traditionalist interpreters disagreed was whether the Flood described in Genesis 6–8 had covered the whole earth or only the inhabited parts of it.

Faced with such diversity of opinions, readers may be forgiven for feeling somewhat bewildered. Two positive points emerge, however. The first is that, even as far back as the time of Augustine in the fifth century AD (quoted by Maurice), Christians have accepted that the discoveries of the natural sciences were to be welcomed and that they presented no direct challenge to Christian belief about the divine origin of the universe. The second point is that, in order to be "faithful" to the Bible, it is not necessary to read it literally. Biblical interpretation is a sophisticated matter requiring a number of skills. The world cannot be divided into two clearly identifiable camps: those who believe the Bible (i.e., interpret it in a particular way) and those who do not (i.e., interpret it differently from those in the first camp). The history of biblical interpretation can deliver readers from the tyranny of those who claim that their interpretation of the Bible is the only valid one and that anyone who differs is unbelieving. The fact that the last word in this chapter was given to Colenso is a reminder that a prime task of biblical interpretation has always been to look beyond the letter and to seek to hear the voice of the living God in and through it. That voice has much to say to us about the creation and our duties toward it.

NOTES

1. Charles Lyell, *Life, Letters and Journals of Sir Charles Lyell, Bart.* (London, 1881), 2:341.

2. F. Temple, R.Williams, B. Powell, H.B. Wilson, C.W. Goodwin, M. Pattison, B. Jowett, *Essays and Reviews* (London: Longman, Green, Longmans, and Roberts, 1861).

3. T. H. Horne, *An Introduction to the Critical Study and Knowledge of the Holy Scriptures*, 5th ed. (London, 1825), 1:163.

4. This was not the view of the discoverer of the cave, the Reverend William Buckland, according to Chris Stringer in *Homo Britannicus* (London: Allen Lane, 2006), 20. Apparently, Buckland thought that the animals represented by the bones had lived in Britain and that their bones had survived the flood by being in the recesses of the cave.

5. Horne, *Introduction*, 1:171.

6. Berossus was a Babylonian priest, c. 300 BC, whose writings were cited by writers such as Josephus and Eusebius of Caesarea.

7. F. Delitzsch, *Die Genesis Ausgelegt*, 2nd ed. (Leipzig, 1853).

8. For Delitzsch's criticism of Hengstenberg, see *Genesis*, 42–43.

9. Delitzsch, *Genesis*, 66–67. See J. G. Herder, *Aelteste Urkunde des Menschengeschlechts*, in *J. G. Herder: Sämmtliche Werke*, ed. B. Suphan (Berlin: Weidmannsche Buchhandlung, 1884), 7:1–171.

10. Delitzsch, *Genesis*, 254–255. My translation: "Our faith rests upon the witness of tradition, in particular on the historical witness of holy scripture."

11. Lyell, *Life, Letters*, 1:185.

12. Delitzsch, *Genesis*, 255. My translation:

> Granted that geology can use this and other evidence to build up a case of irrefutable persuasiveness against the absolute universality of the flood, we are under no apologetic obligation to assert the opposite as an article of faith. What scripture affirms is the universality of the flood in a particular, not a general sense; the universality of the flood for the earth as populated, not for the earth as such. For scripture has no interest in the universality of the flood for its own sake, but only in the universality of the judgment that it carries out.

13. F. D. Maurice, *The Patriarchs and Lawgivers of the Old Testament*, 2nd ed. (London, 1855), 33–49.

14. Maurice, *Patriarchs and Lawgivers*, 42.

15. Maurice, *Patriarchs and Lawgivers*, 44.

16. Maurice, *Patriarchs and Lawgivers*, 44–45.

17. Maurice, *Patriarchs and Lawgivers*, 35.

18. Maurice, *Patriarchs and Lawgivers*, 37.

19. Maurice, *Patriarchs and Lawgivers*, 39.

20. Maurice, *Patriarchs and Lawgivers*, 40.

21. Maurice, *Patriarchs and Lawgivers*, 41–42.

22. M. M. Kalisch, *Historical and Critical Commentary on the Old Testament: Genesis* (London: Longman, Brown, Green, Longmans, and Roberts, 1858), 41.

23. Kalisch, *Genesis*, 35–36.

24. Kalisch, *Genesis*, 35.

25. C. Wordsworth, *Genesis and Exodus: With Notes and Introductions* (London, 1866), xxxii.

26. Wordsworth, *Genesis and Exodus*, 18.

27. T. Whitelaw, *Genesis: The Pulpit Commentary*, ed. H. D. M. Spence and J. S. Exell (London: Kegan Paul, Trench, Trübner, 1897), xviii.

28. Whitelaw, *Genesis*, 2.

29. Whitelaw, *Genesis*, 12.

30. Whitelaw, *Genesis*, 28, quoting from T. H. Huxley's article "Biology" in the ninth edition of the *Encyclopaedia Britannica*.

31. Whitelaw, *Genesis*, 28.

32. Whitelaw, *Genesis*, 121.

33. Whitelaw, *Genesis*, 120. See Ibn Ezra, *Perush Ha Torah* (Jerusalem: Mossad Harav Kook, 1976), 1:40. Ibn Ezra, commenting on Genesis 7:23, opposes "our brothers who say that the flood was not upon the whole earth" (my translation). Matthew Poole, *A Commentary on the Holy Bible* (Edinburgh: Banner of Truth Trust 1962), 1:21, considers "Peradventure this flood might not be simply universal over the whole earth, but only over all the habitable world."

34. Whitelaw, *Genesis*, 98.

35. S. R. Driver, "Evolution Compatible with Faith," in his *Sermons on Subjects Connected with the Old Testament* (London: Methuen, 1892), 1–27. S. R. Driver, "The Cosmogony of Genesis," *Expositor* (1886): 23–45, was reissued with some abridgement in Driver's *The Book of Genesis* (London: Methuen, 1904), 19–33. See also S. R. Driver, *An Introduction to the Literature of the Old Testament* (Edinburgh: Clark, 1891).

36. Driver, "Evolution," 8.

37. Driver, "Evolution," 9–10.

38. Driver, "Evolution," 14.

39. Driver, "Evolution," 18.

40. See John Rogerson, "Colenso in the World of Nineteenth Century Intellectual Ferment," in *The Eye of the Storm: Bishop John William Colenso and the Crisis of Biblical Interpretation*, ed. J. A. Draper (London: Clark International, 2003), 127–135.

41. J. W. Colenso, "On Missions to the Zulus," in *Bringing Forth Light* ed. R. Edgecombe (Pietermaritzburg and Durban: University of Natal, Killie Campbell Africana Library, 1982), 205–238.

42. Colenso, "Missions to Zulus," 233. Charles Lyell, *Life, Letters and Journals of Sir Charles Lyell, Bart.* (London, 1881), 2:341.

6

Genesis and the Scientists
Dissonance among the Harmonizers

John Hedley Brooke

Looking back over what for the Christian faith had been a momentous century, the distinguished Oxford historian of religion J. Estlin Carpenter offered this early twentieth-century retrospect:

> Theories [about the Bible] once ardently cherished have been overthrown. Conceptions that had exerted immense influence for centuries, can no longer be maintained. On the other hand, the true value of the Bible has been enhanced. We have ceased to ask of it what it cannot give us; we cherish all the more highly what it can.[1]

On that positive note, Carpenter declares that "here is the testimony of men who have striven and suffered, men who have believed and hoped; and the power of their faith, their utterance, their character, shines out for us with illustrious value."[2]

In this chapter, I shall mainly be concerned with a historical process—the process that led to the realization that one thing the Genesis text cannot give us is a scientifically or historically accurate account of creation. However, I want to tell the story in a rather different way from the usual narrative. Standard accounts routinely stress the progressive advance of scientific knowledge and its challenge to a literal reading of scripture, culminating in the formidable challenge to Christian teaching posed by Darwin's theory of evolution. From a long-enough perspective, this streamlining of history can be very persuasive. But I would like to offer a finer-grained analysis, in which the following points assume importance:

Harmonization between new sciences and the Bible was almost always possible. Indeed, a lot of ink was spilled in exploring how best this could be achieved. As a contributor to the *British and Foreign Evangelical Review* in 1861 ingenuously and revealingly put it, "Half a dozen schemes of harmony are better than one."[3]

Second, the need to harmonize long preceded the time of Darwin. It is interesting that, when discussing the implications of science for biblical exegesis, Carpenter mentioned the earlier impact of geology but not the Darwinian theory per se.[4]

Third, a recurrent problem was that the harmonization could work too well—creating an embarrassing situation when the science moved on.

Fourth, the harmonization program was largely responsible for its own destruction. It has often been noted how, in the eighteenth century, the legend of Noah's ark lost its credibility as vast numbers of hitherto unknown animal species were discovered. Harmonization, initially at least, was not impossible. But as the pressure on space intensified, ever inflatable arks became ever more unfloatable. The harmonizers sank their own ship.[5] Something akin to this happened during the nineteenth century through repeated reinterpretations of the creation narratives.[6]

Finally, advances in science reinforced a trend already in place in biblical scholarship. This was the recognition of many different genres of literature in the books that constitute the Bible.[7] This in turn would facilitate the conclusion that the Genesis text principally speaks to our human existential condition, asserting both our uniqueness as a species and our ultimate dependence on the source of all creative processes.

Genesis and the Geologists

Questions concerning the compatibility of scripture with the latest science long preceded Darwin. In seventeenth-century Europe, there had been frequent recourse to the principle of biblical accommodation in order to make room for theories of the earth's mobility. If biblical language had been deliberately accommodated by the Holy Spirit to the limitations of the human mind, it should not be expected to contain technical scientific information that would have rendered it incomprehensible to the vulgar. Consequently, it should not be invoked to contest truths established by reason and the empirical methods of the sciences.[8] During the eighteenth century, a far greater challenge had appeared to conceptions of our place in the universe. This came from the French naturalist Buffon who, by placing the appearance of humans in the last of several epochs of earth history, challenged the almost-universal assumption that earth's history and human history were coextensive.[9]

A great expansion in the age of the earth accompanied the development of geology, not least because of the realization that, if the forces sculpting the earth's surface in the past were similar in kind and intensity to the forces acting today, then huge swathes of time were needed to account for the excavation of deep river gorges and the buildup of volcanic cones from their lava flows. Long before Darwin published, Georges Cuvier in France had demonstrated the extinction of large fossil quadrupeds.[10] The sobering implications of extinction for human self-perception could be deeply dispiriting, as Tennyson realized in his poem *In Memoriam*. There had once been consolation in the thought that, while nature was careless of the individual, it was "careful of the type"—but no longer. Tennyson's poem, with its famous depiction of "nature red in tooth and claw," was published in 1850. This was nine years before Darwin's *Origin of Species*, and Tennyson had begun it still earlier, in the 1830s, under the influence of Charles Lyell's *Principles of Geology*.

None of these developments was so devastating as to preclude attempts at harmonization. The successive epochs of Buffon's scheme could be identified with the successive "days" of the Genesis text. A universe far older than traditionally supposed could be construed as a grander creation, providing a more extensive theater for divine creativity. Furthermore, a natural theology was still possible. Lyell, for example, argued from the history of living forms that, whenever an environment had developed that would support life of a certain kind, that very form of life had come into being to occupy the niche. A "Presiding Mind" was implied by the plenitude and adaptation of living things.[11] Even the litany of extinction that could be read from the fossil record did not rule out the possibility that, in wishing to create every creature it was possible to create, the Deity had sometimes had to remove some to make room for others. This, at least, is how Oxford's geological enthusiast William Buckland rationalized the geological revelation.[12] His opposite number in Cambridge, Adam Sedgwick, saw in the fossil record data that, in his opinion, would defeat the atheist. Species had not existed from eternity. There was a time when each and every one had not existed. Records of multiple creative acts were inscribed in the strata.[13]

This means that we should not exaggerate the difficulties. But what of the biblical text? Several moves were repeatedly made. In his inaugural lecture at Oxford, Buckland sought to defuse anxiety by vindicating geology from the charge of irreligion. One of the strategies in his *Vindiciae Geologicae* (1819) was to argue that many features of the earth's surface, smooth U-shaped valleys, for example, were simply inexplicable without postulating a deluge, whose receding waters had carried great boulders over large distances. He has sometimes been mocked for such a contrived harmonization with the Genesis Flood, but it is sometimes forgotten that we, too, have recourse to a geologically recent event—an ice age—to explain the same phenomena. In the 1820s and early 1830s, there was nothing to suggest that the human race was other than of recent origin, as Lyell himself was able to argue. Given that biblical history is concerned with human history, there was no necessary collision on this particular point. As the Scottish naturalist John Fleming insisted in 1822, "among the wildest theories of geologists, there is not one who has ever thought of giving the human race a higher antiquity than that which is assigned by Scripture, and which is amply confirmed by every thing that we know of the progress of human society, arts, and language."[14]

If the issue was the massive age of the earth, it was possible to create more time for the biblical account by postulating a large gap in time between "In the beginning" and the events of the first Genesis "day," when the rudiments of a world began to be molded toward their present configuration. Alternatively, highly elaborate schemes of concordance were conceived in which the rendering of days as epochs resulted in claims that the order of creation in Genesis broadly matched that given by geology. A particularly striking example occurs in the writings of the Scottish evangelical Hugh Miller, who prided himself on having found a loophole in David Hume's famous critique of natural theology. Hume's insistence on the principle that causes must always be proportionate to their effects, if applied to the fauna of the earliest strata, would permit an inference only to a Creator powerful enough to create the simple creatures of those earliest epochs. But, as Miller triumphantly observed, Hume's principle would lead to a false inference because we know from the more complex creatures of subsequent epochs that the Deity was capable of exercising a greater power.[15]

Ingeniously, Miller found in geology another resource with which to combat Hume's skepticism. The logical difficulties arising from the fact that we have only one universe on which to base any inference to a designer were brushed aside with the claim that geology provided what Hume had lacked— experience of plural creations, of successive worlds, as it were.[16] In defending his beloved geology from its Mosaic detractors, Miller cited the great beauty of fossil forms, suggestive of a common aesthetic sensibility in the human mind and in that of its Creator.[17] And to cap his arguments for congruence between Genesis and geology, he gave a double significance to the days of creation. Not only did they correspond to the order of creation as disclosed by the fossil record; they could also be interpreted as the successive days on which the author of the inspired text was vouchsafed a vision of how the earth had been during each of its critical stages.[18]

Dissonances before Darwin

If the need for harmonizing schemes was felt before Darwin, their very success released new opportunities for both dissonance and dissidence. This becomes clear from one of the contributions to *Essays and Reviews* (1860), a book that more than Darwin's *Origin of Species* rocked the English church precisely because among its authors were Oxford divines arguing that the Bible should be read like any other book. Looking back over sixty years of harmonizing strategies, Charles Goodwin declared that the repeated attempts to reconcile Genesis with geology had led to failure.[19] In retrospect, it was possible to see that it had been a misguided strategy and one that had imposed on scientists themselves a burden they should not have been asked to carry. Goodwin pointedly identified problems with each of the harmonizing schemes. Both Buckland in Oxford and Sedgwick in Cambridge had been obliged to retreat from the claim that geology provided proof of a universal flood. Even when Buckland had discussed the relics of the deluge in 1823, the hyena den that he postulated to make sense of the bones in the Kirkdale cave was not one into which the biblical Flood had swept the animal remains from afar. They had been there before and after the Flood, a consideration that also challenged contemporary opinion on how the deluge had happened. It could not have been by the interchange of land and sea if the animals whose remains were found in the cave had lived on land that was dry both before and after the Flood.[20] Among Buckland's most vehement critics was John Fleming, who took the view that there was nothing in the biblical account of Noah's Flood to indicate that it had any geological consequences. References to dissonance among the commentators can hardly be exaggerations when Sedgwick could say of Fleming's censure that he had "often heard of the tomahawk and the scalping knife in warfare, but this was the first time he had ever seen it employed in scientific literature."[21]

A rough concordance between the order of creation in Genesis and the order discernible from the fossil record might be affirmed, but there was dissonance in the details. Goodwin observed that in Genesis the birds preceded the reptiles, whereas in geology it was the reptiles that came first. The alternative strategy of protecting the literal days by expanding the time between an initial chaos and the first day proved to be unsustainable with advances in stratigraphy that undermined belief in the almost simultaneous creation of all living things. But the point on which Goodwin liked to dwell was the discord *between* the various attempts to preserve scientific authority for the Bible. The "trenchant manner" in which "theological geologists overthrow one another's theories" spoke volumes and was a sure indication that the authority of scripture should be reserved for its moral jurisdiction, not for any scientific provenance.[22] "No one contends," he wrote in conclusion, that the Bible "can be used as a basis of astronomical or geological teaching." Straining to bring it into accord with scientifically established facts was to "despoil it of its consistency and grandeur, both of which may be preserved if we recognize in it, not an authentic utterance of Divine knowledge, but a human utterance, which it has pleased Providence to use in a special way for the education of mankind."[23] That was perhaps the most radical way of disposing of the claim, implicit in the harmonization program, that the Bible spoke science, albeit in summary or in elliptical forms. The more conservative tactic was to reappropriate the principle of accommodation, which in earlier periods had allowed astronomers their autonomy. Conflict between these metalevel exegetical principles created yet further scope for discord. It therefore makes sense to say that Darwin's theory compounded problems that already existed, which is not to say that it was not divisive in additional respects.

The Divisiveness of Darwinism

Superimposed on the divisions created by one historical science, geology, were those created by another, evolutionary biology. Darwin's own position in 1859 was neither Christian nor atheist. The roots of his eventual agnosticism are visible in his correspondence, but he had no hesitation in referring to a Creator who had impressed laws upon the universe, the outcome of which conformed to our idea of the highest good, namely, the production of the highest animals.[24] Since Darwin had rejected the authority of revelation but still believed that the laws of nature were not self-explanatory, he is best described as a "deist" when *Origin* was published. The main thrust of his argument was that no miracles were required to explain how new species originated; there were no "independent acts of creation," as he frequently put it. New species derived from preexisting species by long, gradual processes of change as advantageous variations accumulated under what Darwin called the law of natural selection. In the competition for limited resources, advantaged variants would tend to displace their immediate progenitors. Darwin knew, of course, that his vision of the history of life would be shocking to many. His hope, however, was that a philosophy of nature in which the wonderful variety of living things was the result of "designed laws" would not be theologically objectionable. Quotations from Francis Bacon, from William Whewell, and, in the second edition of *Origin*, from Joseph Butler gave theological sanction to the view that there was nothing sacrilegious in invoking natural causes rather than divine intervention to account for the plenitude of life. As for the first form or forms of life from which all species were ultimately derived, Darwin was not averse to using what he called "Pentateuchal language," referring to a Creator who had breathed life into the primordial forms.[25] Explicit in his second edition was the statement that his theory should not offend the religious views of anyone.

The reasons that Darwin's optimism in this respect was to prove misplaced are well known. There was the primary issue of human dignity and uniqueness if one accepted continuity with the animals. What of the human soul and the prospect of a life after death? If the remarkable structural adaptations celebrated by William Paley were simply the result of the perfecting process of natural selection, was the appearance of design in nature anything more than an illusion? And there were, of course, the biblical considerations. Did it make sense to speak of our fallen state if the human race had actually risen from an animal ancestry? For evangelical commentators, there was an obvious concern: how could Christ be the second Adam sent to redeem humankind if there had never been a first? Although the Genesis text implied that creation had taken place in stages, the account of the creation of woman was hard to square with Darwin's naturalism. For these and other reasons, the Darwinian theory would be a divisive force within Christendom. Darwin's old friend Adam Sedgwick reproached him for disconnecting the natural from the moral, which had traditionally been bound together by the perception of final causes and divine purposes in nature.[26]

Darwin was deeply hurt by Sedgwick's censure, describing himself as a martyr. But not all clergymen were so censorious. It is the dissonance between their respective evaluations that is most striking and that deserves special attention. For example, another of Darwin's Cambridge mentors, John Henslow, went so far as to rebuke Sedgwick for his attack:

> I got up and stuck up for Darwin as well as I could, refusing to allow
> that he was guided by any but truthful motives, and declaring that
> he himself believed he was exalting and not debasing our views of
> a Creator, in attributing to him a power of imposing laws on the
> organic world by which to do his work, as effectually as his laws
> imposed upon the inorganic had done it in the mineral kingdom.[27]

The dissonance is also audible between Sedgwick and an Oxford divine, Baden Powell, the professor of geometry in the university. Sedgwick complained of passages in Powell's contribution to *Essays and Reviews* that "would astound Cambridge men." Powell had affirmed Darwin's theory, boldly announcing that it would cause a revolution in how God's relation to nature should be understood. For Sedgwick, this was simply an uncritical capitulation.[28]

Other contrasting reactions show how divisive the theory was. The altercation between Samuel Wilberforce, bishop of Oxford, and Thomas Henry Huxley at the 1860 meeting of the British Association for the Advancement of Science is often taken to epitomize a conflict between religion and science in the early Victorian period. There is much that is unsatisfactory in standard accounts of this legendary encounter.[29] But a crucial point is that Wilberforce was not the only representative of Anglican opinion at the Oxford meeting. The official sermon was preached by Frederick Temple who, years later, would become archbishop of Canterbury. Temple saw no problem in principle with the extension of natural law, arguing that theologians had too often made the mistake of erecting their theologies in the gaps not yet filled by scientific knowledge. For Temple, the more one could explain by recourse to *natural* laws, the greater the support for belief in a world governed by *moral* laws. The discord between Wilberforce and Temple became a public issue in Wilberforce's review of *Essays and Reviews* and was particularly poignant because Temple had been one of Wilberforce's ordinands.[30]

There was dissonance in North America as well as in Britain. At Harvard, Louis Agassiz fought a rearguard action to protect his view that the history of life on earth was the unfolding of a divine plan. For Agassiz, the connections between species were nonmaterial.[31] By contrast, Asa Gray delighted Darwin not only by showing a thorough understanding of natural selection but also by divesting the theory of antireligious connotations. Here were two Harvard scientists taking opposing stands. Gray even suggested that an evolutionary perspective could help theologians with their greatest problem—the extent of pain and suffering in the world. If a struggle for existence had been the motor of evolution, making it possible for human beings to emerge, then other consequences of the competitive process were the price that had to be paid.[32]

At Princeton, a division occurred between Presbyterian theologians. In his book *What Is Darwinism?* (1874), Charles Hodge was clearly worried by what he saw as the evacuation of design, which for him rendered Darwin's theory effectively atheistic. By contrast, James McCosh, who later became president of the university, was more receptive, arguing that the prevalence of accidents in the Darwinian mechanism could not be accidental. It could be seen as inherent within a mechanism designed to be creative.[33] In short, there was a background of division and dissonance against which differences over biblical exegesis were played out.

Dissonance among Harmonizers

In each of these disputes, the antagonists were not suggesting that, in some general sense, science and religion were locked in inescapable conflict. They all believed that peace was possible with the appropriate modification of views. This important point has been recognized by Bernard Lightman who, with reference to Victorian sciences and religions, speaks of "discordant harmonies."[34] His point is that the conflict was not so much between science and religion as between disputants with their own recipes for concord. As polemical a Darwinian as T. H. Huxley, who was certainly antiestablishment, anticlerical, and no friend to theology, wanted peace between science and religion. There was room for both as long as religious presuppositions were kept out of science. Consonantly with that view, Huxley insisted that the exclusion of teleology from scientific explanation did not mean that there was no "higher teleology" giving meaning to the great vista of evolution. There was space for both science and religion because, in the last analysis, science was neither Christian nor anti-Christian but extra-Christian. Thus, he could emphasize, surprisingly perhaps to his modern acolytes, that "the antagonism between science and religion, about which we hear so much, appears to me to be purely factitious." It was "fabricated, on the one hand, by short-sighted religious people who confound a certain branch of science, theology, with religion; and, on the other, by equally short-sighted scientific people who forget that science takes for its province only that which is susceptible of clear intellectual comprehension."[35]

In contrast to Huxley were eminent Victorian scientists who believed that harmony was to be achieved by integrating insights from theology and science. An example would be William Thomson (later, Lord Kelvin), whose understanding of energy resonated with his biblical theology. For Thomson, the principle of energy conservation was a reminder that only God could create and destroy the energy inherent in the universe, while the principle of energy dissipation was a potent reminder of a sense of direction in earth history and the transitory nature of our world. There was a "tendency in the material world for motion to become diffused."[36] The reference was not actually to Genesis but to Psalm 102: "Of old hast thou laid the foundation of the earth: and the heavens are the work of thy hands. They shall perish, but thou shalt endure: yea, all of them shall wax old like a garment." Between Huxley and Thomson, there was an underlying discord. For the latter, harmony could be achieved by integrating insights from both science and scripture; for the former, harmony was to be achieved by avoiding such harmonization.

Biblical Theology and Darwin's Theory

Serious attempts were made by Christian thinkers to assimilate as far as possible the idea of evolution and to rethink their theologies of nature accordingly. One of Darwin's earliest converts was a clergyman, Charles Kingsley, whose popular novels played a large role in familiarizing a Victorian audience with the idea of evolution. Kingsley delighted Darwin with a letter in which he approved the idea that species resulted from a creative process of evolution rather than from so many conjuring tricks.[37] As Kingsley later put it, there had been wisdom in a Deity who could make all things, but there was now a greater wisdom to be seen—in a Deity who could make things make themselves. When Asa Gray saw theological advantages in Darwin's science, he welcomed, as we have seen, a new perspective on the problem of pain and suffering. But in his eyes, there were additional advantages. The Darwinian theory substantiated belief in the unity of the human species since all human beings ultimately derived from a common ancestor. For Gray, Darwin, and Alfred Russel Wallace, here was a valuable corrective to polygenic ideas that could so easily lend support to slavery. As Gray put it, in the light of Darwinian theory, those who "recognize several or numerous human species, will hardly be able to maintain that such species were primordial and supernatural in the ordinary sense of the word."[38] It is a mistake to imagine that all evolutionary thinkers were materialists. Even Wallace, who had conceived the mechanism of natural selection independently of Darwin, would become increasingly attracted to the idea that the course of evolution had been under the guidance of some kind of spiritual power. Wallace, like Darwin, had rejected Christianity, but he could not bring himself to believe that the finer attributes of the human mind—mathematical prowess, musical ability, and other aesthetic sensibilities—were explicable by natural selection alone. They could not be reduced to their survival value. Wallace gradually diverged from Darwin in his willingness to take seriously the relevance of a world of spirit, creating distance and dissonance between them.[39]

From Darwin's correspondence, it is clear that anxieties about biblical interpretation were raised in letters to him. Here is an early example from a clerical naturalist, his friend Leonard Jenyns:

> I am not one of those in the habit of mixing up questions of science
> and Scripture, but I can hardly see what sense or meaning is to be

attached to Gen 2:7 & yet more to vv. 21–22, of the same chapter, giving an account of the creation of *woman*,—if the human species at
least has not been created independently of other animals.[40]

There clearly were new exegetical problems to add to those arising from the
scholarly claim that there were two distinct creation narratives in Genesis 1
and 2.

Appeal to biblical authority certainly lay behind many attacks on Darwin's
theory, though, as James Moore showed in his penetrating study *The Post-
Darwinian Controversies*, reservations were often framed in broader cultural
and philosophical terms, with frequent references to Darwin's desertion of
sound Baconian method.[41] Darwin appears to have felt that it was clerical dab-
blers in natural history rather than biblical theologians themselves who gave
him the most trouble.[42] Interestingly, even among his critics, there was a lack
of unanimity. Darwin wryly observed that his "revilers" were "tearing each
other to pieces."[43]

What kind of accommodation could be achieved? In very general terms,
it was perhaps not too difficult to achieve a limited rapprochement. After all,
the Genesis text did not say "Let there be man" but "Let us make man." Again,
if one were looking for some general congruence, one might observe that
Genesis describes life appearing in stages, which is what evolutionary science
describes in detail. In America, George Frederick Wright was an influential
proponent of theistic evolution, who saw no problem with the Genesis account:
"the language of Genesis may properly be regarded as the language of theistic
evolution." And he pointed to the biblical phrase "Let the earth bring forth" as
an implicit avowal of organic evolution.[44]

Such moves still assumed correspondence of a kind between biblical and
scientific understandings. An alternative approach, increasingly adopted by
liberal Christian thinkers, was to reevaluate the concept of revelation. Instead
of seeing the Bible as a once-for-all and definitive revelation of divine truth, the
concept of evolution was applied to human understanding itself. On this view,
revelation was an ongoing process, and spiritual understanding was progressive. After all, a progressive understanding was visible within the Bible itself,
and it was not difficult to extrapolate the process to include revelation through
human history and religious experience. Accordingly, another American commentator, Newman Smyth, could write that "the same powers of development,
the same law of evolution, seem to have been followed, alike, in nature and in
the Bible."[45] By the end of the nineteenth century, this had become a widely held
view. A Congregational clergyman, Washington Gladden, recalled that he, like
many other Christians, had gradually come to perceive that God's revelation

had occurred by a "continuous process" that paralleled his "work of creation."[46] At this metalevel, harmonization was clearly possible; but, once again, the harmonies resolved into dissonance. The question remained whether divine truth revealed in other realms of human experience supplemented the revelation contained in the Bible or, in effect, superseded it.

Ways Forward

We are used to thinking of linear scientific progress and of a decisive impact of Darwin on the previously harmonious relations between science and religion. By focusing on dissonances both before and after Darwin, and within both scientific and theological groups, I have tried to show that it was never that simple. There are real dangers in trying to streamline the history to fit some preconceived model of the secularizing effect of the sciences.[47] There are other reasons, too, that a linear model fails. For example, Darwin's mechanism of natural selection did not prevail during the second half of the nineteenth century—certainly not as the predominant factor in evolutionary change.[48] Nevertheless, in conclusion, I shall identify three positions that emerged from the complexity of debate and that did offer promise for the future. One concerns the scope of biblical authority, the second the viability of natural selection, and the third the wisdom of tying biblical exegesis too closely to the latest scientific theories.

My first position is also discussed by Professor Rogerson in his contribution to this book. It is illustrated by the efforts of Samuel Driver to show that evolution is compatible with faith. In an Oxford sermon of 1883 preached from Genesis 2:7, Driver created the space for a nonliteral reading of the text. He did this by emphasizing the many different literary genres in the Bible, including poetry, parable, and allegory. The creation narrative was neither history nor science. But, emphatically, this did not mean it was vacuous. It emphasized the dependence of the universe on a transcendent power and the dangers of idolatry. Biblical texts could still be said to be inspired without meaning a direct process of divine communication to the biblical authors. Rather, there had been a "divine intuition," which had allowed them to infuse ordinary human sources with insights drawn from their religious life and traditions. This was a way of looking at the relations between science and theology that avoided collision and, in Rogerson's words, "was said to have saved the faith of a generation."

My second position was taken by two Oxford scientists at the close of the nineteenth and beginning of the twentieth century. Their names were Edward Poulton and Frederick Dixey. They are remarkable because they "kept the

Darwinian faith" in natural selection at a time when it was in danger of eclipse. They are particularly remarkable because they also kept the faith as Christian men of science whose friends included the theologian Aubrey Moore. In a theology that stressed the absolute centrality of God's incarnation in the person of Christ, Moore made room for Darwin's theory. In a much-cited aphorism, he declared that, under the guise of a foe, Darwin had done the work of a friend.[49] Darwin was a friend to the Christian religion because he had purged it of a semi-deistic position in which God was supposedly active only when intervening to create new species. This deus ex machina was not the Christian God, and Darwin had done Christianity a good turn by getting rid of it. The significance of this story lies in the fact that both Poulton and Dixey were influenced by Moore's theology, making it easier for them to defend an undiluted account of natural selection.[50] It is an interesting example because it shows how theological reasoning could still be relevant to the world of science, even if it had ceased to pose technical questions at the cutting edge of scientific research.

My third way forward is illustrated by a British scientist of the nineteenth century who ranks with Darwin as a giant: James Clerk Maxwell. I conclude with him because he was a great scientist who still took his Bible seriously. In a letter to the bishop of Gloucester, written in November 1876, Maxwell explained why trying too hard to harmonize science with the Bible was not the best way of achieving peace and concord. The context was not, in this case, Darwinian evolution. Maxwell was concerned by a statement, which he had seen "printed in most commentaries," that the fact of light being created before the sun was in striking agreement with the "last result of science." What worried him was that this last result was no longer the last result. As he explained to the bishop, it is "certainly older than the time when any notions of the [wave] theory became prevalent."[51]

Now, it gets more interesting. Maxwell offered a possible scenario by which a harmonization could be achieved:

> If it were necessary to provide an interpretation of the text in accordance with the science of 1876 (which may not agree with that of 1896), it would be very tempting to say that the light of the first day means the all-embracing aether, the vehicle of radiation, and not actual light, whether from the sun or from any other source.

But another question then reared its head. Could the biblical author possibly have had such a sophisticated intention? Maxwell thought not: "I cannot suppose that this was the very idea meant to be conveyed by the original author of the book to those for whom he was writing." What then was? "He tells us of a previous darkness. Both light and darkness imply a being who can see if there is light, but not if it is dark, and the words are always understood so. That light and darkness are terms relative to the creature only is recognized in Psalm 139:12."

Maxwell was a theologically literate scientist warning about the dangers of introducing sophisticated and transient theories of science into efforts of harmonization. Ultimately, the harmonization program defeated itself—partly because of the dissonance between the harmonizers, but also because the more successful the harmonization, the more trouble it caused when the science moved on. Here is Maxwell again, in the same letter to Bishop John Ellicott:

> I should be very sorry if an interpretation founded on a most conjec-
> tural scientific hypothesis were to get fastened to the text in Genesis,
> even if by so doing it got rid of the old statement of the commenta-
> tors which has long ceased to be intelligible. The rate of change
> of scientific hypothesis is naturally much more rapid than that of
> Biblical interpretations, so that if an interpretation is founded on
> such an hypothesis, it may help to keep the hypothesis above ground
> long after it ought to be buried and forgotten.[52]

There speaks the scientist; but, in 1876, the bishop could agree with him: "I cordially agree with you as to the light question. Theologians are a great deal too fond of using up the last scientific hypothesis they can get hold of."[53] One would like to think the lesson has been learned.

Acknowledgments

I wish to thank the directors of the Institute of Advanced Studies at Durham University for a visiting fellowship during 2007 that enabled work on this chapter to be completed.

NOTES

   1. J. Estlin Carpenter, *The Bible in the Nineteenth Century* (London: Longmans, 1903), 453.
   2. Carpenter, *The Bible*, 453.
   3. Quoted in Alvar Ellegard, *Darwin and the General Reader* (Gothenburg, Sweden: Gothenburg University Press, 1958), 164.
   4. Carpenter, *The Bible*, 454–463.
   5. Janet Browne, *The Secular Ark* (New Haven, Conn.: Yale University Press, 1983), 26–27.

6. Francis Haber, *The Age of the World from Moses to Darwin* (Baltimore, Md.: Johns Hopkins University Press, 1959), 199–219.

7. Alan Richardson, *The Bible in the Age of Science* (London: SCM, 1961), 62–76.

8. This was one of Galileo's arguments in self-defense, and it was also found among Protestant astronomers who followed Calvin in insisting that "the Holy Spirit had no intention to teach astronomy; and in proposing instruction meant to be common to the simplest and most uneducated persons, he made use by Moses and the other prophets of popular language, that none might shelter himself under the pretext of obscurity." See Kenneth J. Howell, "Styles of Science, Calvinism and the Common Good in the Early Dutch Republic," in *Religious Values and the Rise of Science in Europe*, ed. John Hedley Brooke and Ekmeleddin Ihsanoglu (Istanbul: IRCICA, 2005), 111–130, esp. 123–124.

9. Martin J. S. Rudwick, "The Shape and Meaning of Earth History," in *God and Nature: Historical Essays in the Encounter between Christianity and Science*, ed. David Lindberg and Ronald Numbers (Berkeley: University of California Press, 1986), 296–321.

10. Martin J. S. Rudwick, *Bursting the Limits of Time* (Chicago: University of Chicago Press, 2005), 364–388.

11. Richard Yeo, "The Principle of Plenitude and Natural Theology in Nineteenth-Century Britain," *British Journal for the History of Science* 19 (1986): 263–282.

12. Nicolaas Rupke, *The Great Chain of History: William Buckland and the English School of Geology 1814–1849* (Oxford: Oxford University Press, 1983), 173.

13. John Hedley Brooke, "The Natural Theology of the Geologists: Some Theological Strata," in *Images of the Earth: Essays in the History of the Environmental Sciences*, 2nd ed., ed. Ludmilla Jordanova and Roy Porter (Oxford: Alden Press for the British Society for the History of Science, 1997), 53–74.

14. Cited by James Burns, "John Fleming and the Geological Deluge," *British Journal for the History of Science* 40 (2007): 205–225, on 209.

15. Hugh Miller, *The Testimony of the Rocks* (1857; Edinburgh: Nimmo, 1869), 184–187.

16. Miller, *Testimony*, 184.

17. John Hedley Brooke, "Like Minds: The God of Hugh Miller," in *Hugh Miller and the Controversies of Victorian Science*, ed. Michael Shortland (Oxford: Oxford University Press, 1996), 171–186.

18. Miller, *Testimony*, 155–168.

19. Charles Goodwin, "On the Mosaic Cosmogony," in *Essays and Reviews*, ed. Frederick Temple et al. (1860; London: Longman, 1861), 207–253.

20. Rupke, *Great Chain*, 39–40.

21. Cited in Burns, "John Fleming," 214.

22. Goodwin, "Mosaic Cosmogony," 238.

23. Goodwin, "Mosaic Cosmogony," 253.

24. Charles Darwin, *On the Origin of Species* (London: Murray, 1859), 488.

25. The breathing metaphor was present in the first edition of *Origin* (490), to which was added the explicit reference to a Creator in the second and subsequent editions.

26. Adam Sedgwick to Charles Darwin, 24 November 1859, in Frederick Burkhardt, ed., *The Correspondence of Charles Darwin* (Cambridge: Cambridge University Press, 1991), 7:396–398 (hereafter, *Darwin Correspondence*).

27. John Henslow to Joseph Hooker, 10 May 1860, in *Darwin Correspondence*, 8:200–201.

28. *Darwin Correspondence*, 8:201.

29. For corrective accounts, see John R. Lucas, "Wilberforce and Huxley: A Legendary Encounter," *Historical Journal* 22 (1979): 313–330; Sheridan Gilley, "The Huxley-Wilberforce Debate: A Reconstruction," in *Religion and Humanism: Studies in Church History*, ed. Keith Robbins (Oxford: Blackwell, 1981), 17:325–340; John Hedley Brooke, "The Wilberforce-Huxley Debate: Why Did It Happen?" *Science and Christian Belief* 13 (2001): 127–141; and Frank James, "An 'Open Clash between Science and the Church'? Wilberforce, Huxley and Hooker on Darwin at the British Association, Oxford, 1860," in *Science and Beliefs: From Natural Philosophy to Natural Science, 1700–1900*, ed. David Knight and Matthew Eddy (Aldershot, England: Ashgate, 2005), 171–193.

30. Samuel Wilberforce, *Essays Contributed to the Quarterly Review*, 2 vols. (London: Murray, 1874), 1:114–121.

31. Jon Roberts, *Darwinism and the Divine in America* (Madison: University of Wisconsin Press, 1988), 34–37.

32. Asa Gray, *Darwiniana*, ed. A. Hunter Dupree (Cambridge, Mass.: Harvard University Press, 1963), 310–311.

33. James R. Moore, *The Post-Darwinian Controversies* (Cambridge: Cambridge University Press, 1979), 245–250.

34. Bernard Lightman, "Victorian Sciences and Religions: Discordant Harmonies," in *Science in Theistic Contexts: Cognitive Dimensions*, ed. John Hedley Brooke, Margaret J. Osler, and Jitse Van der Meer (Chicago: University of Chicago Press, Journals Division, 2001), 343–366.

35. Thomas Henry Huxley, *Science and Hebrew Tradition* (London: Macmillan, 1904), 160–161.

36. Crosbie Smith and Norton Wise, *Energy and Empire: A Biographical Study of Lord Kelvin* (Cambridge: Cambridge University Press, 1989), 330.

37. Charles Kingsley to Charles Darwin, 18 November 1859, in *Darwin Correspondence*, 7:379–380.

38. Gray, *Darwiniana*, 144. On the complex relations among monogenism, polygenism, and racial stereotyping, see Robert Kenny, "From the Curse of Ham to the Curse of Nature: The Influence of Natural Selection on the Debate on Human Unity before the Publication of *The Descent of Man*," *British Journal for the History of Science* 40 (2007): 367–388.

39. James Moore and Adrian Desmond, "Introduction," to Charles Darwin, *The Descent of Man* (1879; London: Penguin, 2004), xxxviii–xliii.

40. Leonard Jenyns to Charles Darwin, 4 January 1860, in *Darwin Correspondence*, 8:13–14.

41. Moore, *Post-Darwinian Controversies*, 193–216.

42. Charles Darwin to Asa Gray, 22 May [1860], in *Darwin Correspondence*, 8:223.

43. Charles Darwin to John Henslow, 8 May [1860], in *Darwin Correspondence*, 8:194–195.

44. Roberts, *Darwinism*, 148.

45. Roberts, *Darwinism*, 162.

46. Roberts, *Darwinism*, 162.

47. John Hedley Brooke, "Science and Secularization," in *Reinventing Christianity: Nineteenth-Century Contexts*, ed. Linda Woodhead (Aldershot, England: Ashgate, 2001), 229–238.

48. Peter J. Bowler, *The Eclipse of Darwinism* (Baltimore, Md.: Johns Hopkins University Press, 1983), and *Reconciling Science and Religion* (Chicago: University of Chicago Press, 2001), 122–159.

49. Arthur Peacocke, "Biological Evolution and Christian Theology—Yesterday and Today," in *Darwinism and Divinity*, ed. John R. Durant (Oxford: Blackwell, 1985), 101–130, esp. 110–111.

50. Richard England, "Natural Selection, Teleology, and the Logos: From Darwin to the Oxford Neo-Darwinists, 1859–1909," in Brooke, Osler, and Van der Meer, *Science in Theistic Contexts*, 270–287.

51. James Clerk Maxwell to Charles John Ellicott, 22 November 1876, in *The Scientific Letters and Papers of James Clerk Maxwell*, vol. 3, *1874–1879*, ed. Peter Harman (Cambridge: Cambridge University Press, 2002), 416–418, on 417 (hereafter, *Maxwell Letters*).

52. Maxwell to Ellicott, 22 November 1876, in *Maxwell Letters*, 3:418.

53. Ellicott to Maxwell, 24 November 1876, in *Maxwell Letters*, 3:418.

7

Science and Religion in Nineteenth- and Twentieth-Century Landscape Art

David Brown

In this chapter, I will explore how changes in scientific understanding of the origins of the world and of humanity affected artists, in particular their approach to landscape painting. The natural world had so often been treated in the past as God's first book of revelation that inevitably these changes also had an impact on how and, indeed, whether artists continued to express belief in divine creation in and through their landscape painting. As a way of measuring how far their responses changed and developed, the chapter is in three parts. The first explores attitudes prior to Darwin's breakthrough; the second, what happened in the later nineteenth century; the third, continuing developments in the twentieth century.

It is important to note that, in confining my attention to land-scape art (even if broadly understood), limitations of space mean that I deliberately preclude other types of relations between science and art or between religion and art that also left their mark during this period. So, on the former, nothing is said about the influence of science on art more generally, despite some fascinating cases. Among them might be mentioned, for example, how Munch's famous *Scream* (1893) in part reflects his revulsion at the new world of microbes and the effect of microbes on his own family. Both his mother and sister died from tuberculosis in the year that its bacterial cause was first detected (in 1882).[1] Again, there is nothing on Magritte's treatment of the relativity of time in his familiar picture of a steam engine coming out of a fireplace with the mantelpiece clock fixed at a set time.² Equally, I have ignored the positive evaluation of religion in the context of the relationship between religion and science where this has nothing to do with landscape. For example, American postwar abstract art is often interpreted as an attempt to restate spiritual values in the face of nuclear power, but this was not achieved through landscape. Again, while Constantin Brancusi is concerned in many of his works to reestablish some sort of connection between this world and the divine, his chosen medium is sculpture, not landscape art.³

Landscape Art before the Crisis

While it is untrue that there was no interest in landscape art before the Renaissance, medieval art had in general a quite different approach. Birds, animals, and the contexts in which they were placed were given largely symbolic values, and so appearance as such was of less interest than specific associations, as indicated in bestiaries and so on.⁴ This gradually changed with the Renaissance, but even then it took well into the seventeenth century before landscape art was allowed an independent existence. The French artists Nicholas Poussin (d. 1665) and Claude Lorrain (d. 1682) still had to pretend to some historical or biblical theme, whereas someone like Jacob van Ruisdael (d. 1682) and his Dutch contemporaries could offer their patrons landscape in its own right. Although historians dispute how far this is true, it is possible to detect, to varying degrees, in all three the desire to treat their landscape art as an exercise in natural theology.⁵ Not that this is achieved by any slavish copying of the scene before them. Rather, much as other artists might be motivated by purely aesthetic considerations to produce balance and proportion or particular effects of light, such artists see themselves as justified in modifying the landscape before them in order to clarify a sense of divine presence or action upon the environment. In the early part of the nineteenth century, this was achieved in two contrasting ways. On the one hand, landscapes of immanence suggested the near presence of God within the world itself; on the other, those where transcendence was stressed invited awe at the wonder of what God had achieved in the creation.

Let me take immanence first. The extent to which the literal truth of Genesis was assumed at this time is well illustrated by the way in which the figure of Moses is set at the center of one of a pair of J. M. W. Turner's paintings in which he explores Goethe's rival theory of the origin of colors, exploiting it as an image for the post-Flood world.⁶ Whereas probably no deep religious motives lie behind Turner's action, his contemporary John Constable (d. 1837) offers a quite different scenario. Constable was a committed High Church Anglican, and there seems little doubt that quite a number of his landscapes were intended to evoke a sense of divine presence in nature.[7] Indeed, in respect to his series centered on Salisbury Cathedral, we know not only of his concern to avoid overly simplistic presentations of that message but also of his use of such a landscape to convey his pleasure at what he saw as the deliverance of the Church of England from near disaster. Thus, whereas Bishop John Fisher had complained of too many clouds in an early depiction of the building in its natural setting, in an 1831 version even more clouds are used in conjunction with a rainbow to suggest that the worst dangers from the proposed Reform Bill are now past.[8] While his younger contemporary Samuel Palmer (d. 1881) was less subtle with his explicit use of biblical imagery, his paintings do have an engaging, mysterious quality about them. His later work, however, lacks the visionary quality of what he produced at Shoreham (1823–1835). While impact from the new science might have been to blame, the more likely explanation lies in the responsibilities of married life and the traumatic death of his son.[9]

Quite different is the work of Caspar David Friedrich (d. 1841) and the American Hudson River school, which includes Thomas Cole (d. 1848) and Frederic Church (d. 1900). Here, it is the majesty of the creation that is usually at the center of their concerns. With Friedrich, we know that he was influenced both by the writings of Schleiermacher and by Kosegarten's *Uferpredikten* (Shore Sermons), in the main in a transcendent direction.[10] For instance, his *Winter Landscape* of 1811 uses tall pine trees and a cathedral tower in the hazy distance to suggest awe, but also shows divine action in an abandoned crutch lying in the snow.[11] Although in many respects quite distant from the views of Calvin, Schleiermacher was in fact a Calvinist minister, and it is to Calvinism that we must also look in explaining the background of the Hudson River school and also in part its late twentieth-century reemergence from obscurity.[12] While Cole died without witnessing the impact of Darwin, with F. E. Church, as we shall see, it is possible to identify various changes in his approach. In those earlier times, though, both used the scale of the American landscape to say something about the majesty and grandeur of God as its Creator. Cole's *Garden of Eden* (1828) and *Voyage of Life* (1840) and Church's *Above the Clouds at Sunrise* (1849) and *Niagara Falls* (1857) may all be used to make that point.[13]

Even so, it is important not to isolate Darwin, as though his *Origin of Species* of 1859 was unrelated to other developments, scientific and otherwise, that were already taking place during this period. Contemporaneous with the artists mentioned above were major geological disputes about how the origin of the world should be understood. Although Sir Charles Lyell is nowadays usually seen as the most significant figure, at the time William Buckland at

Oxford and Adam Sedgwick at Cambridge probably had more influence. While both sought to reconcile their findings with scripture, they did call for its reinterpretation.[14] Likewise, German scholars such as Strauss and Bauer were calling into question the historical reliability of the Bible and in the process giving birth to the whole field of biblical criticism.[15] While the new methodologies were slow to have an impact in Britain, it was only a year after the *Origin of Species* that there appeared Anglicanism's first major attempt to deal with the issue, *Essays and Reviews* of 1860. So Darwin should be seen as the culmination of new challenges rather than as an isolated or unique phenomenon.

Artistic Responses to Darwin

In the previous section, I was concerned to emphasize that Darwin needs to be set against a wider pattern of changing conceptions. Not all were unprepared, and so we find some perhaps surprising examples of endorsement, among them John Henry Newman, who speaks of being prepared to "go the whole hog with Darwin."[16] Indeed, Darwin himself did not see what he had discovered as an argument for atheism, and in the *Origin of Species* he is still prepared to talk of a divine role. Nonetheless, for some, it was a deeply traumatic time, not least because his theories appeared to require for God a diminished and more distant role, perhaps in some ways more like eighteenth-century deism. Among those thus affected was the century's greatest art critic, John Ruskin. He had first met Darwin in the house of Buckland, whose fascination with geology he shared.[17] From 1858 onward, the more radical implications of Darwin's ideas began to work their effect.[18] His once deeply held Christian faith tottered, only ever to recover spasmodically.[19] It is not difficult to understand why. Although other reasons might easily have come to mind, his unstinting support for Gothic architecture had largely been expressed in terms of the way in which, on his view, its curves and points best reflected the handiwork of God in designing the intricate details of nature, such as leaves.[20] Darwin's God, though, seemed only distantly involved, if at all.

But my focus here is on the artists themselves. I suggest differentiating three types of response, beginning with a tendency to set apart the human figure from the rest of nature. Presumably, the idea here is that such a contrast can still hint at a relative degree of distinctiveness for human beings: as originating from nature but also with a unique divine endowment in their souls. Perhaps the point can best be made by setting the work of two contemporary artists against each other: Edgar Degas and William Dyce. Degas's reaction to Darwin's suggestion of continuity with the animal world seems to have been one of depression, a retreat from the idealization of the human figure into a stress on its frailty and, indeed, simian features. The latter is particularly obvious in one of his ballerina sculptures.[21] Originally intended for the Fifth Impressionist Exhibition of 1880, he eventually substituted his now more famous *Young Spartans*.[22] Although the date of its final form is controversial, it is clear that an earlier version that assumed classical proportions for the bodies has given place to ungainly girls and boys. In this, his views echo those of the novelist Émile Zola who, in a preface to his novel *Thérèse Raquin* (1867), defended the animal lust of the two principal characters as reflecting a "scientific goal," that is, portraying the world as it was now known it to be.[23]

In marked contrast to Degas, William Dyce is now virtually unknown as an artist apart from in his native Aberdeen. But he was hugely popular in the latter half of the nineteenth century, and reproductions of his portrayal of Christ as an isolated figure in an unwelcoming landscape in *Man of Sorrows* (1860) found its way into many a Victorian home. The allusion (despite the title) seems to be to the temptations in the wilderness.[24] Like his *David in the Wilderness* of the previous year, the background landscape is probably based on the topography of the island of Arran.[25] Whereas David stands confident and assertive, unlike the seated and reflective Christ, what both paintings share is a sense of figures set apart from their surroundings. Indeed, to the modern eye, Christ appears almost like a cut-out figure, easily removable from the rest of the painting. It was one way of insisting that humanity remains distinct from its natural setting as a special divine creation. That is not necessarily to suggest unyielding opposition to Darwin. Unlike so many of the Tractarians, whose piety he shared, Dyce did display genuine interest in science. But even here, there is perhaps a new hint of caution, a sense of distance between God and his creation, as can be seen from another painting from the same year, *Pegwell Bay*.[26] Situated near Ramsgate, it was believed to be where Augustine of Canterbury first landed in England. Yet, on this occasion, there is no allusion to this fact. Instead, the focus is on gathering shells, usually a pleasant diversion on a typical Victorian seaside holiday. But the colors are muted and, as comparison with an earlier sketch makes clear, the potential for highlighting the majesty of the creation is played down.[27] A comet in the sky is scarcely visible, while the erosion of the chalk cliff face seems to witness more to the ineluctable march of iron laws than to a hidden divine hand. As one commentator observes, such features had become "a background against which human life itself might seem no more than an afternoon's sea-shell gathering."[28]

If one response to Darwin, as Dyce's work appears to suggest, was the attempt to maintain some measure of distance between humanity and the rest of the creation, another was to search for evidence of divinity at work within the landscape itself. Although it is quite hard to prove specific influence, it seems quite likely that the new interest in pictures of the Holy Land had this motive as one of its sources of inspiration. The opportunity such a focus offered was reassurance that God had indeed walked this earth, however different in the light of evolution his own nature now appeared to be from our own. Whereas in the past, visitors or pilgrims to Palestine had sought confirmation in liturgical ritual or in relics, now the land as such came to be the medium through which deeper awareness of the reality of the incarnation was sought.[29] Among the pre-Raphaelites, Holman Hunt is an interesting case in point. Like Thomas Seddon, who accompanied him on his first trip to Palestine in 1854, Hunt wanted to produce an accurate record, and that explains the enormous efforts he expended on his best-known painting from that time, the famous Scapegoat.[30] But unlike Seddon, he did not deem this to be enough. He was also equally concerned to conjure up particular atmospheric impressions, as can be seen not only from Scapegoat but also from some of the results from two further trips in 1869 and 1873.[31]

Of course, it could be argued that none of this is a response to Darwin as such, not least because such preoccupation with the landscape of the Holy Land predates his major writings. The pious Presbyterian David Roberts (d. 1864) is justly famous for a number of romantic views that he produced as a result of his eleven-month journey in the area between 1838 and 1839.[32] But I would argue that the approach is an attempt to meet the new science more generally on its own terms: in other words, an empiricist response to empirical discoveries within which Darwin's discoveries were only one element. Frederic Church, to whose work I referred earlier, is known to have been worried by Darwin's discoveries. Although, like Darwin, inspired by the scientific work of Alexander von Humboldt to take an early lively interest in the natural world, he and his wife, Isabel, continued to espouse a simple creationist faith in the face of Darwin's new account.[33] While his reaction included searching for even more awesome scenery than was available in his native United States, these trips abroad also included, significantly, a visit to the Holy Land (in 1868), where a similar pattern of engagement emerges.[34]

As a third type of response, note needs to be taken of those who, even as their faith in the details of Christianity tottered, resorted to a more general mysticism. Here, the obvious example is Vincent van Gogh (d. 1890). Caution, though, is necessary in exploring his development. Many a popular book notes that his father was a Reformed minister in a small country parish, Vincent himself a missionary among miners in Belgium, and presumes his later work in Arles to be in total revolt against an earlier fundamentalist Christianity.[35] The truth is more complex. In his studies in Amsterdam, he became embroiled in attempts within the Dutch church to come to terms with scientific advances, as Christianity became denuded of its supernaturalism and Renan's classic *Vie de Jésus* became a popular, if controversial, text.[36] Experience replaced dogma, and so van Gogh's later nature mysticism is more continuous with his earlier thinking than it might initially appear. If the replacement of Christ by the sun in his adaptation of Rembrandt's *Raising of Lazarus* (1890) might seem to entail a total rejection of Christianity, the prominent position of the church in *Starry Night* (1889) and the halo around the worker in the field in *The Sower* (1888 version) suggest a more complex dynamic.[37] The kind of transformation Christ offered is now seen as mediated through an aesthetic experience that complements rather than conflicts with science.

Even those who remained Christians sometimes found this vaguer form of affirmation a helpful defensive strategy. Thus, despite his return to the practice of Roman Catholicism in 1891 (he died in 1906), Paul Cézanne's position is not dissimilar to that of van Gogh. Enigmatic or caustic remarks were his usual reaction to those who sought justifications for his new stance. Instead, in a series of brilliant paintings, he used one of the mountains of Provence (Mont Sainte-Victoire) to explore at his own pace the range of possible relations between the Creator and this world; its colors are in some paintings quite separate from the landscape below, while in others they invade and intermingle with it.[38]

New Responses in the Twentieth Century

The variety of responses that characterized the later nineteenth century repeated itself in the twentieth. Unfortunately, the most significant religiously and the most significant artistically do not quite correspond. I shall mention the latter first, where two key movements are worth noting: the abstract art influenced by theosophy at the beginning of the century and the later interest in land or environmental art.

Theosophy saw itself as offering a "scientific" response, but its ideas would now seem to most of us to smack more of pseudo-science. At the time, however, they were taken seriously by a number of artists. The most lasting influence was upon Piet Mondrian (d. 1943), who seems never to have quite disengaged himself from its perspective. Like van Gogh, he was the son of a Reformed minister, and his earliest landscapes utilize Christian symbolism.[39] But he was soon captured by the principles of theosophy into believing that the ordinary perceptual processes conceal from us the simple principles imposed by the Creator on the world for its right ordering. The job of the artist is to make these plain, and this he sought to achieve initially in paintings that exhibited the gradual dissolution of both natural and manmade structures into simpler forms, as with apple trees, churches, or the Paris skyline.[40] Later, the same aim was sought in simple paintings of balanced rectangles in different primary colors. Toward the end of his life, his emigration to the United States did lead to one major modification, which was a more dynamic understanding of such principles, seen most obviously in a painting like *Broadway Boogie Woogie* (1943), where, despite the abstraction, one almost feels the bustle of the New York streets.[41] Clearly, such a painting stands at a huge remove from his early landscapes, even those in which the influence of theosophy was already present.[42] But it is important to note that it was still a form of abstraction, which had emerged out of landscape and continued to show some of its concerns. A parallel development can be seen in his contemporary Wassily Kandinsky (d. 1944). Kandinsky initially also, like Mondrian, toyed with theosophy, but he soon abandoned its restraints while still sharing with Mondrian the desire to locate an overall coherence to the world in its divine origin. Three distinct phases in his abstract career correspond to three different types of media in conveying that message.[43] Colors that complemented and balanced one another eventually gave place to simple forms that, in their turn, as with Mondrian, eventually yielded to a livelier dynamic: in Kandinsky's case, the biomorphism of living forms were used to suggest movement.[44] That last phase could in some sense be seen as a return to the landscape of his early years.

Although no longer drawing on theosophy, after the Second World War, attempts to use science to argue for the truth of religion continued. So, for instance, following his conversion to Catholicism in 1950 (he had been brought up as an atheist), Salvador Dalí did not hesitate to appeal to nuclear physics as a way of arguing for the plausibility of an immaterial world existing alongside our own. *Madonna in Particles* (1952) is an overt statement of the theme.[45] Mary's body dissolves into particles as a way of underlining his view that modern science was moving to a more immaterial understanding of the universe and so closer to comprehending its source in a spiritual reality. In his famous *The Sacrament of the Last Supper* (1955), this is achieved more subtly and through inclusion of a landscape in the background (the seascape of Port Lligat, where he then lived).[46] The much-criticized figure who presides is made deliberately frail so that the body that dominates the upper frame (to whom he points) is seen to be absolutely central.[47] Superficial appearance thus conceals a greater reality, and the same holds also for the way in which the communion and background landscape are framed. They are placed within a twelve-sided solid figure (a dodecahedron) that is inherently unstable. Expand its parameters, and there is nowhere flat to stand. The apparent solidity of this world once more dissolves.

In terms of continuing interactions between landscape art and religion or spirituality into the present day, it is undoubtedly environmental or land art that has achieved the highest profile among both professional art critics and the general public, no doubt in part fueled by the current ecological crisis. Commentators suggest that, in some ways, it marks a return to more primitive forms of art, such as the building of the megaliths and pyramids or ritual enactments on the ground, and with that, a spiritual search for the value of human placedness and of the world as our home.[48] In that context, some have chosen to express the aim as being "to supplant science," as a refusal to accept scientific theory as offering the last word.[49] Such, for example, was the view of Robert Smithson (d. 1973), best known for his *Spiral Jetty*, a human-made projection into Great Salt Lake, Utah, whose spirals were intended to reflect an ancient myth of there being a whirlpool at the lake's center. Smithson deliberately allowed the jetty's structure to be of such a kind that it appears and disappears, depending on the movement of the lake's waters, thus suggesting the transience both of nature and of human beings' relation to it.[50] Again, both James Turrell and Michael Heizer have expressed willingness to speak of a religious dimension to their work, especially in generating a sense of awe. The former's now-famous *Roden Crater* (begun in 1972 in Arizona) sought to achieve this through the sky alone being visible from within the hollowed-out crater, and that fascination with light has continued into his most recent work, the transformation of the Old Deer Shelter in Yorkshire Sculpture Park into *Skyspace* (2006). Heizer, in his *Complex City* (1976) in the Nevada desert, used the very scale of the sculptured mass itself "to create a transcendent work of art."[51] All three of these artists are American. In a similar way, the landscape photographer Ansel Adams (1902–84) described some of his portraits as intended "to sanctify a religious idea."[52] In Britain, however, the term "spiritual" is very much the preferred term. How far that also entails a difference of meaning is unclear. In earlier decades, Richard Long (b.1942) was the best known, not least for the tracking of his footsteps and his gathering of natural materials into (usually) circular patterns.[53] While occasionally, he has expressed his aim in terms of reflecting a scientific understanding of the world, more commonly the closest relation is with Zen Buddhism and a search for the underlying unity to all things.[54] More recently, Andy Goldsworthy achieved greater prominence, perhaps largely because of the greater range of his imagination. To give two twenty-first-century examples, icicles were set up on the banks of a Scottish river, while in New York saplings were planted in great boulders placed on the roof of the new Museum of Jewish Heritage.[55]

Although he has been praised for his scientific curiosity, it would perhaps be truer to say that he is inspired by neither science nor religion, but by a much vaguer sense of reverence for nature.[56]

While such movements have had the most impact artistically, of greater interest to many Christians will be continuing attempts to situate Christ or the divine more generally within the landscape. In most cases, such attempts have little, if anything, to do with science. There are, for example, the numerous *Crucifixions* of Craigie Aitchison (b. 1926), where Christ crucified is set against a dramatic but simple landscape in which Aitchison's favorite dog breed, a Bedlington terrier, is often positioned as a puzzled but interested observer.[57] Although a son of the manse, Aitchison is not concerned to advocate any specific Christian beliefs, but rather the mystery of hope even in adversity, for which, he believes, landscape can provide an appropriate metaphor.

For most recent artists, landscape has been much more incidental to their oeuvre. Carol Weight (d.1997), for instance, reinforces the crowd's reaction to Jesus by setting him at the apex of a human pyramid behind which lies a tumultuous sky.[58] In 2004, Maggi Hambling interrupted her normally more representational series of annual Good Friday painting meditations to produce one suggestive of her marvelously evocative seascapes.[59] Although almost all of the work of Sir Stanley Spencer (d. 1959) creates some sense of divine immanence, this is usually achieved through means other than landscape. An exception is his series on *Christ in the Wilderness*. In one, Christ almost fills the desert frame, as he gently cradles a scorpion in his hands. In another, he is praying in a ravine, which on closer inspection becomes the petals of a flower bursting into bloom.[60] In such paintings, landscape succeeds in mediating two worlds.

Yet none of this engages directly with the scientific issue. Perhaps the nearest to do so among contemporary artists is the German Anselm Kiefer (b. 1941). Although he has rejected the Catholicism of his youth, his interest in religion remains. For him, Christianity became too dogmatic quite early in its history and so really closes eyes rather than opens them.[61] But the same fault can, in his view, also occur in science. Scientists should really see themselves as like artists, seeking to link earth and heaven.[62] "Heaven" here stands as a metaphor for another order of reality, a world different from surface appearances. As a painting like *Falling Stars* (1991) seeks to illustrate, it is a dream that we all have, but it is all too easy for each of us as a result to fall into our own private world (*Jeder Mensch steht unter seiner Himmelskugel*, 1970).[63] Then, the potential of the landscape to reveal an alternative order of reality will lead merely to a closed door: the most likely meaning of *Resurrexit* (1973), in which a snake rises to look at the pathway before it into a beautiful forest only to find a stairway to heaven, at the end of which is a closed door.[64] The rich mythic world of Kabbalah can, however, he believes, be used to hint at these alternative possibilities, with microcosm paralleling macrocosm, and so sunflowers are also capable of revealing the world of the stars.[65] As this brief summary indicates, Kiefer's response to the changing character of scientific theory is to insist that it too has a mythic quality and that all visions become tainted, scientific no less than religious, once they lay claim to absolutes.

Concluding Remarks

Because painting is such a different sort of activity from the abstract thinking involved in science and theology, it is very easy to suppose no deep relation. But there is no such thing as uninterpreted perception. Each of us approaches the world with various antecedent presuppositions that ensure that anything we see is a product or mixture of both what is out there and what is in our minds, as it were. So it is with the artists here surveyed. Their paintings propose to us particular world views, sometimes compatible with one another, sometimes not. Contrast, for example, Degas and Dyce. Certainly, the science and theology deployed can at times be naïve, but the great advantage of art is the way in which, instead of requiring assent, it gently invites reflection. Whatever other aesthetic merits the art may have, that challenge to dogmatism in both science and religion is salutary and necessary.

NOTES

1. For further details on this preoccupation of Munch, see L. Gamwell, *Exploring the Invisible: Art, Science and the Spiritual* (Princeton, N.J.: Princeton University Press, 2002), 122–123.

2. *Time Transfixed* (1938). For illustration and further discussion, see Gamwell, *Exploring*, 252–253.

3. As in his series on birds or his *Endless Column* of 1938. For illustrations and discussion, see E. Shanes, *Brancusi* (New York: Abbeville, 1989), 29–41, 82–97.

4. For a survey and evaluation of this and other types of approach to landscape, see David Brown, *God and Enchantment of Place* (Oxford: Oxford University Press, 2004), 84–152, esp. 98–104.

5. Contrast the lack of interest in the religious dimension in Seymour Slive, *Jacob van Ruisdael: Master of Landscape* (London: Royal Academy of Arts, 2005); and Martina Sitt et al., *Jacob van Ruisdael: Die Revolution der Landschaft* (Hamburg: Hamburger Kunsthalle, 2002).

6. *Light and Colour (Goethe's Theory)—The Morning after the Deluge* (1843). For illustrations and discussion of how Goethe challenged Newton's views, see Gamwell,

Exploring, 23–26. For Turner's own knowledge of the Bible, see M. Omer, *Turner and the Bible* (Oxford: Ashmolean Museum, 1981).

7. Implied, for example, by the addition of a small church in the distance to what is otherwise an actual view in *The Cornfield* (1826), which is illustrated in J. Sutherland, *Constable* (London: Phaidon, 1971), 108–109.

8. For this and the earlier painting from 1823, see J. Walker, *Constable* (London: Thames & Hudson, 1991), 88–89, 108–109.

9. For the death of his son in 1861, see W. Vaughan et al., *Samuel Palmer: Vision and Landscape* (London: Lund Humphries, 2005), 193.

10. For these influences, see J. L. Koerner, *Caspar David Friedrich and the Subject of Landscape* (London: Reaktion, 1990), 59, 77–78.

11. Now in the National Gallery in London; illustrated in E. Langmuir, *National Gallery: Companion Guide* (London: National Gallery, 1994), 282.

12. Native American pride has also played its part. For stress on the Calvinist dimension, see G. E. Veith, *Painters of Faith: The Spiritual Landscape in Nineteenth Century America* (Washington, D.C.: Regnery, 2001), e.g., 56–58; J. F. Cooper, *Knights of the Brush: The Hudson River School and the Moral Landscape* (New York: Hudson Hill Press, 1999), e.g., 60–61.

13. For Cole illustrated, see Veith, *Painters*, 44–47, 65; for Church's paintings, see Veith, *Painters*, 39; Cooper, *Knights*, 56.

14. Both Buckland and Sedgwick were clerics. For a brief survey of this aspect of the period, see O. Chadwick, *The Victorian Church*, 3rd ed. (London: SCM, 1971), 1:558–568.

15. Bruno Bauer conceded even less historical content than D. F. Strauss in his *Leben Jesu* of 1835. Their dating of the Gospels to the second century provoked the necessary work that proved them wrong.

16. Quoted in full with reference in my introduction to D. Brown, ed., *Newman: A Man for Our Time* (London: SPCK, 1990), 5.

17. J. Batchelor, *John Ruskin: No Wealth but Life* (London: Pimlico, 2001), 41.

18. Though not alone. The Colenso affair also had some influence.

19. T. Hilton, *John Ruskin: The Later Years* (New Haven, Conn.: Yale University Press, 2000), 49–52, 310–311, 549, 562.

20. John Ruskin's *Modern Painters* (London: George Allen, 1906) is full of such comments, e.g., 3:222 on "the law of the ivy leaf" and cathedral entrances.

21. Illustrated in E. Hüttinger, *Degas* (Naefels, Switzerland: Bonfini, 1977), 58.

22. Illustrated with commentary in K. Roberts, *Degas*, 2nd ed. (London: Phaidon, 1982), 36–37.

23. Preface to the second edition.

24. In the past, *Man of Sorrows* paintings had almost invariably alluded to the crucifixion.

25. For illustrations of these two paintings, see C. Bebington et al., *William Dyce and the Pre-Raphaelite Vision* (Aberdeen: Aberdeen Art Gallery, 2006), 172–175.

26. For illustrations and commentary, see A. Staley and C. Newall, *Pre-Raphaelite Vision: Truth to Nature* (London: Tate, 2004), 188–189.

27. For the earlier sketch, see Bebington et al., *William Dyce*, 166. Here, I disagree with Jennifer Melville's comments in 'Faith, Fact, Family and Friends in the Art of William Dyce' in Bebington et al., *William Dyce*, 38–45, esp. 44.

28. Malcolm Warner, 'Commentary on Illustration No. 106' in L. Parris, ed., *The Pre-Raphaelites* (London: Tate, 1984), 182–3, esp. 183.

29. Egeria's famous account of her pilgrimage to the Holy Land focuses on liturgical remembrance. Again, the collection of relics (including pebbles and soil) in the sancta sanctorum at St. John Lateran in Rome illustrates the other common pattern.

30. Easily seen in the contrast between Hunt's painting and Thomas Seddon's *Valley of Jehoshaphat*; for illustrations and commentary on both, see Parris, *Pre-Raphaelites*, 151–155.

31. The colors in *Scapegoat's* landscape are quite wonderful. Edward Burne-Jones praised Hunt's later *Plain of Esdraelon* for its unforgettable beauty.

32. A magnificent facsimile reproduction of the first edition of 1842 is currently available as David Roberts, *The Holy Land* (London: Studio Editions, n.d.).

33. J. K. Howat, *Frederic Church* (New Haven, Conn.: Yale University Press, 2005), 44, 133.

34. *Jerusalem from the Mount of Olives* is one of the best known. Note should also be taken of his Andes series and of the awesome *Iceberg* (1861); for illustrations, see Howat, *Frederic Church*, 105, 142.

35. His father had a small parish of fifty-six souls at Zundert.

36. It was seen as correct in its rejection of supernaturalism, but too extreme in its conclusions. For a detailed account of the Dutch discussions, see D. Silverman, *Van Gogh and Gauguin: The Search for Sacred Art* (New York: Farrar, Straus & Giroux, 2000), 144–179; cf. 306.

37. For illustrations, see I. F. Walther and R. Metzger, *Van Gogh: The Complete Paintings* (Cologne: Taschen, 1997), 452–453, 520–521, 626.

38. Sometimes line and/or color mark a dividing line; sometimes not. Compare the six examples in U. Becks-Malorny, *Cézanne* (Cologne: Taschen, 1995), 73–79.

39. As in *Windmill* (1905), where the cross-like character of the mechanism is emphasized; for an illustration, see H. L. C. Jaffé, *Mondrian* (New York: Abrams, 1985), 57.

40. For the gradual dissolution of apple trees, see the illustrations in Jaffé, *Mondrian*, 67, 83, 85, 97. For similar treatment of the church at Domberg, see S. Deicher, *Mondrian* (Cologne: Taschen, 1995), 26, 40. For the Paris skyline, see Y.-A. Bois, *Piet Mondrian* (Boston: Bulfinch, 1995), 152.

41. Illustrated in Bois, *Mondrian*, 292.

42. As in the evocative *Wood near Oele* of 1908, illustrated in Deicher, *Mondrian*, 19.

43. Analyzed in Brown, *God and Enchantment of Place*, 144–147.

44. For good examples of the three stages, see *Composition IV* (1911); *On Points* (1928); and *Sky Blue* (1940).

45. Illustrated in R. Descharnes and G. Néret, *Dalí* (Cologne: Taschen 1997), 458. Other examples include *Celestial Coronation* (444) and *Nuclear Head of an Angel* (459).

46. Illustrated in Descharnes and Néret, *Dalí*, 488–489.

47. Paul Tillich was among those who criticized the painting on these grounds when it was first exhibited.

48. For the return to more ancient forms, see T. McEvilley, 'The Rightness of Wrongness: Modernism and its Alter Ego', in J. Kastner and B. Wallis, eds., *Land and Environmental Art* (London: Phaidon, 1998), 207–8, esp. 207. For the ritual analogy, see Lucy Lippard, 'Overlay: Contemporary Art and the Art of Prehistory', in Kastner and Wallis, *Land*, 238–239.

49. Smithson interview reprinted in Kastner and Wallis, *Land*, 202–205, esp. 204.

50. For illustrations, see Kastner and Wallis, *Land*, 56–59.

51. For illustrations and commentary, see Kastner and Wallis, *Land*, 92–93, 200.

52. Quoted in Kastner and Wallis, *Land*, 251.

53. For a largely photographic record, see R. Long, *Walking the Line* (London: Thames & Hudson, n.d.), e.g., 28, 190–191.

54. For moving stones reflecting subatomic physics, see Long, *Walking*, 69; for Zen, 39, 42.

55. Both from 2003; illustrated in A. Goldsworthy, *Passage* (London: Thames & Hudson, 2004), 18–25, 59–73.

56. For scientific curiosity, see Long, *Walking*, 69. For reverence for nature, see T. Friedman and A. Goldsworthy, *Hand to Earth: Andy Goldsworthy Sculpture 1976–90* (Leeds: Henry Moore Centre, 1990), 164: "it is an intensely spiritual affair that I have with nature"; see also 18, 99, 127, 161, 167.

57. For a few examples, see A. G. Williams, *Craigie: The Art of Craigie Aitchison* (Edinburgh: Canongate, 1996), nos. 25, 27, 68, 76, 78–80, 107–108, 117.

58. In *Jesus and the People* (1963), illustrated in R. V. Weight, *Carol Weight: A Haunted Imagination* (Newton Abbot, England: David & Charles, 1994), 56.

59. *Good Friday* (2004) in A. Lambirth, *Maggi Hambling: The Works* (London: Unicorn, 2006), 163. For seascapes, 222–230.

60. For illustrations of the series, see K. Bell, *Stanley Spencer* (London: Phaidon, 1992), 154–159.

61. M. Auping, ed., *Anselm Kiefer: Heaven and Earth* (New York: Prestel, 2006), 166.

62. Auping, *Kiefer*, 176.

63. "Everyone stands under his own dome of heaven"; for both paintings illustrated, see Auping, *Kiefer*, 54, 97.

64. Illustrated in Auping, *Kiefer*, 61. The snake that sloughs its skin is presumably used here as a symbol for possible transformation.

65. This theme is developed from the writings of the mystical philosopher/scientist Robert Flood (d.1637): see Auping, *Kiefer*, 98–99.

PART III

Exploring the Contemporary Relevance

8

Reading Genesis 1–3 in the Light of Modern Science

David Wilkinson

In his bestseller *The God Delusion*, Richard Dawkins makes it abundantly clear that the relationship of science and the Bible is one of conflict, and there is only one winner.[1] For Dawkins, there is no point in reading Genesis in the light of modern science except in order to dismiss the biblical literature as irrelevant and complete nonsense.

However, Dawkins is not the only distinguished scientist who speaks on the relationship of science and the Bible. Francis Collins, director of the Human Genome Project, in the same year also published a book, which takes a very different view.[2] Collins suggests that the Bible enriches our view of science and that science enables us to come to a better interpretation of the meaning of the scriptures. Such a view is shared by a large number of other scientists in fields ranging from biology to physics and from astronomy to psychology.[3] None of these scientists would have any time for scientific creationism, which enlists the book of Genesis as a scientific text to prove its case. These mainstream scientists want to read the early chapters of Genesis in the light of modern scholarship and, indeed, the Darwinian legacy. Yet they still find in these chapters the opportunity for an enriching dialogue between science and theology. In this chapter, I will suggest that this is a fruitful way forward, avoiding the extremes of six-day creationism, on the one hand, and Dawkins's scientific reductionism, on the other. I will suggest that the theological themes in Genesis 1–3 of origin, order, human

significance, and awe go beyond a biblical literalism and find significant resonances in the questions raised by modern science. Indeed, the battles of the
Darwinian controversies may free us to pursue a deeper and more authentic
dialogue between the text of Genesis and the discoveries of evolutionary cosmology and biology.

The Legacy of Darwin in Reading Genesis

It is interesting that both Dawkins and Collins see the importance of the question
not just for the academic sphere but also for the public sphere. Their books were
written with the wider lay audience in mind and have been promoted through
television programs and interviews. The question of the relationship of science
and the Bible has always had this public dimension to it. When we consider the
legacy of Darwin, we encounter not only the academic discussion but also how
this discussion has played out in the media and in public debate. In fact, in the
popular mind, it is all too easy to say that the legacy of Darwin is Dawkins. The
story goes that church leaders in the nineteenth century were all biblical literalists who found their understanding of origins in Genesis 1. That is, they all
believed that the universe was 6,000 years old and that Genesis 1 gave a scientific
description of creation. Then along came Darwin, who demonstrated that the
universe was far older and that the history of origins was very different from that
in Genesis 1. The result of this was that very quickly Genesis 1–3 was completely
discounted by scientists and theologians, apart from a few fundamentalist church
leaders who were not bright enough to understand the science.

Such a story appears often but is highly misleading. First, there was a
complex response among scientists and theologians to Darwin.[4] There were
some within the Christian churches who did oppose Darwin for a variety of
reasons. Canon Henry Baker Tristram, F.R.S. (1822–1906), a distinguished
ornithologist, was extremely skeptical about Darwinian evolution on scientific
grounds rather than theological grounds. However, there were many others
who suspended judgment or who became great proponents of Darwin's theory.
In Durham, at the same time as Tristram, the Reverend Temple Chevallier
(1794–1873), the first Professor of Astronomy and Reader in Hebrew, was more
open to evolutionary thinking. He was one of 717 "gentlemen," many of whom
were the leading scientists of the day, who signed "The Declaration of Students
of the Natural and Physical Sciences" (1865):

> We, the undersigned Students of the Natural Sciences, desire to
> express our sincere regret, that researches into scientific truth are

perverted by some in our own times into occasion for casting doubt upon the Truth and Authenticity of the Holy Scriptures. We conceive that it is impossible for the Word of God, as written in the book of nature, and God's Word written in Holy Scripture, to contradict one another, however much they may appear to differ.... We cannot but deplore that Natural Science should be looked upon with suspicion by many who do not make a study of it, merely on account of the unadvised manner in which some are placing it in opposition to Holy Writ. We believe that it is the duty of every Scientific Student to investigate nature simply for the purpose of elucidating truth, and that if he finds that some of his results appear to be in contradiction to the Written Word, or rather to his own *interpretations* of it, which may be erroneous, he should not presumptuously affirm that his own conclusions must be right, and the statements of Scripture wrong; rather, leave the two side by side till it shall please God to allow us to see the manner in which they may be reconciled.[5]

This declaration responded in part to the earlier Oxford Declaration, organized by a group of High Church Anglicans, which gathered signatures to demand that the Church of England hold to the inspiration and divine authority of the Bible.[6] Chevallier and others who were scientists and Christians wanted to resist the tendency to denounce science for the sake of defending scripture. Rather, they wanted to affirm science as a gift from God and to lay science and the scriptures side by side, believing that the author of both would not allow them to ultimately contradict. Some scientists who were committed Christians, such as Michael Faraday, did not sign it for a variety of reasons, although they agreed with the principle. However, the declaration illustrates very well the point that the responses to Darwin were complex.

As John Brooke has often noted, it is very easy in the discussion of science and religion to oversimplify history in order to make your point.[7] Darwin faced a diversity of opposition; as George Bernard Shaw commented, "Darwin had the luck to please everybody who had an axe to grind."[8] Some of it was scientific and some was theological, but it was not uniform. "The Declaration of Students of the Natural and Physical Sciences" also shows a model of the relationship of science and scripture which points beyond biblical literalism. It notes a commitment to finding reconciliation in a way which respects the integrity of both the nature of science and the nature of scripture. We shall return to this point later in the chapter.

Second, Darwin was not the first and only challenge to a literal view of the Bible. As we have seen in this volume, early Jewish and Christian readings of

Genesis 1 did not see it as a scientific textbook. Early church theologians, such as Gregory of Nyssa and Augustine, pointed out very clearly some of the problems that exist with taking the seven days of Genesis 1 literally, for example, the fact that night and day are spoken of before the creation of the sun and moon.⁹ Augustine here introduced an interesting and important principle to the effect that, with regard to matters of natural order that do not impinge on the heart of revelation, scriptural interpretation should bow to the findings of natural reason and adopt a symbolic interpretation of the text.

Therefore, many Christians in the nineteenth century were quite happy to hold the authority of scripture alongside the new scientific discoveries. As Michael Roberts has shown in his discussion of the rise of geology, few church leaders in the 1860s were biblical literalists in the sense of believing in a creation in 4004 BC.¹⁰ Since 1790, geology had demonstrated the vast age of the earth. Roberts shows that, before 1800, many Christian writers, probably a majority, accepted that the earth was older than 6,000 years. Some argued that God had first created chaos and then much later ordered the earth in six days. As far back as the Newtonian era, British scientists such as Edward Lhwyd, Robert Hooke, and Thomas Burnet questioned a Mosaic time scale. In the nineteenth century itself, there was disagreement in geology between the uniformitarianism of Charles Lyell and Christians such as Adam Sedgwick, William Buckland, William Conybeare, and William Smith, who favored catastrophism, but there was no disagreement on the vast age of the earth. Those Christians who did oppose the vast age of the earth, such as Dean Cockburn of York, the Plymouth Brethren, B. W. Newton, and Philip Gosse, were the exception rather than the rule.

Third, Darwin's description of the mechanism of origins was not entirely new. The work of Buffon, Cuvier, and Lamarck on the fossil record was already moving toward evolutionary theory and questioning the Aristotelian philosophy of the fixity of biological species. Robert Chambers's *Vestiges of the Natural History of Creation* (1844), published anonymously, had already argued that the development of life could be described by natural laws and that God worked through natural laws.

Fourth, and perhaps most important, the main problem that Darwin presented for Christian belief was not an attack on the literal reading of Genesis 1; it was more to do with the undermining of the design argument coupled with the question of what makes human beings special. The growth of the design argument on the back of the scientific revolution had seen a decisive shift for many Christian thinkers away from revelation to reason as the source of knowledge of God. While Hume and Kant had provided a devastating critique of the argument, it still held a great deal of influence in the popular and academic minds. Darwin, in his understanding of natural selection, gave an alternative explanation of the complexity of the natural world to the explanation of a Creator's design. This provided a fatal blow to the security of the argument, leaving those Christians who had moved away from revelation in a vulnerable position. Alongside this, Darwin's theory, especially as it was propounded in *The Descent of Man* (1871), was perceived to be an attack on human dignity. Whatever did happen between the bishop of Oxford, Samuel Wilberforce, and T. H. Huxley at the 1860 British Association for the Advancement of Science meeting (and the records of the debate are not as clear as some would think), it does seem that the oft-quoted "was it on Huxley's grandfather's or grandmother's side that he was descended from an ape?" was a key issue for Wilberforce. Certainly, for Christian believers and scientists Lyell and Sedgwick, a "natural" origin for humanity meant the relegation of moral matters to by-products of physical matter.

Yet, even here, there were other Christian reactions. Botanist Asa Gray and author Charles Kingsley saw God at work in the process of evolution. David Livingstone has discussed in *Darwin's Forgotten Defenders* an even more surprising reaction.[11] B. B. Warfield and James Orr, the founders of the Princeton school of theology, which would lead to American fundamentalism, were quite relaxed about Darwinian evolution. Warfield commented, "I do not think that there is any general statement in the Bible or any part of the account of creation, either given in Genesis 1 and 2 or elsewhere alluded to, that need to be opposed to evolution."[12] The reason for this positive embrace of Darwinism was that these issues were not new. Questions about the interpretation of scripture in the light of scientific discovery went back a long way for those who took the Bible seriously. Further, a sense that God is revealed supremely in the life, death, and resurrection of Jesus meant that Christian faith was not dependent on the design argument. For those Christians who took the Bible as authoritative, there was a great commitment to believing that the author of the word and the world could be trusted to bring the scriptures and science into harmony.

The real legacy of Darwin was to push Christians to a deeper engagement with the text of Genesis. Of course, this was part of a more general picture in the nineteenth century as biblical scholars were exploring the nature of the biblical texts and in particular their contexts and sources. Darwinism reinforced that work, not least in the way it demanded that the task of reading Genesis needed to be done on the wider public stage.

This was encouraged by the way in which the legacy of Darwin was used politically. T. H. Huxley (1825–1895), "Darwin's bulldog," saw the Darwinian controversies as an opportunity to move science out of the political control of the church. Science was controlled by the Church of England through university appointments. The British Association for the Advancement of Science, between 1831 and 1865, had forty-one Anglican clergy in key leadership positions. In 1864, Huxley and nine others formed the X-Club,[13] with the aim of the secularization of society. Out of this was created the conflict hypothesis of the relationship of science and religion, which continues to have great influence today. The complex history of science and religion was rewritten in simple conflict terms in popular books by Draper[14] and White,[15] a view which is represented in the current work of Richard Dawkins. Huxley was a great popularizer and knew that the battle for the control of science was not simply about academic argument but also about the popular mind.

This background leaves three main options for reading Genesis and modern science today.

Reading Modern Science in the Light of Genesis 1–3

The first option is that of six-day creationism, which uses Genesis 1–3 to read modern science. This view sees Genesis 1–3 as literal history, that is, giving a description of how the universe was created over a six-day period a few thousand years ago.[16] The time of the creation can then be estimated by tracing back the genealogies in Genesis to Adam and Eve, and in this way an age of a few thousand years is derived. Part of the attraction of this approach is that identifying all of the text as history means that little interpretation is needed as to what is history and what is not.

The influence of this movement should not be underestimated. While creationism may have, for the moment, lost the public battle for its teaching to be presented as an alternative theory to evolution in school science classes, in the sphere of evangelical churches, it continues to grow in influence. While the theory of intelligent design has attempted to move the public debate away from any reference to Genesis 1–3, creationist Christians still see the battle for orthodoxy in the church as centered on whether one reads these early chapters as scientific evidence.[17]

What is the role of science in this? Is science simply discounted in this view? The answer to this is a little more complex than some would think. Some of the earliest objections to Darwin were not theological but scientific, and it was these scientific arguments that were used by theologians such as Wilberforce. Darwin was criticized for his scientific methodology, in particular for missing links in his chain of evidence. Further, his inability to explain the persistence of apparently useless structures and, before genetics, the mechanism of how natural selection actually worked, generated strong arguments against evolution.

One major problem was the time scale involved. The process of natural selection, according to Darwin's best estimate, required a minimum of 200 million years. Darwin also made a geologically based estimate of 340 million years for the earth's age. However, Lord Kelvin, assuming that the earth has cooled to its present condition from an initially molten state and using measurements in mines of how fast heat is escaping from the earth's interior, concluded that the earth is little more than 20 million years old. This was a major problem for Darwinian evolution, until it was realized that Kelvin got it wrong. Once the radioactivity of the rocks themselves was taken into account, one obtained a much longer time scale. Nevertheless, Kelvin is an interesting case study. He found Darwin's proposal that life evolved to its present state from simple forms too much of an attack on the argument of design.

We see here the use of science to provide arguments for attacks that were in part theologically motivated. The same is true today. Starting from a commitment to a scientific reading of Genesis 1–3, certain scientific arguments against the age of the earth and the mechanism of evolution are then employed. This began with so-called flood geology, which attempted to explain the fossils and geological structures through the pressure caused by a worldwide flood.[18] It continues today with arguments about missing transitional species, evidence that dinosaurs and humans existed at the same time, and the use of the second law of thermodynamics against complexity being able to evolve.[19] Thus, Genesis 1–3 means that the majority of modern scientists have got it wrong, and there are elements within science which point to a universe which is only thousands of years old.[20]

It is here that we note the continuity between creationism and intelligent design. While not necessarily wanting to argue for a creation only a few thousand years ago, intelligent design employs scientific arguments with a theological motivation to prove the existence of a Creator. Thus, Phillip Johnson accepts micro-evolution but not macro-evolution, pointing to the paucity of transitional forms, the sudden explosion of creatures in the early Cambrian period about 570 million years ago, and the argument that random mutations cannot produce coordinated functioning, such as in the appearance of the eye or wings.[21] Michael Behe has famously argued that complex long sequences of biochemical interactions in cells could not have evolved by natural selection.[22] All of these arguments have been strongly rejected by the majority of the scientific community.[23]

If one option is to use science selectively and often incorrectly to prove the time scale of 6,000 years, there is another argument often used by creationists. This is incompatible with the approach described above but sometimes appears in the debate. It is the argument that the universe only *appears* to be old. That is, the universe appears to science to be billions of years old, but that is because God created it old. On this view, fossils were put into the rocks to mislead us. It was first argued in Philip Gosse's *Omphalos* in 1857, which suggested that God created Adam with a navel.[24] At the time, it made little impact, but the theory does reappear from time to time. Logically, it is irrefutable, but theologically, it makes out God to be a deceiver.

We see in all of this a number of important themes. First, these approaches ironically share with Dawkins and others a conflict model of science and religion. In this case, scriptural truth has primacy over scientific truth. If Dawkins wants to use science to interpret and, indeed, dismiss scripture, then creationism uses scripture to interpret and dismiss science. Yet such a view of the relationship of scientific and religious truths is grossly oversimplified, and this can be demonstrated by a careful exposition of the history and philosophy of science and religion. The warfare model popularized by Huxley and taken over by the creationists in their perceived battle with "secular science" does little justice to the contributions that theology has made to the growth of science and, indeed, the contributions science has made to the growth of theology. We will see some of those contributions in the final section of this chapter.

Second, creationism depends on a commitment that Genesis 1 is meant to be read as a scientific text. Of course, the majority of biblical scholars point to the clear figurative elements, poetry, liturgy, and theology within the text.[25] However, these arguments are unheard by creationists, who couple a commitment to biblical authority with one particular interpretation of Genesis 1–3. The fact that this interpretation is only a century old and was codified in the North American context of the post-Darwinian controversies is rarely acknowledged. Here, the legacy of Darwin has led to an interpretation of scripture which allows a battle with science to be clearly engaged. In addition, the defense of Genesis 1–3 as literal scientific history means that the rest of scripture can also be defended as historically true. This so-called slippery slope argument instills the fear that, if you give up on the "history" of Genesis 1–3, then where do you stop with respect to the rest of the biblical narratives? Such an argument, of course, ignores that the Bible is made up of many kinds of literature, and correct interpretation has to take this diversity of genres seriously.

Third, creationism is based on a view that creation is, by its very nature, instantaneous. There has always been a deistic tinge to the Christian doctrine of creation. It is interesting to speculate that the scientific revolution itself, through the growth of technology, gave a view of the creation of objects as a single act. Of course, the biblical narratives have a much broader view of creation, with contexts where a long period of time is assumed, for example, in the creation of Israel (Isa. 43:1, 15). The contemporary Western view of creation has often been presented as simply the act of a God who starts the whole thing off, whether it be the universe or human life, rather than the acts of a God who is the Creator/sustainer and who interacts with and upholds every moment of the universe's process and evolution.

Fourth, creationism seriously questions the nature of science itself. The conflict model downplays the strong Christian foundation to science and its importance as a gift of God.[26] The creationist attempt to defend Genesis against the legacy of Darwin ultimately casts science adrift from its Christian moorings. In addition, there is a subtle difference in the methodology of the science used in creation science and what I will call standard science. Creation science employs scientific argument to prove a conclusion it already has. One finds some scientific arguments which one can isolate from the whole in order to prove that the universe is 6,000 years old or, at least, to cast doubt on the universe being billions of years old. Standard science places more weight on the evidence and the whole canvas of scientific arguments in order to reach a conclusion which is able to integrate the evidence and the arguments and which may be surprising. Now, of course, all science is done with possible conclusions in mind. After all, you do not pay millions of dollars for a new telescope if you do not think that, by using it, you will gather evidence for or against a current theory. But it is that openness to the conclusion being different that marks out standard science from creation science.

Finally, creationism is an easy option for popularization. Just as Huxley saw the conflict model as a way to use the legacy of Darwin, creationism uses the conflict model to win the popular mind. The slippery slope argument likewise reduces the biblical material to one form of interpretation, which is much easier to present in Christian apologetics than a diversity of biblical genres and a complex process of hermeneutics.

Despite its growing influence, creationism remains a minority view among Christians. Unconvinced of Genesis 1–3 having to be read as a scientific text, and unconvinced by reading modern science in the light of that interpretation, Christian theologians have pursued other avenues.

Harmonizing Genesis 1–3 in the Light of Modern Science

How Genesis could be read in harmony with modern science was something that was being done long before Darwin, but the nineteenth century again illustrates helpfully some of the methods employed.

The Gap Theory

This attempt to reconcile the text of Genesis with the findings of science was popularized by the nineteenth-century Scottish preacher Thomas Chalmers.[27] During lectures on chemistry given at the University of St. Andrews during the winter of 1803–1804, he argued that Genesis did not tell the age of the universe, only the age of the human species. He attempted to support this by suggesting a "gap" between verses 1 and 2 of Genesis 1. Thus, verse 1 refers to the original creation, which could be billions of years old. However, the fall of Satan was responsible for bringing ruin and destruction upon the creation, and verse 2 is translated as "The earth became formless and void." The rest of chapter 1 is therefore a seven-day work not of creation but of reconstruction, which did happen thousands of years ago. This has been attractive to many people and is still reflected in a marginal note in the New International Version of the Bible. Its problems are twofold. Most scholars do not think that the translation of the word in verse 2 as "became" is allowable, and that is why most modern translations have "The earth was without form and void" (RSV). Second, there is little support elsewhere in the Bible that the fall of Satan had such a ruinous effect.

Days as Ages

Another attempt at harmonization was suggested in the nineteenth century by Hugh Miller,[28] and it still attracts many supporters today.[29] This view sees the Hebrew word *yom* (translated as "day" in modern translations) in figurative terms of an unspecified period of time, such as ages or the millions of years in the evolutionary process. It then argues for a general agreement between the order of the creative acts and the fossil evidence.

However, once again, there are problems. Although *yom* is used as a longer period of time elsewhere in the Bible, it is highly unlikely that the writer of Genesis 1 was using it in that way. This is shown by the days being used as part of a week and with the emphasis on "evening and morning" (e.g., Gen. 1:8). Further, the agreement between the general order of the biblical creative acts and the fossil record is not exact, so that trees appear before marine creatures (Gen. 1:11, 20), and evening and morning appear before the sun and moon (Gen. 1:5, 14).

Days of Revelation

This unusual understanding was put forward in the nineteenth century by a Jesuit priest, Father von Hummelauer, and in the middle of the twentieth century by P. J. Wiseman.[30] It argues that the seven-day week of Genesis 1 is indeed a literal week, but that it is a week not of God creating but of God revealing to Adam how he created. Each day, God reveals a new part of the story. This week of revelation would then have happened thousands of years ago, as indicated by the Genesis genealogies, but the creation itself could have taken place over an unspecified time before that. Wiseman points out that this explains some odd features of Genesis 1. Why, for example, did God rest on the seventh day when other parts of the Bible are clear that God never tires or grows weary (Isa. 45:28)? Wiseman argues that the week is for Adam's benefit and that God "rests" in order for Adam to have time to contemplate what has been revealed. Unfortunately, this understanding relies on Genesis 1:1 being translated as God "made known the heavens and the earth" rather than "made the heavens and the earth." The majority of scholars, however, do not accept this as a valid translation of the Hebrew sentence.

What do we learn from these attempts at harmonization? They want to take science seriously and yet hold on to a relationship which sees the science being brought into direct contact with the Genesis text. While gaps, ages, and days of revelation are beginning to move toward a more literary view of the text, its scientific truth still needs accommodating to the legacy of Darwin. The difficulty is that the text is stretched too far when we try to conform it with science rather than allowing it to speak for itself.

Reading Genesis 1–3 in Conversation with Modern Scientific Questions

If we move beyond modern science being shaped to fit Genesis 1–3 or, indeed, Genesis 1–3 being shaped to harmonize with modern science, there is a third way that Christian theology has dealt with the Genesis text. This is to give both science and the Genesis text respect as different forms of truth about creation and then to look for resonances between scientific understandings of the world and the biblical insights. Or, to put it another way, to see questions which are posed from science to the text, and vice versa, in a way that leads to a fruitful dialogue.

John Polkinghorne is typical of this approach when he says that science helps us to interpret and understand the scriptures.[31] He wants to allow science to bring both questions and insights to the text. At the same time, there will be questions and insights that reflection on the text will bring to science.

Of course, this approach makes a number of assumptions. First, one adopts a literary approach to Genesis 1–3, asking, what kind of literature is this text actually? Focusing on Genesis 1, we see immediately that it has a very different style from Genesis 2 and 3. Further, we see clear elements of theological polemic, for example, the use of the phrases "greater light" and "lesser light" in verse 16 attacks those stories of creation which see the sun and moon as gods. For the author of Genesis 1, they are simply the greater light and lesser light created by the one true God. In addition, the passage has a liturgical form, with repeated refrains, which gives it a feel of a hymn of worship. These elements point us to the essentially theological rather than scientific nature of the account. I have argued elsewhere that Genesis 1 is a subtle and complex interweaving of literary genres, poetry, hymn, and doctrine in narrative mode.[32] It is therefore wrong to think that science can be simply lifted from the text. Second, this approach also assumes a critical realist approach to both science and theology, that is, they are exploring a common reality in different and limited ways. Consequently, third, a relationship of dialogue between science and theology is possible. A defense of all of these assumptions is possible but beyond the scope of this chapter.[33]

What might these areas of dialogue be? Let me pick three of current interest.

Origins

Stephen Hawking in *A Brief History of Time* suggests a model of the beginning of the universe which through quantum theory does not need a "first cause" in the temporal sense to start it off.[34] While Hawking's model is speculative, it has raised questions of whether much theistic thinking in the area of cosmology is in fact a "god of the gaps" argument or whether the dominant view of creation is deistic.[35] The god-of-the-gaps argument is where science is unable to explain certain aspects of the universe, and so then the move is to insert God as the explanation. At present, there is no consensus on how to describe the first 10^{-43} second of the universe's history, and some argue that this is where God comes in. Meanwhile, the deists believe in a God who interacted with the universe only at its beginning. There are interesting parallels here in the way that Darwin demolished the design argument and the way that Hawking attempts to demolish the cosmological argument in temporal form. Hawking's model should be welcomed, for just as Darwin showed us the inadequacy of the design argument, Hawking leads us to an understanding of the Creator which does not reduce God to a god of the gaps nor to a deistic Creator.

It is in this area that we begin to see resonances with the Genesis text. The theological polemic inherent in chapter 1 proceeds on the basis that God is the only Creator and is without peer or competitor. For example, the sun and moon are called the "greater light" and the "lesser light" as a way of saying that the sun and moon are not gods in themselves but part of God's creative work. It is here that the doctrine of *creatio ex nihilo* becomes important. Some have claimed that the notion of "creation out of nothing" is at best ambiguous in Genesis and only came to clear articulation as Christian faith encountered and responded to the questions and challenges of Greek philosophy and gnostic thought.[36] However, the emergence of the doctrine in Christian writers of the second and third centuries, such as Theophilos of Antioch, Irenaeus, Tertullian, and Augustine, was driven precisely by the concern to maintain the biblical affirmations of the basic goodness of the world and of God's utterly unopposed freedom in creating.[37]

Hawking's model does away with a picture of God reaching out his hand and lighting the blue touch-paper of the big bang. In that sense, there is no need for "something" to go bang. Quantum theory allows a universe to emerge from nothing at all, while still maintaining a historical origination of the universe, in that 13.7 billion years ago, the universe did not exist. R. J. Russell suggests that the notion of a historical origination of the universe provides an important corroborative meaning for the logically prior notion of the ontological origination of the universe, although it is not essential to it.[38] He argues that the relationship between the historical and ontological origins lies in the concept of finitude. The fact that the universe has a finite history is not trivial in the sense that a temporal origination of the universe can provide confirming but not conclusive or essential evidence for ontological origination.

The "process" of creation in the seven days of Genesis 1 is also an important corrective to a deistic view of creation. Don Page makes the point that the Judeo-Christian theology of creation means that God creates and sustains the entire universe rather than just the beginning. Whether or not the universe has a beginning has no relevance to the question of its creation, just as whether an artist's line has a beginning and an end, or instead forms a circle with no end, has no relevance to the question of its being drawn.[39]

Thus, the Genesis text lays the foundations upon which the work of Hawking can be welcomed. Hawking's work questions some uses of the text to build a picture of the Creator. At the same time, Genesis 1 raises questions as to the purpose of the universe and to the origins of the laws of physics, questions which lie beyond science itself.

The Basis of Science

T. F. Torrance has argued that the doctrine of *creatio ex nihilo*, and the associated rejection of gnosticism, was important for the development of the natural sciences on account of the affirmation of the fundamental goodness of creation it represents. Creation is distinct *from* God but dependent for its existence *on* God. As such, creation is both to be valued, rather than escaped, and free to be investigated, rather than worshipped. Along with this, God was not constrained in creating by the limitations of preexisting matter but could create freely. Thus, to fully understand the God-given order of the universe, it is necessary to observe it, which is a basic principle of empirical science.[40]

Further, the fundamental ordering of the creation communicated by the Genesis account of origins has been important to the growth of science. Genesis I paints a picture of a clearly structured creation that is created by God's acts of separation and then his filling up the new structures, transforming the creation from being "formless and empty" (Gen. 1:2) to something which is complex and full of life. Many have argued that the concept of the physical laws in the seventeenth century came in part from biblical doctrines.[41] Certainly, the striking elegance, universality, and intelligibility of the physical laws cannot be explained by science itself, but can be understood naturally in the framework of a faithful Creator God who sustains the universe. There is even some merit in the argument that the inherent materialism of the Hebrew tradition, with its emphasis on the importance of the earth, vegetation, and animals, the dust of the ground, and the centrality of the land, provided the basis for experiments on the natural world. It may be no coincidence that the Royal Society founded in 1662 was made up of Protestants and many Puritans, reflecting the Puritan emphasis on the importance of manual work.[42] In the light of this, the Christian tradition needs to recapture its support for and delight in science, rather than fearing it.

What Does It Mean to Be Human?

One of the major contemporary questions of modern science, whether in genetics, artificial intelligence, the search for extraterrestrial life, or neuroscience, is the question of what it means to be human.

The Genesis passages give valuable insight into these debates. They speak of relationship and responsibility as being key to being human. Being made in the "image of God" (Gen. 1:26–27) has been interpreted in different ways in Jewish and Christian thought, including that God is physically embodied and human beings are physically the image of God; and that the image denotes human reason, freedom, or our moral sense. Yet these interpretations do not do justice to the biblical material. Studies in the language and context of the ancient Near East lead to a different understanding of "image" as not so much a part of the human constitution as a pointer to the distinctive place of humanity within the created order. It is less about something we have or do and more about relationship.[43] In contrast to the Babylonian account, where the role of humans is simply one of serving the gods, humanity, in distinction from the rest of creaturely reality, is viewed here as enjoying a relationship of unique conscious intimacy with God. Or, perhaps better, humanity is that part of creation that is capable of being conscious of and responsive in its relationship to the Creator.

If relationship and responsibility, conveyed by the link between image and stewardship (Gen. 1:26–28), is the key to what makes human beings special, then this provides an opportunity for fruitful dialogue with some of the scientific questions. Within the evolutionary framework, are human beings distinct from their evolutionary ancestors since God takes the initiative and gives the gift of relationship and responsibility? Evolution can be welcomed without collapsing into a scientific materialism which has no place for God.[44] If there are other intelligent beings elsewhere in the universe, the special nature of human beings is not undermined by us not being alone. Indeed, Colin Russell points out that the popularity of speculation about other worlds in the seventeenth century was a significant indicator of the ascendancy of biblical values over those of Aristotle. In the Aristotelian universe, position and status were closely associated. The earth was at the center of all things, separated from the rest of the universe by the orbit of the moon. Human beings were special because we were placed at the center. In contrast, the Genesis narratives do not associate status and place. The dignity and worth of human beings come from the gift of our relationship with God.[45] Further, this sense of image as being defined by relationship and responsibility means that we can move away from dualist thinking about the soul and the body to ways of thinking which will allow a more positive affirmation of the material nature of both the human and the universe.

Conclusion

There is enough in the fruitfulness of the dialogue between modern science and the Genesis narratives to convince us that the legacy of Darwin is not to dismiss Genesis 1–3 as worthless. In fact, the legacy of Darwin pushes us to understand and communicate the nature and insights of Genesis 1–3 more seriously. While we have engaged briefly with scientific questions of origins, the basis of science, and the nature of being human, there are many other questions, such as environmental responsibility, anthropic balances in the law and circumstance of the universe that make life possible, and the awe inherent in the scientific enterprise, all of which also could have fruitful dialogue with the Genesis passages.

Christian theologians need to be less fearful and less hesitant of the dialogue with science. Science can help in understanding the text, and science can receive a great deal from the text. This, however, will need theologians to take science seriously in a way that many did in the post-Darwinian controversies. In fact, in *On the Origin of Species*, immediately after the title page, comes a quote from Francis Bacon from his *Advancement of Learning*:

> To conclude, therefore, let no man out of a weak conceit of sobriety, or an ill-applied moderation, think or maintain, that a man can search too far or be too well studied in the book of God's word, or in the book of God's works; divinity or philosophy; but rather let men endeavour an endless progress or proficience [sic] in both.

NOTES

1. R. Dawkins, *The God Delusion* (London: Bantam, 2006), 92.

2. F. Collins, *The Language of God: A Scientist Presents Evidence for Belief* (New York: Simon & Schuster, 2006), 150.

3. A. McGrath and J. C. McGrath, *The Dawkins Delusion? Atheist Fundamentalism and the Denial of the Divine* (London: SPCK, 2007); O. Gingerich, *God's Universe* (Cambridge, Mass.: Belknap, 2006); J. Roughgarden, *Evolution and Christian Faith: Reflections of an Evolutionary Biologist* (Washington, D.C.: Island, 2006); J. Polkinghorne, *Science and the Trinity: The Christian Encounter with Reality* (London: SPCK, 2004); M. Jeeves, "Changing Portraits of Human Nature," *Science and Christian Belief* 14 (2002): 3–32.

4. J. R. Moore, *The Post-Darwinian Controversies: A Study of the Protestant Struggle to Come to Terms with Darwin in Great Britain and America 1870–1900* (Cambridge: Cambridge University Press, 1979).

5. H. Gay, "'The Declaration of Students of the Natural and Physical Sciences,' Revisited: Youth, Science, and Religion in Mid-Victorian Britain," in *Religion and the Challenges of Science*, ed. W. Sweet and R. Feist (Aldershot, England: Ashgate, 2007), 19–41.

6. O. Chadwick, *The Victorian Church* (London: Black, 1970), 84.

7. J. H. Brooke, *Science and Religion: Some Historical Perspectives* (Cambridge: Cambridge University Press, 1991), 5.

8. G. B. Shaw, *Back to Methuselah: A Metabiological Pentateuch* (Harmondsworth, England: Penguin, 1939), xlv.

9. D. A. Young, "The Contemporary Relevance of Augustine's View of Creation," *Perspectives on Science and Christian Faith* 40, no. 1. (1988): 42–45.

10. M. Roberts, "Genesis and Geology Unearthed," *Churchman* 112 (1998): 225–255.

11. D. Livingstone, *Darwin's Forgotten Defenders* (Edinburgh: Scottish Academic Press, 1987).

12. M. Noll and D. Livingstone, *B. B. Warfield: Evolution, Science and Scripture* (Grand Rapids, Mich.: Baker, 2000), 29.

13. C. A. Russell, "The Conflict Metaphor and Its Social Origins," *Science and Christian Belief* 1 (1989): 3–26.

14. J. W. Draper, *History of the Conflict between Religion and Science* (New York: Appleton, 1874).

15. A. D. White, *A History of the Warfare of Science with Theology in Christendom* (New York: Appleton, 1896).

16. For a historical study, see R. L. Numbers, *The Creationists: The Evolution of Scientific Creationism* (New York: Knopf, 1992).

17. L. Witham, *Where Darwin Meets the Bible: Creationists and Evolutionists in America* (New York: Oxford University Press, 2005); S. Coleman and L. Carlin, eds., *The Cultures of Creationism: Anti-Evolutionism in English Speaking Countries* (Aldershot, England: Ashgate, 2004).

18. J. C. Whitcomb and H. M. Morris, *The Genesis Flood* (Grand Rapids, Mich.: Baker, 1961).

19. C. Mitchell, *The Case for Creationism* (Grantham, England: Autumn House, 1995).

20. K. Ham, *The Lie: Evolution* (El Cajon, CA: Creation Life, 1990).

21. P. Johnson, *Darwinism on Trial* (Downers Grove, Ill.: InterVarsity, 1993); P. Johnson *Defeating Darwinism by Opening Minds* (Downers Grove, Ill.: InterVarsity, 1997).

22. M. Behe, *Darwin's Black Box: The Biochemical Challenge to Evolution* (New York: Free Press, 1996), 39.

23. See M. Isaak, *The Counter-Creationism Handbook* (Westport, Conn.: Greenwood; and Oxford: Harcourt Education, 2005); N. Shanks, *God, the Devil and Darwin: A Critique of Intelligent Design Theory* (New York: Oxford University Press, 2004); B. Forrest and P. R. Goss, *Creationism's Trojan Horse: The Wedge of Intelligent Design.* (Oxford: Oxford University Press, 2004).

24. E. Gosse, *Father and Son* (London: Penguin, 1949), 84–88.

25. D. Wilkinson, *Creation* (Leicester: IVP, 2002), 10–20.

26. R. Hooykaas, *Religion and the Rise of Modern Science* (Edinburgh: Scottish Academic Press, 1973), 105; C. A. Russell, *Cross-Currents: Interactions between Science and Faith* (London: Christian Impact, 1997), 76.

27. W. Hanna, *Memoirs of the Life and Writings of Thomas Chalmers, D.D., LL.D.* (New York: Harper, 1852).

28. H. Miller, *The Testimony of the Rocks* (Cambridge: St. Matthews, 2001).

29. D. Kidner, *Genesis* (London: Tyndale, 1967), 56–57.

30. P. J. Wiseman, *Clues to Creation in Genesis* (London: Marshall Morgan and Scott, 1977).

31. J. C. Polkinghorne, *Belief in God in an Age of Science* (New Haven, Conn.: Yale University Press, 1998), 76–100.

32. Wilkinson, *Creation*, 20.

33. See A. McGrath, *A Scientific Theology*, 3 vols. (Grand Rapids, Mich.: Eerdmans, 2001–2003).

34. S. W. Hawking, *A Brief History of Time* (London: Bantam, 1988), 136.

35. D. Wilkinson, *God, the Big Bang and Stephen Hawking* (Crowborough, England: Monarch, 1996), 81–101.

36. G. May, *Creatio ex Nihilo: The Doctrine of "Creation Out of Nothing" in Early Christian Thought*, trans. A. S. Worrall (Edinburgh: University of Edinburgh Press, 1994); F. Young, "*Creatio ex Nihilo*: A Context for the Emergence of the Christian Doctrine of Creation," *Scottish Journal of Theology* 44 (1991): 141.

37. E. Osborn, *Irenaeus of Lyons* (Cambridge: Cambridge University Press, 2001), 65–68; M. W. Worthing, *God, Creation and Contemporary Physics* (Minneapolis, Minn.: Augsburg, 1996), 76.

38. R. J. Russell, N. Murphy, and C. J. Isham, eds., *Quantum Cosmology and the Laws of Nature: Scientific Perspectives on Divine Action* (Notre Dame, Ind.: Vatican Observatory/University of Notre Dame Press, 1993), 293–329.

39. D. Page, "Hawking's Timely Story," *Nature* 333 (1998): 742–743.

40. T. F. Torrance, *The Christian Doctrine of God: One Being, Three Persons* (Edinburgh: Clark, 1996), 207.

41. M. B. Foster, "The Christian Doctrine of Creation and the Rise of Modern Science," *Mind* 43 (1934): 446–468; E. Zilsel, "The Genesis of the Concept of Physical Law," *Physics Review* 51 (1942): 245–279; F. Oakley, "Christian Theology and the Newtonian Science: Rise of the Concepts of the Laws of Nature," *Church History* 30 (1961): 433–457.

42. D. Stimson, "Puritanism and the New Philosophy in Seventeenth Century England," *Bulletin of the Institute of the History of Medicine* 3 (1935): 321–334.

43. C. Westermann, *Genesis 1–11* (London: SPCK, 1984), 1:158.

44. A. Peacocke, "Welcoming the Disguised Friend: A Positive Theological Appraisal of Biological Evolution," in *Evolutionary and Molecular Biology: Scientific Perspectives on Divine Action*, ed. R. J. Russell, F. J. Ayala, and W. R. Stoeger (Notre Dame, Ind.: Vatican Observatory and the Center for Theology and the Natural Sciences/University of Notre Dame Press, 1998), 18.

45. Russell, *Cross-Currents*, 52.

9

All God's Creatures
Reading Genesis on Human and Nonhuman Animals

David Clough

The Christian tradition has barely begun to read Genesis after Darwin. We no longer read Genesis 1 with a pre-Copernican world view, thinking our planet to be the center of the universe. Most of us are happy to read the text as congruent with scientific theories of the origins of the universe in a big bang. But we continue to be resolutely pre-Darwinian in our reading of the creation narratives. We are still operating with understandings of the relationship between human beings and other creatures that are based on Aristotelian rather than Darwinian theories of the natural world. And our hermeneutics similarly and stubbornly refuses to acknowledge the consequences of recognizing that we are part of the created order, rather than suspended above it as some part-creature, part-divine hybrid. In this chapter, I will argue for the theological necessity of displacing the anthropocentric readings of Genesis that have become Christian orthodoxy in order to begin again the project of reading Genesis after Darwin with particular reference to our understanding of the relationship between human beings and other living things. In conclusion, I will gesture toward the consequences of this project for some central themes of Christian doctrine.[1]

An Anthropocentric Tradition

I begin with some orientation in pre-Darwinian readings of Genesis in relation to the created order apart from human beings. An interesting place to begin is with the first-century Jewish theologian Philo of Alexandria, both because of his influence on later Christian interpreters and because the position he outlines broadly characterizes Christian readings of Genesis until the eighteenth century.[2] In his text from AD 50, *De animalibus* (On Animals), Philo discusses the question of whether animals possess reason. The form of the text is dialogic: Philo is in discussion with his apostate nephew Alexander. But the dialogue is of a particular kind: the first seventy-six sections of the text, out of a total of one hundred sections, is a monologue by Alexander, minutely detailing evidence of the purposive and apparently rational behavior of spiders, bees, swallows, monkeys, fawns, elephants, fish, tortoises, falcons—even oysters—alongside many others.[3] The final quarter of the treatise is Philo's response: a brisk judgment that all of these things are done naturally by the creatures, rather than by foresight: while their actions look similar to those of human beings, they are without thought, and the complexity of their actions is attributable to the way they are designed, rather than to their own rationality. He concludes that we should "stop criticizing nature and committing sacrilege" because ascribing serious self-restraint to animals "is to insult those whom nature has endowed with the best part."[4] In his commentary on the text, Abraham Terian finds in this conclusion the aim of the treatise: "In spite of the title of the treatise and the frequent references to animals, the work as a whole is basically anthropological."[5] Philo is discussing animals in order to defend the Aristotelian distinction between humans and other animals on the basis of reason.

When Philo turns to the interpretation of Genesis, he is similarly determinative about the qualitative difference between human beings and the rest of creation, this time giving it a theological significance. In his treatise on the creation of the world (*De opificio mundi*), he argues that the image of God in human beings is not physical but "in respect of the Mind, the sovereign element of the soul...for after the pattern of a single Mind...the mind in each of those who successively came into being was moulded."[6] Later in the same work, he asks why human beings were created last among the creatures and finds four reasons, each of which makes clear human superiority. First, just as the giver of a banquet ensures that everything is prepared before the guests arrive, so God wanted human beings to experience a "banquet and sacred display" of all the things intended for their use and enjoyment. Second, human beings were created last so it might be instructive to future generations that God provided abundantly for their ancestors. Third, God wanted to unite earth and heaven by making heaven first and human beings last, since human beings are "a miniature heaven." Finally, human beings had to arrive last so that, in appearing suddenly before the other animals, the other

animals might be amazed, do homage to their master, and be tamed.[7] Philo
is no less bracing in his *Questions and Answers on Genesis*. He asks why the
animals had to die in the Flood, given that they are incapable of sin, and provides three answers. First, just as when a king is killed in battle, his military
forces are struck down with him, so God decided that, if the king of the animals were struck down, the animals should be destroyed too. Second, when a
man's head is cut off, no one complains that the rest of the body dies too. Since
human beings are the head of the animals, it is not surprising that all other
living things should be destroyed with them. Third, since the beasts were
made for the "need and honour of man," once human beings were destroyed,
it was right for them to be killed too.[8]

Philo's reading of Genesis in the light of Aristotelian natural philosophy was influential for Christian interpretation of the texts, and the qualitative division between human beings and other creatures on the basis of
reason has set the parameters for Christian thought ever since. Augustine,
for example, also found the image of God in the human mind—though he
extended this in a Trinitarian mode with a division among mind, love, and
knowledge[9]—and thought that the lack of a shared rational life between
humans and other animals was grounds for the permissibility of killing
them.[10] Aquinas believed that God, rather than human beings, is the last
end of the universe, but it is only rational creatures that share fully in this
end[11] and are made fully in the image of God.[12] Luther's commentary on
Genesis agrees strikingly with Philo that we can discern God's provident
care for humanity in his making every part of creation with a view to its contribution to a splendid home for human beings.[13] Calvin concurred that it is
understanding and reason that separate human beings from "brute animals"
and echoed Philo's judgment that all things were created for the convenience
and necessities of human beings.[14] In place of Philo's metaphor of a banquet,
Calvin pictured creation as a theater designed so that, beholding the wonderful works of God, human beings might adore their author.[15] Luther and
Calvin considered that the image of God must be understood as what was
original in Adam and restored in Christ, which Calvin understood as excellence in everything good, chiefly located in the human mind and heart but
showing in every part.[16]

If we turn to modern interpreters of Genesis, we find a significant shift
in understandings of the meaning of the image of God in recognition of the
inadequacies in previous accounts. There is a wide consensus that the attempt
to identify particular human faculties that constitute the image of God is misguided: Wenham comments that, in every case, there is suspicion that commentators are reading their own views about what is most significant about

human beings into the text.[17] There is also an impressive consensus about how the image of God should be interpreted: commentators largely agree that the language is the democratization of political terminology in a Mesopotamian context in which the king was called the image of God.[18] While the explanation of the meaning of the image of God has been transformed, however, its function in demarcating a decisive division between human beings and other creatures remains the same. Brueggemann, for example, declaims the privileged status of human beings in terms comparable with Philo's: "There is one way in which God is imaged in the world and only one: humanness! This is the only creature, the only part of creation, which discloses to us something about the reality of God."[19] Brueggemann suggests that God has a "different, intimate relation" with human beings, with whom God has made a "peculiarly intense commitment" and to whom God has granted "marvellous freedom."[20]

While reason has been displaced from the Aristotelian world view in modern accounts as demarcating the line between humans and all other living creatures, Brueggemann's language exemplifies the widespread retention of a view that human beings belong in a different theological category from other living things. It is this view that I take to be indicative of a reading of Genesis that is pre-Darwinian, for the reasons that follow.

Attempts to Reconcile Human Separatism and Evolution

Let us call a view (like Brueggemann's) that places human beings and other living things in different theological categories a "human-separatist" view. My question is whether a human separatist can also believe in human evolution: the theory that human beings evolved from other living creatures. It seems to me that there are two possible ways of reconciling the human-separatist view with belief in human evolution.

First, one could argue that human beings have developed so far beyond any other creature as to make them qualitatively different. The main problem with this line of argument in general is that it is hard to give content to exactly what constitutes this development while retaining its capacity to distinguish between humans and animals. For example, Keith Ward defends the Thomist view that human beings are the exclusive possessors of rational souls and that this is compatible with human evolution: "we might say that, when the brain reaches a certain stage of complexity, the power of conceptual thought, of reasoning and thinking, begins to exist; and that is when a rational soul begins to be."[21] But what are we to understand by rationality here? It is commonly linked to capacities such as intelligence, the possession of beliefs and desires, or autonomy and personhood, but studies of nonhuman species indicate that human beings differ only in degree from other creatures in relation to each of these capacities.[22] The task of distinguishing between humans and other living things on the basis of rationality is so taxing that some have opted to make the distinction by definition: Jonathan Bennett defines rationality as "whatever it is that humans possess which marks them off, in respect of intellectual capacity, sharply and importantly from all other known species."[23] The fact that Bennett is reduced to this strategy shows that the hope of a "sharp" and "important" line marking the difference between human beings and other species may be a forlorn one. Ward concedes that, if other living things apart from humans were found to be rational, they would also have to be granted the protections offered to humans.[24] He fails to account, however, for the complexities introduced if rationality is a matter of degree rather than an absolute category.

Other alternatives that have been offered to distinguish reliably between humans and animals, such as self-consciousness or language, are similarly found on closer inspection to be matters of degree, which some creatures apart from humans possess in part.[25] Even without the benefit of modern scientific evidence about the intelligence and self-consciousness of nonhuman creatures, Charles Darwin set out the key features of an argument against the assertion of a qualitative difference between human beings and other creatures in 1871 in *The Descent of Man*:

> Nevertheless the difference in mind between man and the higher
> animals, great as it is, is certainly one of degree and not of kind.
> We have seen that the senses and intuitions, the various emotions
> and faculties, such as love, memory, attention, curiosity, imitation,
> reason, &c., of which man boasts, may be found in an incipient, or
> even sometimes in a well-developed condition, in the lower animals.
> They are also capable of some inherited improvement, as we see in
> the domestic dog compared with the wolf or jackal. If it be main-
> tained that certain powers, such as self-consciousness, abstraction,
> &c., are peculiar to man, it may well be that these are the incidental
> results of other highly-advanced intellectual faculties; and these
> again are mainly the result of the continued use of a highly devel-
> oped language. At what age does the new-born infant possess the
> power of abstraction, or become self-conscious and reflect on its own
> existence? We cannot answer; nor can we answer in regard to the
> ascending organic scale. The half-art and half-instinct of language
> still bears the stamp of its gradual evolution.[26]

One might think it helpful to reach for the aid of emergence theory at this point. For example, Arthur Peacocke characterizes evolution as a process

> of *emergence*, for new forms of matter, and a hierarchy of organiza-
> tion of these forms, appear in the course of time. These new forms
> have new properties, behaviours and networks of relations which
> necessitate not only specific methods of investigation but also the
> development of epistemologically irreducible concepts in order to
> describe and refer to them. To these new organizations of matter
> it is, very often, possible to ascribe new levels of what can only be
> called "reality" that is, the epistemology implies at least a puta-
> tive ontology. In other words new kinds of reality may be said to
> "emerge" over time. Notably, on the surface of the Earth, new forms
> of *living* matter (that is living organisms) have come into existence by
> this continuous process—that is what we mean by evolution.[27]

In the context of trying to find a reliable marker to establish a discontinuity between the human and nonhuman, however, this is all beside the point.
My argument here is that we lack any identification of a capacity that human
beings have and that all other animals do not. Were we to discover such a
capacity, emergence theory might help to explain how it could have evolved,
but emergence theory does not help with the prior task of identification of a
distinctively human marker.

An example may help our appreciation of the difficulty of distinguishing between human beings and other species in this way. In 1972, Francine
Patterson began teaching sign language to a gorilla called Koko. Koko learned
to use a vocabulary of over 1,000 words and was able to respond in sign language to questions asked in English with a receptive vocabulary of several
thousand words.[28] Some of the conversations that have been recorded with
Koko are predictable:

> "What do gorillas like to do most?" *"Gorilla love eat good."* Or, "What
> makes you happy?" *"Gorilla tree."* "What makes you angry?" *"Work."*
> "What do gorillas do when it's dark?" *"Gorilla listen* (pause), *sleep."*[29]

Other responses are quite unexpected:

> "How did you sleep last night?" (expecting "fine," "bad," or some
> related response). *"Floor blanket"* (Koko sleeps on the floor with
> blankets). "How do you like your blankets to feel?" *"Hot Koko-love."*
> "What happened?" (after an earthquake). *"Darn darn floor bad bite.*
> *Trouble trouble."*[30]

Koko is able to make jokes: the following conversation followed her being shown a picture of a bird:

KOKO   *That me.* (pointing to adult bird)
BARBARA   Is that really you?
KOKO   *Koko good bird.*
BARBARA   I thought you were a gorilla.
KOKO   *Koko bird.*
BARBARA   Can you fly?
KOKO   *Good.* (i.e., yes)
BARBARA   Show me.
KOKO   *Fake bird, clown.* (Koko laughs)
BARBARA   You're teasing me. (Koko laughs) What are you really?
KOKO   *Gorilla Koko.*[31]

Perhaps most surprising are the conversations recorded with Koko about death:

When Koko was seven, one of her teachers asked, "When do gorillas die?" and she signed, *"Trouble, old."* The teacher also asked, "Where do gorillas go when they die?" and Koko replied, *"Comfortable hole bye."* When asked "How do gorillas feel when they die—happy, sad, afraid?" she signed, *"Sleep."*[32]

In 1984, Koko's favorite kitten, All Ball, was run over by a car. When she was told of the kitten's death, Koko cried. Four months later, the following conversation was recorded:

PENNY   How did you feel when you lost Ball?
KOKO   *Want.*
PENNY   How did you feel when you lost him?
KOKO   *Open trouble visit sorry.*
PENNY   When he died, remember when Ball died, how did you feel?
KOKO   *Red red red bad sorry Koko-love good.*[33]

Finally, a gorilla named Michael, who had been Koko's companion for twenty-four years, died of natural causes. In the following weeks, Koko frequently gave mournful cries, especially at night, and, using sign language, asked for the light to be left on when she went to bed.[34]

While Koko's use of language is exceptional, similar experiments have been done with chimpanzees and bonobos,[35] and other studies have shown dolphins to be capable of syntactical analysis.[36] Skeptics might argue that the behaviors are unconsciously cued by the researchers, the conversations recorded could have been selected from a large number that were not considered meaningful, or the apes are merely engaging in behaviors that lead to rewards. However, it is hard to discount the range and depth of the evidence that the apes are able to use language meaningfully, and it is hard to avoid the consequent disruption to what we previously considered an absolute distinction between human beings and other species.[37]

We have seen, then, that the most frequently offered markers of difference—rationality, intelligence, and language—are unable to identify a qualitative difference between humans and other creatures. The example of Koko shows why: we have until recently substantially understated the capacities of our nearest relatives, the great apes. We could multiply discussions of putative distinguishing attributes almost indefinitely: we have seen that Brueggemann, for example, suggests that human beings have a qualitatively different capacity for relationship with God. Others have suggested that only human beings can have autonomy, personhood, morality, or immorality. Once we have realized the fate of other proposed capacities, however, we are properly more skeptical about such loose appeals. It seems likely that, as in the case of language and rationality, we have assumed rather than proved that the difference between human beings and other creatures is one of kind rather than degree. Until further evidence is adduced, we must accept the provisional conclusion that there is no distinctive human capacity that can be used to mark a qualitative difference between human beings and other species: as Darwin argued, the difference is one of degree. If we want to retain a human-separatist view that humans belong in a different theological category from other species, we cannot depend on natural attributes for its support.

There is a second way we could argue for the human-separatist position, however, which is not reliant on identifying a difference in kind between human beings and other living creatures. It argues that we do not need a natural difference to establish a theological difference. One version of this position is congruent with the consensus of Old Testament scholars that the image of God should be understood functionally, rather than metaphysically: what is distinctive about human beings is the task that God has chosen to assign them. God has made human beings to be God's image on earth, to rule over the other creatures in the same way that the sun and moon rule over the day and night. It is this divine vocation for the human species that places it in a theologically different category, independent of arguments about humans' possession of distinctive characteristics. Alternatively, we could use the Barthian language of election: there was no qualitative distinction between Abraham and his fellow human beings, but through blessing him, God chose to elect the nation of Israel as the people of God. In the same way, we could say that, of all the creatures, God chose to elect human beings and give them a particular status amid creation. For Barth, this is closely linked to the doctrine of the incarnation; Brueggemann states that, in the incarnation, "the creator is 'humanized' as the one who cares in costly ways for the world," citing Karl Barth for support.[38] Human beings may have evolved from other creatures, and therefore stand in a relationship of continuity rather than discontinuity with them, but God's identification of them as God's image on earth and God's decision to dignify human beings above all other species through the incarnation establish the qualitative difference demarcating the human that was hard to locate in a comparison of attributes.

I have suggested three alternative construals of this second defense of the human-separatist position on the basis of vocation, election, and the incarnation. In relation to vocation based on an interpretation of the image of God, there seems to be no serious theological objection to the view that God has given human beings a particular role with respect to the created order. But it seems to me that, by itself, the attribution of a particular vocation for human beings is insufficient to ground the qualitative distinction that the human-separatist position requires. Our task and our responsibility before God are, no doubt, particular to the place we find ourselves within God's creation, but the Bible repeatedly affirms that all of creation participates in the praise of God and each living thing has a part in God's purposes.[39] Paul's egalitarian vision of the diversity of tasks and capacities of the members of the body of Christ (1 Cor. 12) together with Martin Luther's affirmation of a wide range of human vocations of equal status[40] and Jesus's reinterpretation of lordship as servanthood should give us pause before we judge that the vocation God has granted to human beings creates a difference in theological status between them and the rest of the creation. The vocation given by God to human beings denotes particularity rather than separation from other species.

If we were to picture God's action in making human beings in God's image as election, however, we would certainly succeed in making the human-separatist case. Through its election by God, Israel is separated from the other nations and given a particular privilege and status. While its election may be to bring light to all nations (Isa. 51:4), God's election sets it apart and places it in a unique relationship with God that is a good parallel with the special relationship Brueggemann pictures between God and humankind. The difficulty with this argument is that we have no biblical or other grounds for believing that God has elected human beings to a particular status that makes them qualitatively different in theological terms from other living creatures.

Brueggemann's arguments are based on Barth's affirmations about the particular dignity of the human, which are in turn based on his interpretation of the doctrine of the incarnation. The argument for the human-separatist view on the basis of God's election of human beings therefore stands or falls with the argument from the incarnation, to which I now turn.

One of the central tenets of Barth's theological project is the affirmation that God is "for" human beings. Barth echoes Calvin's judgment in affirming that "the universe is created as a theatre for God's dealings with man and man's dealings with God."[41] For Barth, all Christian theology must be understood through the person of Jesus Christ, and creation is merely the external basis of the covenant of grace God establishes through Christ with human beings.[42] In Christ, "God is *human*."[43] It is hard to envisage a higher or more absolute distinction that could be established between human beings and the rest of creation. Put this way, the qualitative theological distinction between human beings and all other living things seems glaringly and blindingly obvious.

There is, however, no theological necessity in construing God's purposes in creation and the meaning of the incarnation in the way Barth does, and there are good reasons to doubt his judgment. In relation to his assertion that human beings were God's sole end in creating the universe, we must recognize that there are no biblical or other reasons for narrowing God's purposes in the creation and redemption of the universe merely to the human. As we have seen, this seemed obvious to Philo and Calvin, and they are in the company of a great many others, but there are significant biblical elements that stand in the way of such a narrow interpretation of God's intentions in creation and redemption. In Genesis 1, God pronounces good what he makes on each day with no reference to its fitness for human purposes, and assigns to human beings the task of governing the rest of the created order, rather than becoming spectators, consumers, or disposers of it. God's speech to Job reminds him of the incomprehensible diversity of creation, including elements such as Behemoth and Leviathan, whose existence is a threat to humankind, rather than a service to it (Job 38–41). In the New Testament, in his letters to the Romans, Ephesians and Colossians, Paul affirms the significance of God's redemptive work for the whole of creation.[44]

Barth's argument that the incarnation represents God's privileging of the human seems persuasive until we reflect on attempts earlier in the Christian tradition to particularize the significance of the incarnation. The Acts of the Apostles narrates a dispute between those among the first Christians who thought that Gentiles must conform to Jewish law to become members of the church and those who thought that the Gentiles should be admitted without precondition, in fulfillment of prophecies that foretold that all peoples would come to worship the Lord (Acts 15). If the church had chosen the for-mer position, it would have decided in effect that the best description of the incarnation was that God became a Jew; instead, its decision resulted in the declaration at the Council of Nicaea that God became human. The church therefore broadened its understanding of God's incarnation in Jesus Christ from Jewish human to human. Arguably, however, the church did not fully appreciate the significance of its affirmation at Nicaea; one way of under-standing the struggle of women in the church in the intervening 1,700 years is that the church was frequently operating on the understanding that, in Jesus Christ, God became a male human being.[45] The twentieth century saw a debate in some ways similar to the one that preceded the admission of the Gentiles: discussion of whether women can participate in the church on equal terms with men. In parallel with the Gentile case, we can restate the case for equality as the assertion that the best understanding of the incarnation is to avoid particularizing the maleness of Christ and instead opt for an inclu-sive rendering, deliberately affirming for the first time that, in Christ, God became simply human.

These examples make clear that the boundaries demarcating the signifi-cance of the incarnation have been contested in the Christian tradition and have had to be redrawn in order to reflect a sufficiently inclusive understanding of God's purposes. If it is the case that the church has been led to progressively broader understandings of the significance of the incarnation, it seems to me that the doctrine of the incarnation need not demarcate an absolute distinc-tion between human beings and the rest of creation. If we have widened our understanding from God becoming a Jewish male human, to a male human, to a human, there seems no barrier to broadening our view one step further in claiming that the incarnation is best understood as God becoming a crea-ture. In fact, this is less of an innovation than it seems: in Paul's letter to the Colossians, he links the creation of all things in Christ, the holding together of all things in Christ, and the reconciling of all things in Christ through the cross (Col. 1:13–20), pointing to an understanding of the incarnation as Christ becoming a representative of "all things." Similarly, if we recognize with Paul in Romans 8 that not just human beings but the whole of creation is groan-ing in need of God's redemption, and if we also take account of Gregory of Nazianzus's famous dictum about the incarnation that what Christ did not assume, he did not heal,[46] then we are in urgent need of an understanding of the incarnation that sees it as fundamentally the assumption of creation by its Creator. If this is the case, however, we no longer have grounds for using the incarnation to demarcate an absolute distinction between human beings and other creatures.

Conclusion: Against Human Separatism

I have argued that Christian readings of Genesis 1 remain pre-Darwinian in taking a human-separatist view that posits a qualitative theological difference between human beings and other species of living things. I identified two arguments supporting a human-separatist view in an evolutionary context. The first was that human beings have evolved so far beyond other species as to constitute a new category of living thing, supporting a theological judgment of a difference in kind, and I argued in response that studies of great apes have shown the truth of Darwin's judgment that the difference between human beings and other creatures is of degree only. The second argument I considered was that there is a theological basis for a discontinuity between human beings and other species, despite their respective attributes. The candidates for this theological basis that I considered were the functional interpretation of the image of God as task and vocation, the idea that God has elected the human species, and the doctrine of the incarnation. I agreed that God assigns human beings a particular task, but suggested that this was insufficient to ground the claim that they had become qualitatively different from other creatures as a result. I showed that the concept of human election was dependent on the incarnation, and finally I argued that the doctrine of the incarnation need not and should not be interpreted in such a way as to establish a discontinuity between human beings and other creatures.

My argument, therefore, is that the human-separatist view that posits a qualitative theological distinction between human beings and other species is incompatible with the belief that human beings evolved from other animals. Such a view remains pre-Darwinian in its reading of Genesis and fails to appreciate the full consequences of what the Darwinian revolution means for Christian theology. We therefore stand in need of a reading of Genesis that fully recognizes the relationship of continuity between human beings and other creatures. In closing, I want to identify briefly three key implications of this conclusion.

First, I do not believe that to recognize that the work of Darwin demands a new reading of Genesis is necessarily to allow scientific understandings to determine theological conclusions. When Christians were first challenged by those inside and outside the church about affirming the equality of women, they engaged in a reappraisal of their readings of scripture and the outworking of it within the Christian tradition. They decided that texts such as Genesis 1:27 and Galatians 3:28 could be read as affirming the equality of women and men. As a result, after significant and lengthy internal debates, many churches recognized that the internal and external challenges were in harmony with a strand already present in the Christian tradition that had previously received inadequate attention. This was not a case, therefore, merely of secular ideals forcing a theological accommodation, but of Christians hearing a prophetic voice alerting them to the need to reappraise what they had received. In the case of slavery, the challenge was similar, though some Christians were quicker to recognize that the internal logic of their faith commitments necessitated moral and political change. I suggest that Darwin's theory of evolution is a similar prophetic calling to the church to revisit and reevaluate its theological heritage and to recognize that continuity between human beings and other creatures is deeply embedded in biblical teaching and the Christian tradition. It is the affirmation of God as Creator of all things which makes clearest the essential relationship among all of God's creatures, and I have already indicated key parts of the biblical witness that strongly affirm this view.

If it were a theological necessity to affirm human separatism, we would be faced with an unwelcome choice between creationism—as the only way to undergird theological affirmations that human beings are a different kind of creature—and atheistic Darwinism. Happily, this is not the case. Just as Christianity came to realize in a post-Copernican context that displacing the planet earth from the center of the solar system need not mean discarding Genesis 1 from the scriptural canon, so we in a post-Darwinian context must realize that displacing human beings from a separate theological category of creature can prompt us to better readings of the Genesis creation narrative.

Second, however, I do not want to understate the theological challenge of moving beyond the human-separatist position, which I have argued is unsustainable. For me, this is exemplified most clearly in the words of Psalm 8 that claim God has made human beings a little lower than God and put all things under their feet (vv. 5–6). This assertion of the human-separatist view has strong affinities with Genesis 1 and alongside other texts will clearly have to be read differently if I am right that this position is untenable. My initial proposal here is that we recognize that these and similar texts are proclamations of good news to God's people in exile, desperately in need of reassurance that God remains God and that God values human beings and will not abandon them. Brueggemann makes this point with respect to Genesis 1, and it is instructive that the verses I have cited from Psalm 8 follow the psalmist's pondering of the majesty of God's creation and his questioning why human beings should have any significance from a divine point of view. In his commentary on Genesis, Calvin quickly discounts apparent challenges from contemporary scientific views that recognize that the moon merely reflects the sun's light and, in any case, is very much smaller than Saturn, which is not mentioned at all. He says that Genesis is an account of what is visible and does not attempt "to soar above the heavens."[47] Where Brueggemann pictures Genesis as good news for exiles, Calvin therefore sees Genesis 1 as telling the story of the creation of the universe from a human point of view.

Now, in relation to this point, we could quickly respond that we can never obtain any other point of view than the human, but it might be that telling the human story in particular ways has significant and negative consequences for our appreciation of other parts of God's creation. The twelfth-century Jewish thinker Moses Maimonides is interesting on this point. In contradiction to the Jewish tradition and his earlier views, which both followed Philo in seeing human beings as the end of creation, Maimonides insisted that God intended all creatures for their own sake. He illustrates his point in this way: to think that the world was created for humankind is like a man in a city thinking that the final end of the city's ruler is to keep the man's house safe at night. From his point of view, it looks like this, but once we have seen the bigger picture, the man's view is obviously ridiculous.[48] My sense is that some of the texts and traditions we have received are understandably concerned to render the world theologically intelligible to human beings and announce to them the good news that they are of infinite importance to their Creator. In the light of what Darwin has taught us, however, it is necessary for us to recognize that God's purposes are not exhausted in the creation and redemption of human beings: just as there are other citizens in the city in Maimonides' parable, so there are other creatures over which God's providential care also extends. It is this change of perspective, very much akin to that God demanded of Job, which will guide the hermeneutical and theological innovations we need to make in response to a rediscovery of our solidarity with God's other creatures.

Third, we need to recognize that rereading Genesis 1 in the way I am proposing will have implications for our practice as well as our doctrine. It cannot be otherwise: if we take the view that God's sole aim in creating the universe was the redemption of human beings, we will have justification for using all parts of creation for whatever we need and want, as Calvin recommends. If we take the human-separatist view, we will place human beings in a different moral category from other creatures to match their qualitative theological difference and therefore, appropriately, give far less regard to the well-being of nonhuman creatures. But if we reject these doctrinal views, we will need to rethink our ethics, too. Even given his view that the universe was established for human beings, Barth saw the killing of animals as "something which is at least very similar to homicide" and which is legitimate only under the pressure of necessity.[49] Once we have departed from Barth in recognizing our decisive solidarity with all of God's creatures in creation and redemption, we will have to ask even more seriously: what are our responsibilities to our fellow creatures?

NOTES

1. I do not, of course, mean to claim that I am anything close to the first to notice this question. Among the many works to draw welcome attention to the issue and challenge Feuerbach's view that "Nature, the world, has no value, no interest for Christians" (Ludwig Feuerbach, *The Essence of Christianity*, trans. George Eliot [New York: Prometheus, 1989], 287) are Charles Birch and Lukas Fischer, *Living with the Animals: The Community of God's Creatures* (Geneva: WCC Publications, 1997); Celia Deane-Drummond, *The Ethics of Nature* (Oxford: Blackwell, 2004); Gary A. Kowalski, *The Bible According to Noah: Theology as if Animals Mattered* (New York: Lantern, 2001); Andrew Linzey, *Animal Gospel: Christian Faith as Though Animals Mattered* (London: Hodder & Stoughton, 1998); Andrew Linzey and Dan Cohn-Sherbok, *After Noah: Animals and the Liberation of Theology* (London: Mowbray, 1997); Andrew Linzey, *Creatures of the Same God: Explorations in Animal Theology* (Winchester, England: Winchester University Press, 2007); Charles Patterson, *Eternal Treblinka: Our Treatment of Animals and the Holocaust* (New York: Lantern, 2002); Paul Waldau, *The Specter of Speciesism: Buddhist and Christian Views of Animals* (Oxford: Oxford University Press, 2002); Stephen H. Webb, *Good Eating* (Grand Rapids, Mich.: Brazos, 2001); Stephen H. Webb, *On God and Dogs: A Christian Theology of Compassion for Animals* (Oxford: Oxford University Press, 1998); Robert N. Wennberg, *God, Humans, and Animals: An Invitation to Enlarge Our Moral Universe* (Grand Rapids, Mich.: Eerdmans, 2003); Donna Yarri, *The Ethics of Animal Experimentation: A Critical Analysis and Constructive Christian Proposal* (Oxford: Oxford University Press, 2005). My point is that the standard reading of Genesis as placing human beings in a different theological category from the rest of creation persists in spite of this attention.

2. For a valuable survey of the developments in theological thinking on this issue at the end of this period, see Keith Thomas, *Man and the Natural World: Changing Attitudes in England 1500–1800* (London: Penguin, 1984).

3. Philo of Alexandria, *De animalibus*, trans. Abraham Terian (Chico, Calif.: Scholars, 1981).

4. Philo, *De animalibus*, §100.

5. Philo, *De animalibus*, §112.

6. Philo, *De opificio mundi*, §23, in *Philo*, vol. 1, trans. F. H. Colson and G. H. Whitaker (London: Heinemann, 1929).

7. Philo, *De opificio mundi*, §§25–28.

8. *Philo*, supplementary vol. 1, trans. F. H. Colson and G. H. Whitaker (London: Heinemann, 1929), bk. II, q. 9.

9. Augustine, *On the Holy Trinity*, ed. Philip Schaff (Peabody, Mass.: Hendrikson, 1995), bk. 9.

10. Augustine, *City of God*, trans. R. W. Dyson (Cambridge: Cambridge University Press, 1998), bk. 1, chs. 20, 33.

11. Aquinas, *Summa contra Gentiles*, trans. English Dominican Fathers (London: Burns Oates & Washbourne, 1923), chs. 111–112.

12. Aquinas, *Summa Theologica*, trans. Fathers of the English Dominican Province (London: Blackfriars, 1963), I.93.2.

13. Martin Luther, *Lectures on Genesis, Chapters 1–5*, in *Luther's Works*, vol. 1, ed. Jaroslav Pelikan (St. Louis, Mo.: Concordia, 1958), 39.

14. John Calvin, *Genesis*, ed. and trans. John King (Edinburgh: Banner of Truth Trust, 1965), 96.

15. Calvin, *Genesis*, 64.

16. Calvin, *Genesis*, 95. See J. Richard Middleton, *The Liberating Image: The Imago Dei in Genesis 1* (Grand Rapids, Mich.: Brazos, 2005), 20–21, for a summary of Luther's and Calvin's positions.

17. Gordon J. Wenham, *Genesis* (Waco, Tex.: Word, 1994), 1:30.

18. See, for example, Wenham, *Genesis*, 31; Victor P. Hamilton, *Genesis*, 2 vols. (Grand Rapids, Mich.: Eerdmans, 1990, 1995), 1:135; Walter Brueggemann, *Genesis* (Atlanta, Ga.: John Knox, 1982), 32; Gerhard von Rad, *Genesis*, rev. ed. (London: SCM, 1972), 58; and the detailed discussion in Middleton, *Liberating Image*, 93–145. Westermann is a dissenting voice, preferring Barth's interpretation of the image as a counterpart to God: Claus Westermann, *Genesis 1–11*, trans. John J. Scullion (London: SPCK, 1984), 146–158.

19. Brueggemann, *Genesis*, 32.

20. Brueggemann, *Genesis*, 31.

21. Keith Ward, *The Battle for the Soul: An Affirmation of Human Dignity and Value* (London: Hodder and Stoughton, 1985), 53.

22. See discussions in Yarri, *Ethics of Animal Experimentation*, 21–55; Marc Bekoff, *Minding Animals: Awareness, Emotions, and Heart* (New York: Oxford University Press, 2002); Carolyn A. Ristau, ed., *Cognitive Ethology: The Minds of Other Animals* (Hillsdale, N.J.: Erlbaum, 1991).

23. Cited in Yarri, *Ethics of Animal Experimentation*, 33.

24. Ward, *Battle for the Soul*, 152–153.

25. See Yarri, *Ethics of Animal Experimentation*, 27–32, 43–49.

26. Charles Darwin, *The Descent of Man, and Selection in Relation to Sex* (London: John Murray, 1871), 105–106.

27. Arthur Peacocke, "Biological Evolution: A Positive Theological Appraisal," in *Evolutionary and Molecular Biology: Scientific Perspectives on Divine Action*, ed. Robert John Russell, William R. Stoeger, and Francisco J. Ayala (Berkeley, Calif.: Vatican Observatory and Center for Theology and the Natural Sciences, 1998), 358.

28. Francine Patterson and Wendy Gordon, "The Case for the Personhood of Gorillas," in *The Great Ape Project: Equality beyond Humanity*, ed. Paola Cavalieri and Peter Singer (New York: St. Martin's, 1993), 58–59.

29. Patterson and Gordon, "Case for the Personhood of Gorillas," 62.

30. Patterson and Gordon, "Case for the Personhood of Gorillas," 62.

31. Patterson and Gordon, "Case for the Personhood of Gorillas," 66.

32. Patterson and Gordon, "Case for the Personhood of Gorillas," 67.

33. Patterson and Gordon, "Case for the Personhood of Gorillas," 67.

34. "Koko's Mourning for Michael" (Aug. 2, 2000), *Gorilla Foundation*, at http://www.koko.org/world/mourning_koko.html, cited in Adam Kolber, "Standing Upright: The Moral and Legal Standing of Humans and Other Apes," *Stanford Law Review* 54, no. 1 (2001): 174.

35. For a survey, see Kolber, "Standing Upright," 170–174.

36. Louis M. Herman, Stan A. Kuczaj, and Mark D. Holder, "Responses to Anomalous Gestural Sequences by a Language-Trained Dolphin: Evidence for Processing of Semantic Relations and Syntactic Information," *Journal of Experimental Psychology: General* 122, no. 2 (1993): 184–194.

37. As late as 1968, Noam Chomsky was still arguing that Descartes was right that language was a "species-specific human possession" (Noam Chomsky, *Language and Mind* [New York: Harcourt Brace Jovanovich, 1968], 10).

38. Brueggemann, *Genesis*, 33.

39. See, for example, Ps. 148; God's speech to Job, chs. 38–41; or Paul's evocation of the whole of creation groaning for redemption in Rom. 8.

40. For a survey of this topic in Luther's thought, see Paul Althaus, *The Ethics of Martin Luther*, trans. Robert C. Schultz (Philadelphia: Fortress, 1972), 36–42.

41. Karl Barth, *Church Dogmatics*, vol. II, pt. 2, trans. G. W. Bromiley et al. (Edinburgh: Clark, 1957), 94.

42. Karl Barth, *Church Dogmatics*, vol. III, pt. 1, trans. J. W. Edwards, O. Bussey, and Harold Knight (Edinburgh: Clark, 1958), 94–228.

43. Karl Barth, *The Humanity of God*, trans. Thomas Wieser and John Newton (Richmond, Va.: John Knox, 1960), 51.

44. Rom. 8:19–23; Eph. 1. 10; Col. 1:15–20. See below for a further discussion of these texts as they impact on interpretation of the incarnation.

45. The classic statement of this concern is Rosemary Radford Ruether's chapter, "Can a Male Savior Save Women?" in her *Sexism and God-Talk: Towards a Feminist Theology* (London: SCM, 2002), 116–138.

46. Gregory of Nazianzus, 'Letter 101', in *Cyril of Jerusalem, Gregory Nazianzen, Nicene and Post Nicene Fathers*, Series 2, vol. 7, (Edinburgh: T & T Clark, 1989), 440.

47. Calvin, *Genesis*, 85.

48. Moses Maimonides, *The Guide of the Perplexed*, trans. Shlomo Pines (Chicago: University of Chicago Press, 1963), 3:13.

49. Karl Barth, *Church Dogmatics*, vol. III, pt. 4, trans. A. T. MacKay et al. (Edinburgh: Clark, 1961), 350–355.

IO

Evolution and Evil
The Difference Darwinism Makes in Theology and Spirituality

Jeff Astley

A good number of theologians seem to hold the view that reading Genesis after Darwin involves little more than adopting a more sophisticated view of the book of Genesis, treating it as a religious text that neither intends nor implies any particular biological claim. This is often coupled with a metaethical or sociological critique of some of the more challenging aspects of evolutionary reflection. Many of these elements can indeed serve us well in helping to undermine the prejudice that Genesis and Darwinism are engaged in some archetypal conflict of religion versus science. But there is no room for theological complacency. Darwinism remains a dangerous idea for any religious perspective that is expressed in or has developed from accounts of a divine origin of the multiplicity of living things, which are assessed by God as wholly good (Gen. 1:31a): accounts in which the Creator intends that our human species should dwell within this plant and animal creation as its natural and spiritual home (Gen. 2:4–25).

Philip Kitcher, who has produced definitive critiques of both creationist "science" and the more imperialist forms of sociobiology, has written of the way that Darwinism subverts religious belief in a supremely wise and loving Creator who has providentially planned life on earth. Rather, he writes, "we easily might take life as it has been generated on our planet as the handiwork of a bungling, or a chillingly indifferent, god."[1]

But why intrude such a strident voice into the general murmurs of reconciliation that mark so many of the meeting points of evolutionary science with the faith of Genesis? Let us seek a quieter and more pleasant prospect. I used to own a house with a small pond in the garden. I found it comforting to sit beside it and observe the insects skittering across or fluttering over the water, the tadpoles and fish swimming around, and the frogs sitting patiently on its shore. And, if I kept still enough, I was sometimes rewarded by a bird coming to take a drink at my suburban water hole. An idyllic scene.

But surely not. It was a *jungle* out there. Competition, predation, a struggle for existence. And *fear*? The bird's wariness as it approached seemed to be an expression of something akin to human anxiety. As it looked from side to side, hopped forward, and then retreated, I couldn't help but think, "I know how you feel; I'm a bit like that myself." Unlike the bird, however, I am often also aware of the jungle within me, when bacteria and viruses strive for the upper hand and my temperature rises with the heat of the battle.

Anthropomorphic twaddle, of course. Simon Barnes counsels us against it: "Life is no more cruel than it is benign....[L]ife is not there to teach us moral tales, or to uplift us with its beauty or to appall us with its cruelties. Life is."[2]

Yet Darwin voiced similar concerns, slipping into a troubled agnosticism. His big idea was that the descent with modification of all living things was mainly driven by processes of natural selection, in which the overproduction of offspring leads to competition for limited resources, and out of the variety of individuals in a population some are found to be at a "selective advantage" over the others. In his *Origin of Species*, he summarizes the "general law" of natural selection as "multiply, vary, let the strongest live and the weakest die."[3] In the "breathtakingly wasteful and inefficient" process described by Darwinism, "suffering is not a by-product but constitutive of the script the Creator has chosen to write."[4] For, in Darwinism, the natural world is characterized by competition, struggle, suffering, death and extinction.

In fact, the differential *reproduction* of organisms is more significant than their differential survival, and—to quote the reproductive biologist Jack Cohen—"reproduction is nearly all death."[5] So, fourteen out of sixteen starlings die without breeding; and out of 10,000 eggs laid in a frog's lifetime and out of 40 million cod eggs, on average only 2 survive to breed. Human biology hides this apparent "waste." Nevertheless, in an ejaculation of up to 200 million genetically unique sperm, only 1 will fertilize a genetically unique egg, *if* there is an egg around; and only just over a third of fertilized eggs will produce a baby. The explanation of these numbers is to be found not only in predation (not at all in the human case), but also in the number of abnormalities that inevitably arise from genetic (including chromosomal) mutation, which is the fundamental process that drives all evolution and which, insofar as it is largely unrelated to the needs of the organism, may be properly described as "chance."

Now, we can overplay the role of natural selection in the evolutionary process. Random genetic drift and geographical isolation are more benign factors, and sexual selection is not all bloody battles between males. Likewise, cooperation (a process that begins at the level of the cells themselves) is just as necessary for survival as is competition. Not all biologists adopt Tennyson's gloomy view of a "Nature red in tooth and claw" that is "careless of the single life" and even of entire biological taxa—"I care for nothing, all shall go."[6] Thus, Alfred Russel Wallace, the co-discoverer of evolution through natural selection, opined that "the amount of actual suffering caused by the struggle for existence among animals is altogether insignificant."[7] But Darwin wrote of "the war of Nature,"[8] and his supporter T. H. Huxley complained of "the moral indifference" and "unfathomable injustice of the nature of things."[9]

It is unsurprising, then, that many perceive the processes of natural selection as exacerbating the problem of evil for the religious believer.

Problems of Evil

In this chapter, I shall explore some ways in which the problem of evil may be viewed from the standpoint of evolutionary biology. In doing so, I shall keep returning to the perspective of spirituality. It is routine to distinguish between two rather different problems of evil.[10] One is the problem of *explaining evil* in God's creation, sometimes called the cognitive or theological problem of evil, in which the questions are "Is belief in God intelligible in a world that contains evil?" and "Is evil itself intelligible in God's world?" The other is the spiritual, religious, psychological, and pastoral problem of facing and *coping with evil*. Different questions are posed here, which include "Is this a God who can help?" and "What spiritual and religious resources can help us conquer evil?"

Theodicy is that part of theology that deals with the cognitive problem of evil. It has been criticized as a merely theoretical undertaking by those who want something that is more focused on the individual's salvation and her concern to overcome evil, and is more contextualized in human practice.[11] According to Dewi Phillips, the question "Why?"—at least when voiced by the individual sufferer—"does not really seek an answer" but, rather, "reactions or responses to replace the question." The questions posed by our experience of evil seem to seek "for something which explanations cannot give."[12] Phillips thought that too much of theodicy works with philosophical abstractions rather than religious concepts, and in justifying evils it verges on the morally corrupt. If we take a spiritual perspective more seriously, we may be able to avoid these pitfalls.

I am not privileging spirituality because I think that the cognitive problem of evil is unimportant. But we don't know enough about the God of mystery and God's mysterious interaction with and future plans for creation to make any response wholly convincing. I also think that we radically understate the extent to which we find ourselves holding an attitude and then seeking some sort of rational justification for it. In particular, spiritual and religious attitudes come first, and they remain the most important motivators of belief. As powerful engines for living, they may be held in the teeth of apparently conflicting evidence, including the experience of evil. Such a stance can be rationally defended; indeed, it is akin to some aspects of the scientist's conviction that puzzling evidence must have a scientific explanation. But neither of these stances (which are, of course, compatible) is based on reason. A better word here is "faith," even, perhaps, "hope."

Natural Evil and God's Intentions

Natural evil comprises those natural events that give rise to physical pain and mental suffering. The extent to which animals "suffer" pain is disputed, but the biological utility of a response that leads them to avoid tissue damage would have been greatly enhanced by the development of sentience and of more complex conscious processing.[13] Pain has evolved because it has survival value. It is unfortunate that there is no selective advantage in an animal's ceasing to feel pain when it is no longer able to escape the pressure of the predator's fangs or (as is more usual in our own case) a cancerous growth. For similar reasons, humans are subject to the woes of old age because conditions that only arise after we have ceased to breed cannot be selected against.

Given the world we have, however, pain and suffering are inevitable, and natural selection itself is inevitable. This latter inevitability is not always acknowledged. But unless resources are unlimited and predators absent, as is sometimes the case when a species moves into a new habitat, certain events will follow as evolutionary change is fueled by a population burgeoning among limited resources. Like animal breeders, but more blindly, nature *selects*. A soft-hearted Mother Nature who looks kindly on the runt of the litter merely postpones the reckoning. As competition heats up, maladapted descendants will eventually lose the race against their better-adapted relatives and other competitors.

Could God not have ordered nature differently, then? Well, perhaps not any nature that would drive, or even permit, much evolutionary change. In any case, materiality inevitably involves imperfection: a tendency to disorder, decay, fragility, and mortality. Austin Farrer noted the "mutual interference of systems" as "the grand cause of physical evil" and a necessary correlate of physicality. Keith Ward writes of such evil as "an inevitable consequence" of the sort of world we live in.[14] Perhaps no radically alternative world could exist, even without evolution.[15]

But does God *intend* the suffering of nature or is it an unintended concomitant of God's purpose of evolutionary change? Some argue that we should only ascribe those natural events to God's agency "in which he realizes his purposes, and not events which he permits though they are contrary to his positive will."[16] Intention may be a matter of doing something because you want to do it for its own sake or for some further end; but Anthony Kenny says of the foreseen but unintended consequences of our actions that we "want" them only insofar as we consent to them, and that is "quite different from any feeling of desire."[17] So does God create a tough environment in which pain is inevitable for the sake of a greater good that God doesn't just want (intends) but *desires* (really intends)?

Perhaps we should add that some actions are more truly revelatory of our nature than others. (You would learn little of my true character by watching me brush my teeth.) The problem is that a Creator God does too much. Spiritual perception is needed to discern God's characteristic activity, God's *true* acts, amid the ambiguous vastness of nature. To achieve this, we have to know what—and whom—to look for. God's intentions cannot simply be read from nature.

Soul Making and Ambiguity

In John Hick's "vale of soul-making theodicy," natural evil is necessary if we are to develop a worthwhile moral and spiritual character—as opposed merely to flourishing as God's protected and pampered pets. Without pain, there would be no courage and no compassion. But this is a view that must face Phillips's criticism of the "instrumentalist nightmare" of justifying the cost of suffering in terms of the benefit of the virtues it evokes.[18] Expressed as an explanatory theodicy, this criticism is hard to avoid, but interpreting it in terms of a spirituality of suffering provides a different slant. Perhaps the idea is best understood as a lens through which we try to see the point of our own lives more clearly and the sufferings of nature differently.

Yet perception can properly provoke explanation. One of the more profound elements in this viewpoint is the acknowledgment of the apparent gratuity of natural evil. It is spiritually important that we should see suffering in this way. If we were to come to believe that a person's pain was planned for his good, it would be less likely to evoke the courage or the compassion that God really intends to create.[19] Hence, the truth about suffering is to be found on two levels. God intends the evil (at one level, the general level) that he really intends (at another level) that we should work to overcome. In terms of spiritual perception, God's hand in this is *necessarily* hidden.

But what of the animals? "If God watches the sparrows fall," writes Holmes Rolston, "God must do so from a great distance."[20] Hick recognizes that his soul-making defense does not apply in the case of animals without moral personalities. Rather, "sentient Nature supports and serves its human apex.... by helping to constitute an independent natural order to which man is organically related and within which he exists at an epistemic distance from which he may freely come to God."[21] Animals, too, are created at a distance from God's glory, down here in the ambiguous mud; and our origins must lie with them if we are to retain any spiritual choice over against God.

Is this enough? Jürgen Moltmann writes of "the resurrection of Nature" and Jay McDaniel hopes more specifically for a "pelican heaven."[22] Christopher Southgate also looks for some type of afterlife that can serve as eschatological compensation for the individual suffering of animals and for all those "unfulfilled organisms" that may be regarded as "the victims or casualties of evolution."[23] But these are speculative theological steps too far for me, and some are difficult to defend in any detail. We may also note that such options would not have been available for most of the Old Testament period, when the Creator was praised by people who had no positive conception of even a human afterlife.

God's Action in the World

The way we understand natural evil will depend in part on the way we understand God's relationship to the universe. Hick's soul-making theodicy implies that God ought not intervene in nature to protect us from the possibility of pain, let alone to heal our animal cousins.

Others take a different view. Exponents of "intelligent design" argue that complex organelles and biochemical pathways could not be produced by the natural processes of evolution and required additional supernatural intervention to come into being. Not only are its particular claims about "irreducible complexity" often in conflict with scientific evidence, but the whole approach is also vulnerable to the charge of elevating the theological significance of these elements as expressions of God's will *at the expense of* the rest of God's activity in creating and sustaining the world. Most interventionist perspectives seem to conflict with Augustine's view that the regular sprouting of seeds is a greater "daily miracle" than the feeding of the 5,000. Appeals to the miraculous also raise questions about the *limitations* of this more potent divine activity: why does God not make more and better molecular machines? If God intervenes to heal people, why does he not do so more often and to better effect?[24]

Even if the mechanism of evolution is mindless, this does not mean that the whole process is not designed with a meaning, purpose, and intended direction. In *theistic evolution*, God creates new forms "through evolution," although the adaptations of living things may be interpreted as the result of God's activity in a wide variety of ways, depending on their location on the spectrum of theological positions on divine action.[25] At the opposite end of this spectrum from creationism and intelligent design, this takes a wholly deistic form; but it may also be understood in ways that allow the Creator to influence various selection pressures and/or the largely unpredictable or even indeterminate events of genetic mutation (at the quantum level) in some undetectable way—as in Robert Russell's noninterventionist understanding of divine providential action. But those who dislike the idea of God "scrabbling around in the basement of sub-atomic particles, furtively adjusting quarks when no one is looking,"[26] may prefer (as I do) Arthur Peacocke's account. This permits more real chance within nature and denies not only any special intervention by God but also *any* "kind of special guidance....whereby God pushes or pulls evolution in a direction it would not otherwise have taken by its own natural processes and propensities."[27] Biologists often appeal to "top-down," "whole-part," or "system-level" explanations that describe the role, function, and (inherent) purpose of an organism within the larger context of its environment. Only at this level can "why" questions be asked and answered ("Why is the frog jumping away from the snake?" "Why are cheetahs close to extinction?").[28] Peacocke thinks of God interacting with the world in a similar manner, not by jumping into any gaps or modifying the inevitable uncertainties within the natural system, but by a transfer of information "with the world-system as a totality," which exists within God's own self.[29]

But perhaps this interactive panentheism is also a speculation too far.

Spirituality Again

Let us return to a more spiritual framework. One of Darwin's supporters, the Christian naturalist Asa Gray, argued that the process of evolution shows the necessity of waste and suffering. Such a view allows theodicy to incorporate the evolutionary perspective and to confess, with Rolston, that nature is "cruciform" and that the secret of life is a sort of passion play in which all have "borne our griefs and carried our sorrows."[30]

Is this how we look on nature? Richard Dawkins may be wrong about a great deal, but he captures well "the feeling of awed wonder that science can give us," which he describes as "one of the highest experiences of which the human psyche is capable."[31] Simon Barnes's refrain that "Life is" is a part of this. According to Rudolf Otto, religious awe is something of a mixed response. Before the truly holy, the mystery that is "inexpressible and above all creatures,"[32] we are daunted—even terrified—yet fascinated too: repelled and attracted at one and the same time. The shudder of Otherness is an intrinsic part of spiritual experience. Analogously, but at a lower level, nature can also appear both lovely and dreadful, an experience that may be expressed in thoughts of nature as God's servant/destroyer as well as his creative agent. This is the shared dark side of God and nature, which is another thing we need to acknowledge.

The farmer's children are lucky, people say, because they learn earlier than the rest of us a sober realism about muck, sex, food—and death. In this way, too, life just "is." "Shall we receive good at the hand of the Lord, and shall we not receive evil?" the Job of the early prose story rhetorically asks his wife. And in all of this, "he did not sin with his lips" (Job 2:10). Of course, we must also allow the reaction that the later, more poetic Job gives us in spades—what Daniel Migliore has called our "faithful resistance" to evil.[33] We are permitted to protest even on behalf of ourselves, certainly for others, and perhaps for the rest of nature, too. We may shout at the cat before it pounces on the bird. Beyond this, however, we shall have to accept the suffering and the death. The naturalist rarely intervenes, for if you start, where will you stop? It is a deeply spiritual truth that there is really no option, in the end, other than acceptance. For our soul's sake, we have to embrace with St. Francis our omnipresent Brother Death, recognizing with Karl Barth that even our perishing is part of "the good order of God."[34]

John Haught argues that the economy of evolution should be seen as a manifestation of God's humble, self-emptying love, which strives to "let the other be."[35] This kenotic theme is best interpreted not in terms of God's loss of infinite power, but as God granting the existence of other, finite powers. God does this, Philippians 2:5–8 suggests, because grasping at and holding on to power are not what divinity is about. This, too, is primarily a spiritual insight. The self's letting go is the real issue. We may say that this is modeled—as is so much else in the spiritual life—on the image of the Christ-like Creator God.

But we write theology as well as read it; and we dare to speak of God in this way, I suggest, because we have discovered the necessity of letting go for ourselves: letting go of our toys, our friends, our lovers, and especially our children. It is not just Buddhists who speak good spiritual sense about not clinging to transient things: "Selflessly to love the transient and let it go: that is beatitude."[36] Love is best proved in the letting go. This is also a form of acceptance.

A spirituality that includes an acceptance of natural evil, as the way that life is and must be, is likely to shift us along the spectrum of models of divine activity away from the interventionist end. "My grace is sufficient for you, for power is made perfect in weakness," God says in response to Paul's repeated prayer for healing (2 Cor. 12:9). God says this, too, through the cross—and he did not intervene then, either. I simply do not expect that form of divine activity in nature, however much I may hope for it and, indeed (because dishonesty is spiritually impossible in prayer), however much I may ask for it. But spiritual hope is something different from secular expectation or anticipation. It is a matter of desire and the voicing of our deepest valuations that leads to a purification of that desire. It is also a waiting on God for *whatever* God will give, while always knowing that the greatest thing that God can ever give us is himself. If that is not given and received, no amount of balm will heal us.

If natural selection is an inevitable process, then God's special divine activity and, perhaps, his intervention would be repeatedly required for God to remove (or just to ease) the natural evils which it generates.[37] As these evils remain, and remain in such numbers, it does not appear that God *is* so employed. Those who deny this will hear the old troubling question voiced once again: if God is willing to intervene in or steer nature so as to ensure a better evolutionary world, why does God not do so more often?

But should we disown any God who does not intervene or steer nature's development as inactive, absent, and uncaring? I do not believe so. The continuing, universal preserving act, which is the metaphysical whisper behind all natural things and events, is all of the divine activity needed in many people's theology. It is present to all created things as the sustaining thread of God's love, on which everything depends. To know that the Holy Other is in this way always among us—even in the pain—and always desires our good and our response is a way of seeing the world that can change everything, even without miracles.

I would add that the account of nature we adopt should resonate with the fact that there is, for many people, an at-home-ness in the natural world that runs very deep and that carries overtones of our evolutionary origins. After all, nature is the place we have evolved to fit—and to fit in. Edward Wilson coined the term *biophilia* for our innate need to connect with the living world.[38] He relates it to the importance of our stewardship of the environment, and that should be a major theme in any spirituality of nature. If nature is the expressive end product of God's creative will, however, we should expect not only that our relationship with it ought to take the form of caring concern, but also that our study of it will be a sort of revelation and our experience of it a kind of healing. And running the inference backward: if we find ourselves with these attitudes toward nature, and find that they serve to heal us, can we not infer *something* about God's relationship to nature and the character of that relationship?

Moral Evil

Moral evil comprises human wrongdoing and the pain and suffering that it causes. Theists usually explain such evil with the help of a freewill defense (FWD), citing the logical impossibility of God giving us "very serious free will, i.e., the free will to choose between good and wrong, without the natural possibility (unprevented by God) that we will do wrong."[39] Hick writes, "It seems to me that once you ask God to intervene to prevent some specific evil you are in principle asking [God] to rescind our human freedom and responsibility."[40]

Christian theology's reading of Genesis has led many to seek to apply the FWD to the Fall of Adam (Gen. 3), and some have even posited a premundane fall of angels, who then became powerful sources of natural evil as well as of human temptation. According to Augustine, we all share a "seminal identity" with Adam, the first human. Hence, humans "begot perverted and condemned offspring," "for we were all in that one man, seeing that we all were that one man who fell into sin."[41]

Adam's Fall is said to have three results for all human beings: *original sin* (an inherited corrupt tendency to sin), *original guilt* (our inherited guilt for Adam's sin), and *natural evil.*[42] For Calvin, "the whole order of Nature was subverted by the sin of man."[43] Original sin as an innate faultiness—a tendency toward sin and spiritual blindness—is a fact of the moral and spiritual life, whatever its origins. But many have balked, as Ezekiel does (ch. 18), at the idea that a child should suffer for the sins of her father. That view is "clearly to be rejected on moral grounds: I cannot be guilty in respect of the sins of another."[44]

Evolutionary theory also challenges the notion of Adam's Fall by giving *Homo sapiens* a list of ancestors in evolutionary history and by replacing the paradisiacal environment of our origins with one in which suffering and death were already present. While some writers recognize a particular, historical "fall" of a tribe of early hominids, who turned away from God to selfishness, and others have even speculated about God creating Adam "in the body of a Near Eastern farmer comparatively recently,"[45] many prefer to reinterpret the doctrine of the Fall as describing the state *in which* humans were created through evolution: "we appear to be rising beasts rather than fallen angels!"[46] On this latter view, we may be said to have been "created fallen," with selfishness, aggression, and self-assertiveness built into our life at various levels, as features that were necessary for our early evolution. Kingsley Barrett has even described Darwinism as "a demythologised version of the doctrine of original sin."[47] But I am also sympathetic to the view that the Fall is really our awakening into a new consciousness of sinfulness and moral choice.[48]

Certainly, "original sin is part of the biological package. It comes with being human."[49] Interestingly, the atheistic philosopher Daniel Dennett seizes on the metaphor of original sin as an appropriate figure for the failure to achieve perfection in the copying process of nucleic acid replication, a failure that inevitably results in inherited errors (mutations) without which "evolution would grind to a halt."[50] There is a parallel here with the ancient Christian claim that Adam's sin was a "happy fault" because it led to a better state (traditionally understood as the redemption of human beings through Christ). Dennett's view may inform a spirituality of accepting life with all its imperfections, since the imperfections help to drive evolutionary adaptation, and (despite the creationists' claims) natural adaptations are usually imperfect. That is perhaps the sense in which we should confess that the present structure of nature falls short of what God really, ultimately, intends it to be.

Virtue and Biology

Evolution and ethics form an odd couple. In Darwin's day, many fastened on an "evolutionary ethics" of Social Darwinism that took its values from the brutal and competitive processes that they saw in nature. But Huxley argued that we must resist the forces of evolution by helping the weak and suffering, since altruism and sympathy are antithetical to nature's ways. "The ethical progress of society depends, not on imitating the cosmic process, still less in running away from it, but in combating it."[51] Darwin, however, believed that the evolved parental and social instincts of animals would inevitably give rise to the development of conscience, as humans evolved. And cooperation and sociability assuredly offer survival advantages quite as significant as those that competitiveness delivers.

Many argue that our moral sensitivities, even those that seem contrary to nature, are ultimately the product of evolutionary processes; but this is a contentious position. We cannot deny the differences that human thinking and social life make to human morality.[52] It is our motivating feelings that have evolved, rather than any species of higher moral reasoning that is distinctively human (such as the principle of impartiality, which is perhaps the key to true ethics). It may be that some of "the emotions you feel are pure Darwinism,"[53] including your moral sentiments, but any such analysis must allow morality to be regarded both as part of our nature (as a moral disposition) *and* as open to nurture, enculturation, education, and reflection. "We are not hardline 'genetically determined' like (say) ants, who go through life like robots. Nor are our patterns of thinking so fixed by our biology that culture has no effect.... We may not follow these thoughts, but they are there."[54] Some hold that this sort of position lies too close to having your cake and eating it,[55] but I am not sure why. Just as looking at the behavior of children can give us insights into similar behavior in adults, so looking at animal behavior can sometimes teach us something important about ourselves.

Richard Dawkins also believes that we can—and should—rebel against the "selfishness" of our genes. "Let us try to *teach* generosity and altruism, because we are born selfish."[56] However, as he well knows, many of our cooperative, kind, sympathetic, faithful, and charitable dispositions have also evolved as part of our human nature; and, in any case, the word "selfish" may be applied only metaphorically to our genes. It is strange to view ourselves simply as innately depraved. We also need to celebrate the more cooperative and kinder dimensions of our humanity and to promote forms of moral nurture that sometimes cut along the grain of our ("better") nature rather than solely against it. And we must also admit that, even if the motivation that underlies our generosity or kindness has evolved "for" ulterior genetic purposes (in that, if it had not increased reproductive fitness, it would not have developed), nevertheless the motivation is what it is now. Generous people are trying to be *generous*; they are not seeking to maximize the inheritance of their genes.

Human Dignity and Human Humility

At the notorious 1860 meeting of the British Association for the Advancement of Science in Oxford, Bishop Samuel Wilberforce is said to have concluded what may have been a measured critique of Darwin's theory, but was described by some as unfair ridicule, by jokingly challenging Huxley as to whether he claimed to be descended from an ape on his grandfather's or his grandmother's side. This would presumably have been a particularly offensive notion to Victorian sensibilities. Wilberforce indisputably wrote, in what Darwin called an "uncommonly clever" review of *Origin*, of "the degrading notion of the brute origin of him who was created in the image of God, and redeemed by the Eternal Son."[57]

From the first, there was little doubt that Darwin's theory embraced human beings, and Darwin later discussed human origins in *The Descent of Man* (1871), arguing that the differences between humans and present-day apes were differences in degree rather than in kind, both groups sharing common anthropoid ancestors. Compared with the doctrine of a special human creation, and the implied biblical claim that the rest of creation was created by God for the sake of human beings (cf. Gen. 1:26–28), by treating animals as our kith and kin, evolution appears to offer a lower view of the status of our species.

At least, this teaches us humility. The evolutionary perspective is a reminder that, although we are "fearfully and wonderfully made," it is out of the dust of the earth. Etymologically, *humility* derives from *humus*, the ground; it is a spiritual attitude of great significance for the way we look on moral evil.

Both biology and theology insist on a dark side to human nature. Evolutionary accounts can never *justify* selfishness or sneakiness, let alone sexism, racism, or rape and other forms of violence. But if our genetics is no excuse for our evil behavior, neither is our environment; and if the determinism of the one is to be resisted, it seems perverse to welcome the determinism of the other, as some appear to do. We live at the confluence of both streams, astride whatever mechanism it is that chooses which of the motivating waters will gush through into the mill race that helps to turn the wheel of our overt actions. But we are never wholly self-made human beings in the economy of morality. Both our genes and our environment (including education) contribute to what we are and do. So the aphorisms remain appropriate: "There but for the grace of God, go I" and "Judgment is mine, says the Lord." And perhaps also the Thomistic insight that grace perfects nature and does not destroy it.[58] "The point of stressing biological facts," writes Mary Midgley, "is to suggest that our nature matters."[59]

Another positive emphasis in the work of Richard Dawkins is his focus on our ancestors.[60] When a biologist uses this term, she clearly intends to extend it beyond the faded photographs in the family album or the portraits in the baronial hall, back through our genetic history. Along with every organism that ever lived, we can all make the proud claim that we *have* ancestors: forebears who all survived and flourished at least long enough, and well enough, to breed. In Darwinian terms, they "succeeded." In genetic terms, this is largely because they possessed good genes—genes that were good at growing a body that was good enough to survive and reproduce.

We are *descendants* and, to that extent, dependents. Our life and, indeed, our successful reproduction are now dependent on much more than our ancestors; but theists believe that acknowledging dependence in one dimension doesn't preclude our conceding its significant role in another. As I hope the posters in the nursery school still say, there are many "people who help us"—and many without whom we could not survive. Most are hidden from our sight, and the spiritual temptation is to ignore their significance. But no claim to individual autonomy can plausibly ignore our status as dependent, rational animals. Our lives are possible because of mummy and daddy; and the farmers and the shopkeepers; and the doctors, cooks, and all the rest; *and*—in another way—because of our ancestors, stretching back through ancestral forms whose portraits we would not care to hang in any hall.

Humility is a key Christian and human virtue and, perhaps, "the only wisdom we can hope to acquire."[61] According to the ethicist Bernard Gert, this spiritual virtue is "the foundation of all of the moral virtues," for humility involves "a general attitude towards one's place in the world" and an appreciation of the (large) extent to which we depend on others and the (small) extent to which, once again, we may claim to be self-made persons.[62] Humility is a realistic virtue that betokens a realistic perspective on ourselves and others.

One of the dangers we run by ignoring the implications of evolution is that of failing to see that our dignity comes from a God who creates us in and through these other beasts. People sometimes look back on their grandparents' lives and wonder how they survived; they may be grateful to them for their struggle to bring up their children, knowing that life was a lot harder then. It was even harder further back in our ancestry.

We will respect our ancestors even more if we believe that we owe them the foundations of our moral sense. The primatologist Frans de Waal and his coworkers have produced some startling research on patterns of empathy, reciprocation, retribution, and conflict resolution among chimpanzees. Siding with Darwin rather than Huxley, de Waal insists that natural selection does not just give rise to a competitive mindset. He treats the evolution of cooperative impulses, such as "consolation of distressed individuals and protection against aggression," as key to human morality. De Waal writes of "three levels of morality"—moral sentiments, social pressure, and judgment and reasoning—and argues that there are many parallels between humans and apes at the first level, some at the second, but very few at the third. Nevertheless:

> To neglect the common ground with other primates, and to deny the
> evolutionary roots of human morality, would be like arriving at the
> top of a tower to declare that the rest of the building is irrelevant,

that the precious concept of "tower" ought to be reserved for its sum-
mit. While making for good academic fights, semantics are mostly
a waste of time. Are animals moral? Let us simply conclude that
they occupy several floors of the tower of morality. Rejection of even
this modest proposal can only result in an impoverished view of the
structure as a whole.[63]

Some evolutionary biologists use the phrase "evolution deniers" for creationists and advocates of intelligent design. De Waal employs the term "anthro-
podenial" to castigate the "wilful blindness" of those who refuse to admit the
continuity between humans and other animals. He has also coined the term
"Beethoven error" for the claim that "since selection is a cruel, pitiless process of elimination, it can only have produced cruel and pitiless creatures."[64]
You might as well say that Beethoven's dirty and disorderly apartment could
never produce his intricate, beautiful compositions. I suppose that de Waal
is reminding us that a priori, armchair speculation always needs to be tested
against whatever empirical facts we have.

And in the end—the practical end—our *theological* speculations will also
have to be tested, in a broader way. They must be tested against a sane and
salvific spiritual state that permits us to look unflinchingly even on blood-
stained nature and to see it as God's good world. And to find ourselves at
home in it.

NOTES

1. Philip Kitcher, *Living with Darwin* (New York: Oxford University Press,
2007), 126.

2. Simon Barnes, *How to Be a Bad Birdwatcher* (London: Short, 2004), 158–159.

3. *Origin* (1859), end of ch. VII.

4. Kitcher, *Living with Darwin*, 124.

5. Unpublished lecture, University of Durham, February 2006.

6. Tennyson, *In Memoriam* (1850), lv, lvi.

7. A. R. Wallace, *Darwinism* (1889; London: Macmillan, 1905), 37.

8. *Origin*, end of ch. XIV.

9. T. H. Huxley (1893), in Julian Huxley, ed., *Evolution and Ethics 1893–1943*
(London: Pilot, 1947), 68.

10. Thus, Brian Hebblethwaite, *Evil, Suffering and Religion* (London: SPCK,
2000), chs. 2 and 3.

11. Kenneth Surin, *Theology and the Problem of Evil* (Oxford: Blackwell, 1986),
ch. 1.

12. D. Z. Phillips, *Wittgenstein and Religion* (Basingstoke, England: Macmillan,
1993), 160, 166–169; Phillips, *The Problem of Evil and the Problem of God* (London:
SCM, 2004), ch. 6.

13. See Richard Swinburne, *Providence and the Problem of Evil* (Oxford: Clarendon, 1998), 171–175.

14. Austin Farrer, *Love Almighty and Ills Unlimited* (London: Collins, 1966), 50–51; Keith Ward, *Divine Action* (London: Collins, 1990), 55.

15. Hebblethwaite, *Evil*, 85.

16. Vincent Brümmer, *Speaking of a Personal God* (Cambridge: Cambridge University Press, 1992), 122; cf. John Hick, *Evil and the God of Love* (London: Collins, 1968), 110.

17. Anthony Kenny, *Will, Freedom and Power* (Oxford: Blackwell, 1975), 56; Kenny, *Freewill and Responsibility* (London: Routledge & Kegan Paul, 1978), 51.

18. Phillips, *Problem of Evil*, 225, see also 66–71.

19. See Thomas Tracy, "Evolution, Divine Action, and the Problem of Evil," in *Evolutionary and Molecular Biology*, ed. Robert John Russell, William R. Stoeger, S.J., and Francisco J. Ayala (Vatican City State: Vatican Observatory; Berkeley, Calif.: Center for Theology and Natural Sciences, 1998), 524–526.

20. Holmes Rolston, *Science and Religion* (New York: Random House, 1987), 140.

21. Hick, *Evil*, 251–252; see also 345–353.

22. Jürgen Moltmann, *The Way of Jesus Christ* (London: SCM; San Francisco: HarperSanFrancisco, 1990), 296–297; Jay McDaniel, *Of God and Pelicans* (Louisville, Ky.: Westminster John Knox, 1989), 45.

23. Christopher Southgate, *The Groaning of Creation* (Louisville, Ky.: Westminster John Knox, 2008), 40.

24. See Michael Ruse, *Darwin and Design* (Cambridge, Mass.: Harvard University Press, 2003), 322; Kitcher, *Living with Darwin*, 106–110.

25. For a range of views, see David J. Bartholomew, *God of Chance* (London: SCM, 1984); Kenneth R. Miller, *Finding Darwin's God* (New York: HarperCollins, 1999), chs. 8 and 9; A. R. Peacocke, *Creation and the World of Science* (Oxford: Oxford University Press, 2004), 92–97; Peacocke, *Paths from Science towards God* (Oxford: Oneworld, 2001), ch. 5; Ted Peters and Nathan Hallanger, eds., *God's Action in Nature's World* (London: Ashgate, 2006); Ted Peters and Martinez Hewlett, *Evolution from Creation to New Creation* (Nashville, Tenn.: Abingdon, 2003), ch. 6; Russell, Stoeger, and Ayala, *Evolutionary and Molecular Biology*, sec. II (esp. 191–223), 357–376, 418–442, 513–520.

26. Ward, *Divine Action*, 127; see John Polkinghorne, *One World* (London: SPCK, 1986), 71–72.

27. Peacocke, *Paths from Science*, 75.

28. See Steven Rose, *Lifelines* (London: Allen Lane, 1997), ch. 1.

29. Peacocke, *Paths from Science*, 108–114; see also his *All That Is* (Minneapolis, Minn.: Fortress, 2007), ch. 9.

30. Rolston, *Science and Religion*, 144–145; see also his *Genes, Genesis and God* (Cambridge: Cambridge University Press, 1999), 303–307.

31. Richard Dawkins, *Unweaving the Rainbow* (London: Allen Lane, 1998), x.

32. Rudolf Otto, *The Idea of the Holy* (Oxford: Oxford University Press, 1925), 13.

33. Daniel Migliore, *Faith Seeking Understanding* (Grand Rapids, Mich.: Eerdmans, 1991), 116–117.

34. Karl Barth, *Church Dogmatics*, vol. IV, pt. 2, ed. G. W. Bromiley and T. F. Torrance (Edinburgh: Clark, 1958), 469.

35. John Haught, *God after Darwin* (Boulder, Colo.: Westview, 2000), 111–114.

36. Don Cupitt, *After All* (London: SCM, 1994), 92.

37. See Robin Attfield, *Creation, Evolution and Meaning* (Aldershot, England: Ashgate, 2006), 129, 143–150; Ruse, *Darwin and Design*, 330–333; Nicholas Saunders, *Divine Action and Modern Science* (Cambridge: Cambridge University Press, 2002), chs. 5 and 6; Peacocke, *Paths from Science*, 107, 180–181.

38. Edward O. Wilson, *The Diversity of Life* (Cambridge, Mass.: Harvard University Press, 1992), 349–351.

39. Swinburne, *Providence*, 127.

40. In Stephen T. Davis, ed., *Encountering Evil* (Louisville, Ky.: Westminster John Knox, 2001), 70.

41. Augustine, *City of God*, bk. XIII, ch. 15, sec. 14. But Augustine and, especially, Calvin reject the strong view of freewill outlined earlier.

42. This may or may not include death. Yet death is an inevitable corollary of the possibility of (more) life, and the death of plants is assumed in the creation stories; see Richard T. Wright, *Biology through the Eyes of Faith* (Leicester: Apollos, 1991), 23–24. Whether Genesis 3 intends human death to be seen as a punishment for sin is unclear; see Gerhard von Rad, *Genesis* (London: SCM, 1972), 95–96; Gordon J. Wenham, *Genesis 1–15* (Waco, Tex.: Word, 1987), 87; Claus Westermann, *Creation* (London: SPCK, 1971), 109.

43. John Calvin, *Commentary on Genesis*, trans. John King (Edinburgh: Calvin Translation Society, 1847), 177.

44. Swinburne, *Providence*, 41.

45. R. J. Berry, *God the Biologist* (Leicester: Apollos, 1996), 50. See also Neil Messer, *Selfish Genes and Christian Ethics* (London: SCM, 2007), ch. 7; Keith Ward, *Religion and Human Nature* (Oxford: Clarendon, 1998), ch. 8; Wright, *Biology*, ch. 8.

46. Peacocke, "Biological Evolution—A Positive Biological Appraisal," in Russell, Stoeger, and Ayala, *Evolutionary and Molecular Biology*, 373.

47. C. Kingsley Barrett, "Sermon," in P. A. Beecham, ed., *Evolution; or, How Did We Get Here?* (Oxford: Westminster College, 1998), 140.

48. Rolston, *Genes, Genesis and God*, 301.

49. Michael Ruse, *Can a Darwinian Be a Christian?* (Cambridge: Cambridge University Press, 2001), 210.

50. Daniel Dennett, *Darwin's Dangerous Idea* (London: Penguin, 1995), 203.

51. Huxley, *Evolution and Ethics*, 82.

52. The genome is always more of a "recipe book" than any sort of "blueprint," according to Matt Ridley, who recommends that we reject the glib phrase "nature versus nurture" in favor of a recognition of nature *via* nurture. As the notion of an innate human nature with particular instincts must include the instinct to learn things, "none of our instincts is inevitable; none is insuperable." Matt Ridley, *Nature*

via Nurture (London: HarperCollins, 2003), 248; Ridley, *The Red Queen* (London: Penguin, 1993), 305.

53. Ruse, *Darwin and Design*, 237.

54. Michael Ruse, "The Significance of Evolution," in Peter Singer, ed., *A Companion to Ethics* (London: Blackwell, 1993), 503. We should judge sociobiology and evolutionary psychology from their best and most careful formulations, not their worst. David Buss's standard textbook declares genetic determinism and the idea that human behavior is impervious to change as "misunderstandings"; Buss, *Evolutionary Psychology* (Boston: Allyn and Bacon, 2004), 19–20.

55. Keith Ward, *God, Chance and Necessity* (Oxford: Oneworld, 1996), 180–184; Denis Alexander, *Rebuilding the Matrix* (Oxford: Lion, 2001), 387–391.

56. Richard Dawkins, *The Selfish Gene* (Oxford: Oxford University Press, 2006), 3.

57. Samuel Wilberforce, "Art VII—On the Origin of Species...", *Quarterly Review*, Vol. CVIII (July 1860), 258.

58. It does not need to, if nature is not wholly corrupted and is as it is because of *God's* subjecting it in hope—that is, in the "expectation of good." See Rom. 8:20; and James D. G. Dunn, *The Theology of Paul the Apostle* (London: Clark, 1998), 387, n217.

59. Mary Midgley, *Heart and Mind* (London: Methuen, 1983), 31.

60. Richard Dawkins, *River Out of Eden* (London: Orion, 1996); Dawkins, *The Ancestor's Tale* (London: Weidenfeld & Nicolson, 2004).

61. T. S. Eliot, "East Coker," II, in *Collected Poems 1909–1962* (London: Faber and Faber, 1963), 199.

62. Bernard Gert, *Morality* (New York: Oxford University Press, 1998), 306–307.

63. Frans de Waal et al., *Primates and Philosophers* (Princeton, N.J.: Princeton University Press, 2006), 168, 190–191.

64. De Waal, *Primates and Philosophers*, 65, 56.

II

"Male and Female He Created Them" (Genesis 1:27)
Interpreting Gender after Darwin

Stephen C. Barton

Introduction: Darwin on Gender

I would like to begin with a word about pheasants. In a remarkable passage in *The Descent of Man* dealing with sexual selection, Darwin writes the following:

> Many will declare that it is utterly incredible that a female bird should be able to appreciate fine shading and exquisite patterns. It is undoubtedly a marvellous fact that she should possess this almost human degree of taste, though perhaps she admires the general effect rather than each separate detail. He who thinks that he can safely gauge the discrimination and taste of the lower animals, may deny that the female Argus pheasant can appreciate such refined beauty; but he will then be compelled to admit that the extraordinary attitudes assumed by the male during the act of courtship, by which the wonderful beauty of his plumage is fully displayed, are purposeless; and this is a conclusion which I for one will never admit.[1]

Here, we have displayed many of the features of Darwin's writing that make his work so compelling and engaging, not only to his contemporaries, but to many still today: the sharp observation of the natural world, the rhetoric of enchantment and awe in the presence of the ordinary (yet extraordinary) comings and goings of the nonhuman species, and the pervasive use of anthropomorphism, itself an expression of his sense of the connectedness through evolution of all living things. For the theologically inclined, there is also the sense that, intentional or not, Darwin's writing bears all of the characteristics of a natural theology:[2] he imputes intention and design to nature by denying that the "exquisite patterns" of the male pheasant's plumage and "the extraordinary attitudes assumed by the male during the act of courtship" are purposeless.

From the perspective of modernity, however, there is also a shadow side to Darwin's enchanting description. In the context of his larger theory of natural selection and sexual selection, his account of the male and female pheasants' "courtship" hints at Darwin's profound indebtedness to Victorian values, not least its gender norms. Here, so it can be argued, male superiority and female inferiority in humankind are taken for granted and mapped onto nature with all of the authority of science, and, conversely, a nature so gendered serves as a foundation and warrant for hierarchical relations between the sexes in human society. As Cynthia Russett puts it in her account of "the Victorian construction of womanhood":

> Darwinian sexual selection explained physical and behavioural differences between the sexes as advantageous in finding mates. Thus women became fragilely attractive, while men grew muscular and courageous, each sex loving in the other what it did not find in itself. It followed, therefore, that women could never expect to match the intellectual and artistic achievements of men, nor could they expect an equal share of power and authority. Nature had decreed a secondary role for women. The great principle of division of labor was here brought to bear: men produced, women reproduced. This was called complementarity.[3]

All of this has been explored extensively in the scholarly literature on Darwin and the Darwinians.[4] The recognition is widespread that Darwin's position is paradoxical. On the one hand, there is his scientific radicalism and Whig social liberalism—he was, for example, a vigorous supporter of the abolition of slavery—while, on the other hand, there are his conservative views on gender and the "woman question," and he held those views at a time (the second half of the nineteenth century) when the movement for women's emancipation was becoming increasingly active and effective.

How might we explain the paradox? First, the weight attaching to gender arises in part from evolutionary theory itself—in particular, the role attributed to sexual reproduction in the passing on of variability and the role of gender differentiation in natural selection and sexual selection in the struggle for survival. Second, the conventional scientific and social-scientific wisdom among Darwin's contemporaries was that female inferiority was biologically determined. According to one commentator:

> Darwin endorsed and reinforced this work, expressing his conviction not only of female inferiority but also of innate differences in the quality of female thought. He had long believed that women had a greater capacity for religious belief (or a greater credulity) than men. He now claimed that while women were tenderer and less selfish, they were also more emotional and less capable of reasoned thought.[5]

Third, there was, in Victorian bourgeois culture and practice, a pervasive "separate sphere ideology,"[6] according to which the subordination of women to men, with each knowing their own place, was a mark of civilization[7]—and Darwin's practice of a kind of genial patriarchy in his own personal life and household relations shows that he shared this assumption.

The Legacy of Darwin

Although the logic of Darwin's theory of natural selection and sexual selection did not *require* an understanding of male-female relations (at least among humans) as relations of superordination and subordination, it could nevertheless be taken that way. In what Donna Haraway calls "the union of the political and the physiological,"[8] the biology could be made to serve the interests of an ideology where differences of social and cultural power are grounded in nature.

Theories and strategies that fall under the rubric of Social Darwinism are one legacy of this union. Notoriously, one form of Social Darwinism popular well into the twentieth century, the "science" of eugenics, was virtually invented by Darwin's cousin Francis Galton; and there is little doubt that Darwin himself, in moving beyond careful scientific observation of the natural world into cultural issues of race, class, women, and economics, as he does in *The Descent of Man*, shows himself to be deeply enmeshed in the cultural prejudices of his day.[9]

More recently, intense debates have surrounded the disciplines of sociobiology and evolutionary psychology. In brief, at the heart of some of these debates are concerns about the closely related problems of determinism and reductionism. In relation to *determinism*, the issue is whether human behavior, including sexual behavior and gender codes, is determined by our "biological programming." In relation to *reductionism*, the issue is the primacy given to biological or naturalistic explanations, on the assumption that "levels of explanation and analysis for one level of being are adequate for other levels."[10] So, as Elaine Graham puts it in relation to the gender question, "gender differences are reduced to the biological dichotomy of male and female, which is an adequate framework for understanding sexual reproduction, but resembles life less satisfactorily the further we try to extend the analysis into gender roles and characteristics."[11]

This is not the place to explore these debates further. It is sufficient to note that Darwin's discovery of natural selection as the mechanism of the evolution of species gave a profound impetus not only to the natural sciences but, more ambiguously, to the sciences of human culture, economics, and politics as well. I say "more ambiguously" because the pervasive and triumphant "naturalization" of human beings in all their aspects—including the moral, the aesthetic, the religious, and what it means to be male and female—represents a comprehensive understanding of life, and of the human, which, from a theological point of view is, in the final analysis, impoverished.[12]

Gender's Troubled History

What Darwin offered was a naturalistic myth of origins that displaced—even replaced—the myth of origins offered by the Christian religion. As George Levine puts it, alluding specifically to the book of Genesis, "Whichever version of 'natural selection' one takes, Darwin's story of origins has become an inescapable alternative to 'In the beginning...'"[13] But it may be said that Darwin's naturalistic foundationalism, with the sanction it gave in his own day and subsequently to the separate-spheres ideology of gender, is, from where we stand, not surprising. For, perhaps more than ever before, we are aware that gender *has a history*. In particular, the separate-spheres ideology of gender has a history. In brief, whereas in earlier times, the separation of male and female was written into and sanctioned by the cosmological, in later (post-Enlightenment) times, the separation of male and female was written into and sanctioned by the biological.

The Classical Tradition

Something must be said of this history of gender; otherwise, we will not be able to locate our own post-Darwin understandings. There is, crucially, the

profoundly androcentric legacy of the classical tradition. Influential here in
the realm of metaphysics is Plato's *Timaeus* where, according to Andrew Louth,
"the cosmos is understood on the analogy of the human person, or conversely—and this is how it seemed to Plato—the human person is a copy, reflection, image of the cosmos, which is a living creature endowed with soul and
reason."[14] Here, in the hierarchy of spirit over matter, male is to spirit as female
is to matter. Here also, the declension of humanity into male and female is a
fall from the primal unity. Salvation (*sōtēria*) or freedom (*eleutheria)* is found
now by means of the cultivation of the soul through the exercise of reason in
the practice of philosophy with, as a corollary, the control of the body by the
practice of disciplinary regimes of one kind or another.

The hierarchical interpretation of difference is evident also in the physi-
ognomic observations to be found in the ancient medical texts. Here, we find
that the differences between male and female physiognomy are heavily valorized. In a study of "Contradictions of Masculinity" in antiquity, Dale Martin
writes:

> [T]he ideal male occupied the high end of a hierarchical spectrum
> whose low end was occupied by the female. Heat is generally consid-
> ered male, and cold female. The male body is dry; the female moist.
> The male is compact and dense; the female porous. The male body is
> efficient; it properly uses up its fuel and so has no need to expel any
> excess on a regular basis. In contrast, the female body is a location
> of surfeit and excess, signified in its need to slough off excess blood
> and semen each month.[15]

In ancient political philosophy, influential also is the Aristotelian tradition,
where the hierarchical ordering of things, including the polis, is reflected in
the ordering of the *oikos*, or household, with its three sets of primary relations
of superordination and subordination: husband over wife, parents over children, and masters over slaves.[16]

The Biblical Tradition

As well as the classical legacy, there is the legacy of the religion of Israel and of
Hellenistic Judaism. In the priestly redaction of the Pentateuch, and not least
in the story of creation, the series of separations which make life on the earth
possible culminate on the sixth day in the creation of *adam*, humankind, in the
form of male and female: "And God created humankind [*adam*] in His image,
in the image of God He created him; male and female He created them" (Gen.
1:27). In passing, it is worth noting, as Nahum Sarna writes, that "[n]o such

sexual differentiation is noted with regard to animals. Human sexuality is of a wholly different order from that of the beast.... [It is] a blessed gift of God woven into the fabric of life."[17] Noteworthy also is the solemn repetition of this definition of humankind (*adam*) as male and female at the head of the ten-generation genealogy at Genesis 5:1–2. In the priestly scheme of things, then, humankind as male and female is inscribed in creation.[18]

These separations and distinctions, which make life possible, are reinforced in the purity rules of Leviticus. Here, the binary opposition of clean and unclean, with the ritual weight falling more heavily on women than on men due to the menstrual taboo (Lev. 15:19–24), sustains the social and symbolic life of the people while at the same time keeping them in line with a cosmos ordered and sustained by God in his holy transcendence.[19] And, as Robert Hayward and others have demonstrated, the same system of ritual and symbolic separations and distinctions comes also to characterize the ordering of the Jerusalem Temple, itself seen as a microcosm of heaven and earth.[20] The divine sanctioning of the social order, including the order of male and female, could not be clearer.

Hellenistic Judaism

In the Hellenistic Judaism of Philo of Alexandria, rooted in both the Bible and Plato, we find both a strong separate-spheres ideology and, underlying it, a sophisticated androcentric metaphysics. The ideology comes in his famous idealized account of the separation of public and private space along gendered lines where, within an overall assumption of male dominance, the public sphere is the male domain and the private sphere of the household is the female domain.

> Market-places and council-halls and law-courts and gatherings and meetings where a large number of people are assembled, and open-air life with full scope for discussion and action—all these are suitable to men both in war and in peace. The women are best suited to the indoor life which never strays from the house, within which the middle door is taken by the maidens as their boundary, and the outer door by those who have reached full womanhood.[21]

In concert with this separate-spheres ideology, the androcentric metaphysics is all-pervasive. In his commentary on Genesis, for example, the differences between Genesis 1 and 2 are exploited in such a way as to allow Philo to posit two distinct acts of creation, according to which the first Adam is an entirely spiritual, androgynous (male/female) being, and the second is the carnal male

Adam from whom the female is constructed. Hermeneutically stunning here is the way scripture and Platonic cosmology are brought into such imaginative engagement. Here, the primacy of spirit over matter, of the real self over the embodied sexed self, of oneness over duality, of male over female are affirmed and sanctioned by being given foundational authority in the scriptural account of how things were "in the beginning."[22]

Early Christianity

What of the legacy of early Christianity? A large part of the story, told so well by Peter Brown in *The Body and Society* (1988) and developed by Elizabeth Clark in *Reading Renunciation* (1999), is that of the "divided self" of early Christian anthropology and eschatology, with its doctrine of "flesh" (*sarx*) as evil in a constant struggle with "spirit" (*pneuma*) as good and the corollaries of sexual asceticism, on the one hand, and the control—even the demonization—of women and the body, on the other.[23] The early Christian picture overall is mixed, moving between approval of the discipline of Christian marriage and approval of the discipline of sexual renunciation and the celibate life.[24]

What are we to say, for example, of Jesus?[25] In spite of the modern desire to sexualize Jesus, either in heterosexual terms by imaginings about his relationship with Mary Magdalene or in homosexual terms by imaginings about his relationships with the twelve or with the "disciple whom Jesus loved," the disconcerting thing is that Jesus, like John the Baptist, practiced what Geza Vermes aptly called "prophetic celibacy."[26] In the context of early Judaism, this was not unprecedented.[27] Josephus tells us that the Essenes "disdain marriage" (*Jewish War*, 2.120), and the texts from Qumran on the whole presuppose a celibate male community organized as a spiritual temple. With his profound sense of eschatological vocation to call Israel to repentance and renewal in view of the breaking in of the kingdom of God, Jesus remained single. As he says in a statement that is very likely self-referential, "there are those who have made themselves eunuchs for the sake of the kingdom of heaven" (Matt. 19:12). For Jesus, therefore, sexual discipline takes the form of singleness and celibacy, as an expression of his devotion to God and to God's people, Israel. Quite consistent with this are his reserved attitude toward sexual desire in his teaching in the Sermon on the Mount (Matt. 5:27–30) and his stringent teaching on the discipline of marriage (Mark 10:2–12).

The apostle Paul practiced celibacy also; and as with Jesus, his motivation was overwhelmingly theological and eschatological (1 Cor. 7). With Jesus' death and resurrection, the age of the Spirit has begun, and a new creation is coming into being. In the formula of Galatians 3:28, with its "no male and

female" through union with Christ, there is a radical affirmation of "new creation" identity, understood as the transformation of the originating creational
identity of male and female depicted in Genesis 1:27. Nevertheless, the Paul
who authored Galatians 3:28 is the same Paul who, in another context and
this time by appeal to the second creation story, insists, after something of
a rhetorical song and dance, on the maintenance of conventional head sym-
bols of gender differentiation (1 Cor. 11:2–16, esp. vv. 8ff.). It is as if the two
creation stories are being played off against each other or, better, are being
made to do different and complementary work: the first supports the work of
unification; the second supports the work of differentiation and, inevitably, of
hierarchy.[28]

Moving beyond Paul, in the moral exhortations on household life in
Ephesians, Colossians, 1 Peter, and elsewhere, we are struck by a very significant "Christianizing" of the household code, on the one hand, and, on the other,
the evident satisfaction with the traditional binary distinctions (husband-wife,
parents-children, master-slave) and hierarchical ordering that are characteristic of conventional social norms.[29] In the pastoral epistles, furthermore, any
egalitarian tendencies in gender relations in the first generation of Christianity
disappear completely in the second generation with the deliberate accommodation of ecclesial morality to patriarchal household morality. Significantly,
the divine sanction for this is, once again, the second creation story; and now,
although not for the first time (2 Cor. 11:2–3), the fateful hermeneutical step is
taken to place the blame for the primal sin on Eve, the archetype of all women.
The crumb of comfort offered is that salvation for women is still possible—*if*
they fall into line and fulfill their preordained marital and reproductive roles
(1 Tim. 2:8–15, esp. 14–15).[30]

Of course, we know from other sources, like the Gospel of Thomas or the
Acts of Paul and Thecla, that salvation for Christian women was possible by
an alternative—and, to us, most paradoxical—way: that of becoming "male"
through a life of holy virginity in which gender differentiation (specifically,
female difference) was erased by being transcended in language and lifestyle.
Note, however, that the radical and liberative potential of gender transcendence—of becoming "like the angels in heaven who neither marry nor are
given in marriage" (Luke 20:34–36)—is not absolute. The life of the spirit and
life in the Spirit genderized as male remain normative. As Daniel Boyarin
acutely observes: "The transcendent androgyne is male. This paradoxical figure of a transcendence of gender that is still, as it were, male is not a factitious
by-product of male domination but is...crucial to the whole structure of gender transcendence itself. All theories of transcendence are already appropri-
ated by the male."[31]

Reflections

Now, before leaping to the modern period and while acknowledging the danger of oversimplifying a nuanced and complex history, let me offer a few general observations. First, it is clear that ideas of the (gendered) self in its relation to other selves and to the cosmos as a whole play a crucial role, especially where the self in relation to the cosmos is understood in static and fundamentally mimetic terms. Second, it is clear also that the pervasive valorization of the binary opposition, male-female, according to which male is valorized positively (as spiritual, rational, strong, active, hot, nonporous, etc.) and female negatively (as material, emotional, weak, passive, cold, porous, etc.), has been enormously influential and, we must say, enormously impoverishing and destructive for both women and men. Third, this history shows that the body, especially (but not only) the female body, bears a particularly heavy burden, marked, literally and symbolically, as the primary locus of the human quest for identity, meaning, and transcendence. Fourth, myths of origins—not least, the accounts of creation in Holy Writ—are enormously influential in providing foundational warrants for particular world views and social patterns, including what it means to be male and female. Fifth, in the eschatological horizon of early Christianity, shaped by the life and teaching of Jesus and by reflection on his death and resurrection, possibilities of personal and social transformation open up—however tentatively—including new understandings of what it means, as members of "the body of Christ," to be male and female.[32]

Gender and (Post)modernity

Although deeply rooted, institutionally and culturally, in the past, the story of male and female has taken new turns and been affected by new developments in modernity and late or postmodernity. Indeed, it can be argued, with Richard Roberts, that, with late modernity, "an inversion of historic Western priorities of rational soul over sensual body has begun to take place."[33] Roberts's vivid personal testimony to the changes that modernity has brought to how we conceive and practice "the body" is worth quoting:

> We live in an age of extremes: in my own lifetime we have moved
> from the residual consciousness of the so-called Victorian ethos of
> repression and of denial to bodily and sexual over-exposure. Now we
> are rapidly entering an era in which constant re-description of the
> body is giving way to its re-creation: the possibilities raised by the

human genome project (which opens up the way to the profitable and comprehensive "perfecting" of "nature") and virtual reality (with its paradoxical juxtapositions of alienation and intimacy) enlarge the contemporary imaginary in ways that break with all prevenient constraints. The very idea of a natural "human" is dissolved and recongeals. As ever, the rational and the sensual struggle with each other; but now they operate within fluid boundaries. In individualised, late modern society intimacy is burdened with high expectations whilst the ambient framework of such relationships is degraded. We are in multiple crises.[34]

The various contributory factors behind these crises, especially as they bear on the issue of gender, deserve elaboration, however briefly.

The Impact of Post-Enlightenment Philosophy

First, there is the legacy of modern philosophy from Descartes on. Mary Midgley, among others,[35] has drawn particular attention to the problems arising from the highly atomistic and individualistic understandings of the self characteristic of post-Enlightenment thought, whether the rationalism of Descartes, the social contract theory of Rousseau, the anarchism of Nietzsche, or the existentialism of Camus.[36] Such understandings, so it is argued, may make a positive contribution in relation to the struggle for equality and the rights of the individual, including the right to choose. They are less helpful, even pernicious, to the extent that they ignore significant difference in the interests of standardization, allow "the lure of the universal" to distract attention from the particular (the needs of children or the weak and vulnerable, for example), and make women invisible by assuming as normative the individual as male[37]—with "male" understood as rational rather than emotional, solitary and self-sufficient rather than social and interdependent.

Along the way, Midgley makes what strikes me as a most acute observation. Reflecting on her account of the mind/body problem in modern philosophy, where she has been so bold as to allow the problem of gender to obtrude, she says:

> Then why...do I persist in talking about the relations between the
> sexes instead of getting down directly to the mind/body problem?
> I answer: *because mind/body problems, being queries about ourselves,*
> *never do present themselves to us directly.* They are always seen
> reflected indirectly in some mirror or other, and the distortions
> of the particular mirror are crucial to understanding them. They

always appear in our lives in terms of myth, and the current myths
are shot through with dramas about gender.[38]

The suggestion that "dramas about gender" are one of the ways we mirror,
indirectly and in distorted ways, profound questions about the nature of the
self is surely fruitful and in continuity with observations made earlier. More
specifically, we might want to say that the ways in which the male-female
dichotomy is made so often to be the line of demarcation along which all kinds
of cultural battles are fought is a pervasive theme from the premodern period
to the modern and postmodern.

Postmodernity and the Destabilizing of Gender

It may seem astonishing that, up to this point in the chapter, no definition of
"sex" or "gender" has been offered. The discussion so far has proceeded on the
comforting assumption that we all know what we are talking about, that the
meanings of "sex" and "gender" are stable. Indeed, in social-scientific discourse
until the late twentieth century, the conventional and generally helpful understanding has been that the sex of a person is what is given in nature and the
gender of a person is what is given in culture.[39] Put succinctly: sex is to nature
what gender is to culture. I say that this has been helpful because it expresses
in a convenient way the widely observed phenomenon in human groups and
societies across the world that masculinity and femininity by no means follow
directly from (respectively) maleness and femaleness. An important corollary
of this is that gender identity is not biologically determined; rather, it is socially
constructed. As such, it is relative, fluid, and contingent; and the realization
that men and women are "made not born" is an idea that, by moving from an
essentialist to a constructionist position, has been seen to have considerable
potential for personal empowerment and cultural creativity.

But what if "nature" itself is a cultural product? If so, the convenient
nature-culture dichotomy may be a misleading interpretation arising out of
the legacy of deeply ingrained essentialist—even misogynist—ways of seeing.
Gender may be in more trouble than we had previously imagined! This indeed
is the argument of materialist feminist Judith Butler in her work of 1990,
Gender Trouble.[40] The radical force of her attempt to critique gender essential-
ism (especially what she terms "compulsory heterosexuality") and to subvert
the weight of conventional gender binaries is evident in the following:

> Perhaps the problem is more serious. Is the construction of the
> category of women as a coherent and stable subject an unwitting
> regulation and reification of gender relations? And is not such a

reification precisely contrary to feminist aims? To what extent does
the category of women achieve stability and coherence only in the
context of the heterosexual matrix? If a stable notion of gender no
longer proves to be the foundational premise of feminist politics,
perhaps a new sort of feminist politics is now desirable to contest the
very reifications of gender and identity, one that will take the vari-
able construction of identity as both a methodological and normative
prerequisite, if not a political goal.... If the immutable character of
sex is contested, perhaps this construct called "sex" is as culturally
constructed as gender; indeed, perhaps it was always already gender,
with the consequence that the distinction between sex and gender
turns out to be no distinction at all. It would make no sense, then,
to define gender as the cultural interpretation of sex, if sex itself is
a gendered category. Gender ought not to be conceived merely as
the cultural inscription of meaning upon a pregiven sex (a juridi-
cal conception); gender must also designate the very apparatus of
production whereby the sexes themselves are established. As a result,
gender is not to culture as sex is to nature; gender is also the discur-
sive/cultural means by which "sexed nature" or "a natural sex" is
produced and established as "prediscursive," prior to culture, a politically neutral surface *on which* culture acts.[41]

Here, then, we have a thoroughgoing hermeneutic of suspicion—the work of
Michel Foucault is a constant reference point—which seeks to denaturalize sex
by positing "natural" sex as the work of gender and the (usually hidden) "apparatus of production." As one commentator sums up: "Accordingly now when
we study gender within a given historical or existing culture, we understand
that we are investigating the praxis and process by which people are interpel-
lated into a two- (or for some cultures more) sex system that is made to seem
as if it were nature, that is, something that has always existed."[42]

In terms of the recent history of gender, what Butler's work represents is a
significant shift: from the quest for *sexual* liberation in the 1960s and later to
the quest for *gender* liberation at the end of the twentieth and into the twenty-
first century. Her work seeks to do so by moving the discussion beyond the
polarizations of essentialist and constructionist positions in the direction of
an identity politics.[43] The goal here is—by means of subversive and parodic
discourses, practices, and performances of one kind or another—to recreate
gender by the reappropriation of gender difference in ways that escape stereo-
type and enable "personal transformation beyond normal human expectations
and restrictions."[44]

Reflections

Having said something about the fate of male and female in modernity and late or postmodernity, a further pause to take stock may be in order. First—and we saw this in the case of evolutionary theory also—the way in which abstract, universalizing ideas about the self or about the freedom, equality, and progress of humankind may serve to render the Other mute, invisible, or oppressed by a process of standardization is striking. And when such ideas have a notion of the heterosexual male as the normative human, the apparently inevitable consequence is that women, children, sexual minorities, and minorities of all kinds suffer. If this is so, then new ways of seeing and new ways of speaking that are not afraid of difference, of the local and the particular, need to be found. In talking of new ways of seeing and speaking, we are moving, of course, into the realm of hermeneutics, and here I am struck by the potential of hermeneutical approaches of a reflexive, nonfoundational, communal character, of the kind opened up in literary theory by Stanley Fish and developed in theological and ecclesial contexts by Mary McClintock Fulkerson, Stanley Hauerwas, and others.[45]

Second, recent and current anxieties about the "aporia [perplexities] of the body" (Richard Roberts) and "dramas about gender" (Mary Midgley) are important, both in their own right and as reflections of wider issues: for the body and gender relations mirror society and social relations, as Mary Douglas has helped us to see.[46] What I want to suggest here is that we see in the identity politics and subversive gender performances of Judith Butler and others a secular version of the critique of idolatry and of the quest for personal transcendence, a critique and a quest with which the religiously minded must have considerable sympathy.[47]

"Male and Female He Created Them": Reading Wisely

I have spoken of Darwin and the legacy of Darwin's naturalistic alternative to "In the beginning." I have spoken also of the troubled history of gender from antiquity to the present day. Let me speak now, however briefly, of reading Genesis, in particular, reading Genesis 1:27: "male and female He created them."

The Ambiguous Potential of Scriptural Accounts of Origins

First, in learning to be wise readers, we need to be aware of the ambiguous potential of scriptural—and therefore authority-bearing—accounts of origins. For sociological and psychological reasons, as well as religious ones, the attraction of accounts of how things have been from the beginning is that they provide us with *foundations* and, therefore, potentially at least, with a sense of security. We *find ourselves*—in the potentially anarchic realm of sex and gender and with all the contingencies of our sheer bodiliness and the struggle for survival—inscribed in scripture in a divinely revealed order of creation. This makes life possible. It gives our lives shape and meaning and dignity by writing us into a larger story, the story of *adam* (humankind) made in the divine image as male and female, the story of Adam and his co-regent in creation, Eve.[48]

But we have lost our innocence. We know from historical, cultural, and feminist criticism that the Genesis accounts of creation offered divine sanction to a social order in ancient Israel where holiness and power were ordered along priestly and patriarchal lines and where the gender binary of male and female was part of an elaborate symbolic world distinguishing Israel from its neighbors as pure from impure. We know also that, from earliest times up to the present day, the story of Adam and Eve has been and is used to give divine sanction to a separate-spheres ideology and to patterns of superordination and subordination in relations between men and women which are, at the very least, highly controversial—life giving to some, death dealing to others.[49] I say "life giving to some" because I recognize—in line with a growing ethnographic literature[50] and developments in hermeneutics[51]—that, paradoxically, many women in Christian churches, denominations, and sects find personal empowerment in patterns of sociality where a separate-spheres ideology operates and where power overall lies with men.[52]

The point remains, however. The idea, prominent in certain circles, that there is such a thing as "biblical manhood and womanhood" authorized by the biblical creation story and universally normative, is profoundly mistaken, however well intentioned. As well as lacking historical and exegetical credibility,[53] it imputes agency and intention to the text (or its imagined authors) alone, neglecting the fact that agency and intention lie also with the guardians of meaning within the interpreting community.[54]

Interpreting Genesis in the Light of Christ

Second, in learning to be wise readers of Genesis, we need to follow (although not slavishly) the example of our forebears, from Augustine to Barth,[55] and interpret the text from a Christian theological point of view—which is to say, *christologically* and *eschatologically*. Darwin's account of origins is not the only alternative to Genesis, for the testimony of the New Testament is that the order of creation is what has been revealed in Christ. On this view, to interpret Genesis literally is to interpret it in terms of Christ.

So, for example, the "In the beginning" of Genesis has now to be read in the light of the "In the beginning" of the prologue of the Gospel of John. And it is noteworthy, though often overlooked, that in John's creation narrative, itself a christological reinterpretation of the Genesis narrative, the generative power that is at work is a power that transcends male and female. Those who become "children of God" are said to be born "not of blood or of the will of the flesh or of the will *of the male* [oude ek thelēmatos andros], but of God" (1:13). And what is interesting is how this plays out in the narrative following: first, Jesus' "natural" father plays no part; second, women are portrayed positively as recipients of significant christological revelations—think of the mother of Jesus, the Samaritan woman, Mary and Martha, and Mary Magdalene—and third, a particular point is made of Jesus' implicit challenge to the androcentric assumptions of his disciples, as when, in the story of the Samaritan woman in John 4, the returning disciples "were astonished that he was speaking with a woman" (4:27). Nor is it insignificant that the first person to whom the risen Christ appears is a woman, Mary Magdalene (John 20:11–18). It is, then, as if the gospel narrative is elaborating and developing in an imaginative and symbolic way what the new "In the beginning" might mean for male and female in the light of Christ.[56]

Or, take the case of Paul. Once again, the first creation is reinterpreted in the light of the new creation. Thus, in Romans, the first Adam is seen in the light of Christ, the eschatological Adam, the revelation of the new humanity (Rom. 5:12–21). In Galatians, as noted earlier, in a striking reversal of Genesis 1:27, Paul says that, in Christ, there is "*no* male and female" (Gal. 3:28). As in John, human identity is being reimaged. A new, eschatological identity has been made possible by the breaking in upon the world of a new order of things. One of the reasons that Paul is so angry with the believers in Corinth is that their sexual practices and gender relations are still so mired in the patterns of desire and domination identified as *porneia* (1 Cor. 5–7) that they fail so signally to embody their participation in the eschatological "body of Christ."

In sum, John and Paul help us to see what it means to be wise readers of Genesis. They do so by performing readings of creation in the light of Christ and the eschatological Spirit.

Reading in Communion

Third, and finally, learning to be wise readers of Genesis, of what it means (from a Christian viewpoint) to be male and female *in Christ*, is something we cannot do on our own. Given that being male and female is about sex *difference* and its ongoing interpretation and expression in human relationships over time and space, it makes sense that learning what it means to be male and female is a communal activity where the narratives, practices, and performances of gender may be played out and tested over time. For the Christian, it is the *koinōnia* (fellowship, participation) of the church, understood eschatologically as the body of Christ, where this may best take place.[57]

Of course, such a proposal may evoke little more than a hollow laugh. The church, past and present, does not present itself as the place whose narratives, practices, and performances are such as to shape us to be wise in being male and female. With some notable exceptions, the church, like society at large, has not performed gender difference well.

Nevertheless, it may still be the case that the community we call the church offers life-giving resources for "making the difference."[58] At the simplest and deepest level, there is, at the very heart of what the church is about doctrinally and sacramentally, a celebration of *life as grace and gift*. From her vantage point in moral philosophy, Mary Midgley makes an observation that is pertinent here:

> On any view of causes, a great deal in the life of each of us is completely out of our power, and our freedom must consist in the way we handle that small but crucial area which does actually come before us for choice. This situation is far more benign than people obsessed with freedom make it sound, because what comes to us by no choice of our own is a gift—a whole world which we could not possibly have made and at which, in spite of all its horrors, we can on the whole only bow our heads in wonder. Moralists able only to think of autonomy, of the active imposition of the will on what is round us, miss the essential values of receptivity, of contemplation, of openness to the splendours of what is not oneself. Our inheritance, both social and natural, is not a shocking intrusion on our privacy and freedom, but a realm for us to live in.[59]

The phrase "openness to the splendours of what is not oneself" strikes me as the best possible starting point for learning together the habits, disciplines, and practices that might allow us to be a little less afraid of sex differences and to perform gender in ways that begin to do justice to "the body's grace"[60] in a story of grace that is not yet finished.

NOTES

1. *The Descent of Man*, 2.93, cited in George Levine, *Darwin Loves You: Natural Selection of the World* (Princeton, N.J.: Princeton University Press, 2006), 196–197.
2. Cf. Levine, *Darwin Loves You*, 197–198.

3. Cynthia Eagle Russett, *Sexual Science: The Victorian Construction of Womanhood* (Cambridge, Mass.: Harvard University Press, 1989), 11–12. The book as a whole is very relevant as a thorough history of nineteenth-century scientific controversies over sexual difference.

4. For what follows, see Fiona Erskine, "*The Origin of Species* and the Science of Female Inferiority," in *Charles Darwin's* The Origin of Species: *New Interdisciplinary Essays*, ed. David Amigone and Jeff Wallace (Manchester, England: Manchester University Press, 1995), 95–121.

5. Erskine, "*The Origin of Species* and the Science of Female Inferiority," 99.

6. Erskine, "*The Origin of Species* and the Science of Female Inferiority," 102. The point is developed effectively on 115:

> Separate sphere ideology could not be relinquished lightly: it gave women a defined role as protectors and guarantors of Victorian civilization and distanced that civilisation both from the lower classes and the lower races, amongst whom the sexuality of the women as much as the brutality of the men was a distinguishing mark of inferiority. If the social and racial hierarchies upon which their civilisation depended entailed an acceptance of sexual hierarchy, and if such a sexual hierarchy were threatened by the demands of women, many were prepared to relinquish their demands and accept that hierarchy. For the liberal bourgeois social order, from whose ranks were drawn the reformers, separate sphere ideology provided the necessary complement to the competitive ideology of the marketplace. The public world promoted economic prosperity, the private guaranteed domestic and social harmony. The public world provided work for the middle-class man, suited to business; the private for the middle-class woman, fitted for the transmission of the values of bourgeois society to her own household and to the wider community. There was scant support for any philosophically articulated feminism: women's rights campaigners argued for greater access to social influence within the broadly consensual social framework of patriarchy.

7. This is a significant theme in Victorian literature. Witness, for example, in George Eliot's *Middlemarch*, how detrimental this ideology is to the relation between Casaubon and Dorothea.

8. Donna Haraway, *Simians, Cyborgs and Women: The Reinvention of Nature* (London: Free Association, 1991), 7, cited in Elaine Graham, *Making the Difference: Gender, Personhood and Theology* (London: Mowbray, 1995), 84.

9. For evidence of Darwin's eugenicist tendencies, see *The Descent of Man*, 1.168, cited in Levine, *Darwin Loves You*, 61.

10. Graham, *Making the Difference*, 86.

11. Graham, *Making the Difference*, 86.

12. Note the sobering admission of George Levine, an enthusiastic defender of Darwin, in *Darwin Loves You*, at 64. Speaking of the eugenicist tendencies in Darwin's thought, Levine says:

> Nothing in the theory of descent by modification through natural selection entails this kind of [eugenicist] social analysis and program. When cultural

assumptions are unquestioned, natural selection can be slotted in to do all kinds of work, and when social structures are taken as natural ones, in the sense that hierarchies within it are understood as analogous to or the same as hierarchies in uncivilized nature, natural selection stops being a metaphor.

13. Levine, *Darwin Loves You*, 59.

14. Andrew Louth, "The Body in Western Catholic Christianity," in *Religion and the Body*, ed. Sarah Coakley (Cambridge: Cambridge University Press, 1997), 112.

15. Dale B. Martin, "Contradictions of Masculinity: Ascetic Inseminators and Menstruating Men in Greco-Roman Culture," in *Generation and Regeneration: Tropes of Reproduction in Literature and History from Antiquity through Early Modern Europe*, ed. Valeria Finucci and Kevin Brownlee (Durham, N.C.: Duke University Press, 2001), 81–108.

16. See David L. Balch, *Let Wives Be Submissive: The Domestic Code in 1 Peter* (Chico, Calif.: Scholars, 1981).

17. Nahum M. Sarna, *The JPS Torah Commentary: Genesis* (Philadelphia: Jewish Publication Society, 1989), 13. I have used Sarna's translation of the Genesis text here.

18. For an insightful analysis, see Phyllis A. Bird, "'Male and Female He Created Them': Genesis 1.27b in the Context of the Priestly Account of Creation," in Bird, *Missing Persons and Mistaken Identities: Women and Gender in Ancient Israel* (Minneapolis, Minn.: Fortress, 1997), 123–154.

19. On the symbolism of blood taboos, see Leonie Archer, "'In Thy Blood Live': Gender and Ritual in the Judaeo-Christian Tradition," in *Through the Devil's Gateway: Women, Religion and Taboo*, ed. Alison Joseph (London: SPCK, 1990), 22–49.

20. C. T. R. Hayward, *The Jewish Temple: A Non-Biblical Sourcebook* (London: Routledge, 1996).

21. Philo, *De specialibus legibus*, 3.169. See on this, Jorunn Økland, *Women in Their Place: Paul and the Corinthian Discourse of Gender and Sanctuary Space* (London: Clark International, 2004), 58ff., esp. the section "Discourses of Space."

22. See the profound essay of Daniel Boyarin, which is simply entitled "Gender," in *Critical Terms for Religious Studies*, ed. Mark C. Taylor (Chicago: University of Chicago Press, 1998), 117–135, esp. 119–122. For a more extended examination, see Thomas H. Tobin, "Interpretations of the Creation of the World in Philo of Alexandria," in *Creation in the Biblical Traditions*, ed. Richard J. Clifford and John J. Collins (Washington, D.C.: Catholic Biblical Association of America, 1992), 108–128.

23. See Peter Brown, *The Body and Society: Men, Women and Sexual Renunciation in Early Christianity* (London: Faber, 1988); Elizabeth Clark, *Reading Renunciation: Asceticism and Scripture in Early Christianity* (Princeton, N.J.: Princeton University Press, 1999).

24. For a valuable account, see Elaine H. Pagels, "Adam and Eve, Christ and the Church: A Survey of Second Century Controversies Concerning Marriage," in *The New Testament and Gnosis*, ed. A. H. B. Logan and A. J. M. Wedderburn (Edinburgh: Clark, 1983), 146–175.

25. For a nonfoundationalist answer to this question, see Dale B. Martin, *Sex and the Single Savior: Gender and Sexuality in Biblical Interpretation* (Louisville, Ky.: Westminster John Knox, 2006), 91–102. In my view, Martin's account of the application of historical reason to the question of Jesus' sexuality is unjustifiably cavalier.

26. See Geza Vermes, *Jesus the Jew: A Historian's Reading of the Gospels* (London: Collins, 1973). See also Dale C. Allison, *Jesus of Nazareth: Millenarian Prophet* (Minneapolis, Minn.: Augsburg Fortress, 1998), ch. 3, "Jesus as Millenarian Ascetic."

27. See P. W. Van der Horst, "Celibacy in Early Judaism," *Revue Biblique* 109, no. 3 (2002): 390–402.

28. See Boyarin, "Gender," 124.

29. See J. D. G. Dunn, "The Household Rules in the New Testament," in *The Family in Theological Perspective*, ed. S. C. Barton (Edinburgh: T&T Clark, 1996), 43–63.

30. See on this, Jouette Bassler, "Adam, Eve, and the Pastor: The Use of Genesis 2–3 in the Pastoral Epistles," in *Genesis 1–3 in the History of Exegesis*, ed. G. A. Robbins (Lewiston, Maine: Edwin Mellen, 1988), 43–65.

31. Boyarin, "Gender," 122.

32. Significant in this connection is Halvor Moxnes, "Asceticism and Christian Identity in Antiquity: A Dialogue with Foucault and Paul," *Journal for the Study of the New Testament* 26, no. 1 (2003): 3–29.

33. Richard Roberts, "The Dis/embodied Trinity: Some Thoughts on Theology and Sexuality," *Crucible* (April–June 1999): 72–87, at 77.

34. Roberts, 'Dis/embodied Trinity', 77.

35. See also the ground-breaking study by Genevieve Lloyd, *The Man of Reason: "Male" and "Female" in Western Philosophy*, 2nd ed. (London: Routledge, 1993).

36. I am drawing here particularly on two essays by philosopher Mary Midgley: "On Not Being Afraid of Natural Sex Differences," in *Feminist Perspectives in Philosophy*, ed. M. Griffiths and M. Whitford (Bloomington: Indiana University Press, 1988), 29–41; and "The Soul's Successors: Philosophy and the 'Body,'" in *Religion and the Body*, ed. Sarah Coakley (Cambridge: Cambridge University Press, 1997), 53–68.

37. Midgley, "Natural Sex Differences," 36, cites Shulamith Firestone's acute observation about "the absurdity of men's viewing themselves as totally detached individuals in relation to the rest of society, while still expecting to go home to a wife who would always have their dinner hot for them in the evening."

38. Midgley, "The Soul's Successors," 64 (author's emphasis). Along interestingly similar lines is the comment of K. R. Soleim in his study of Descartes, "I Doubt: I Am a Man: The Cartesian Subject Exposed to Sexual Difference," in *Feminism, Epistemology and Ethics*, ed. I. N. Preus (Oslo: Oslo University Press, 1996), 137–146, at 141:

> So, if discourse on sexual difference leaps from one dimension to another through the ages, if it leaps from cosmology and metaphysics to the domain of medicine and sociology, the leap may be compared to a symptom changing places across the tormented body. *If sexual difference is expelled from one domain, it is bound to erupt, unexpectedly like a symptom, in another.* (my emphasis)

39. See, for example, Ann Oakley, *Sex, Gender and Society* (Aldershot, England: Gower, 1985).

40. Judith Butler, *Gender Trouble: Feminism and the Subversion of Identity* (London: Routledge, 1990).

41. Butler, *Gender Trouble*, 5, 7.

42. Boyarin, "Gender," 117.

43. I owe this insight to Graham, *Making the Difference*, 187–190.

44. Sarah Coakley, *Powers and Submissions: Spirituality, Philosophy and Gender* (Oxford: Blackwell, 2002), 161.

45. See, for example, Mary McClintock Fulkerson, " 'Is There a (Non-Sexist) Bible in This Church?' A Feminist Case for the Priority of Interpretive Communities," *Modern Theology* 14, no. 2 (1998): 225–242; and Stanley Hauerwas, *A Community of Character* (Notre Dame, Ind.: University of Notre Dame Press, 1981).

46. Mary Douglas, *Purity and Danger* (London: Routledge and Kegan Paul, 1966).

47. See on this, Coakley, *Powers and Submissions*, 153–167.

48. For an excellent treatment, see J. Richard Middleton, *The Liberating Image: The Imago Dei in Genesis 1* (Grand Rapids, Mich.: Brazos, 2005).

49. An important analogy here is the way the scriptures have been used, up until the relatively recent past, to give divine sanction to the institution of slavery. Excellent on this regarding the history of the United States is Elizabeth Fox-Genovese and Eugene D. Genovese, "The Divine Sanction of Social Order: Religious Foundations of the Southern Slaveholders' World-View," *Journal of the American Academy of Religion* 55, no. 2 (1987): 211–233. Note especially the specific link with patriarchal authority on 219ff.

50. See, for example, Nancy Tatom Ammerman, *Bible Believers: Fundamentalists in the Modern World* (New Brunswick, N.J.: Rutgers University Press, 1987); Brenda E. Brasher, *Godly Women: Fundamentalism and Female Power* (New Brunswick, N.J.: Rutgers University Press, 1998).

51. See Fulkerson, "Is There a (Non-Sexist) Bible in This Church?" and her monograph *Changing the Subject: Women's Discourses and Feminist Theology* (Minneapolis, Minn.: Fortress, 1994).

52. The alluring slogan "equal but different" is often heard in these contexts.

53. Especially valuable at this point are essays by Phyllis A. Bird, "Genesis 1–3 as a Source for a Contemporary Theology of Sexuality" and "Genesis 3 in Modern Biblical Scholarship," in Bird, *Missing Persons and Mistaken Identities*, 155–173, 174–193.

54. See on this, Martin, *Sex and the Single Savior*, 1–16, "The Myth of Textual Agency."

55. Relevant here is K. E. Greene-McCreight, *Ad Litteram: How Augustine, Calvin, and Barth Read the "Plain Sense" of Genesis 1–3* (New York: Lang, 1999).

56. See Sandra M. Schneiders, "Women in the Fourth Gospel and the Role of Women in the Contemporary Church," in *The Gospel of John as Literature*, ed. M. W. G. Stibbe (Leiden: Brill, 1993), 123–143.

57. In passing, this is why, theologically speaking, church is more important than family—or, put better, why the believer's primary family *is* the church. See on this, Rodney Clapp, *Families at the Crossroads: Beyond Traditional and Modern Options* (Downers Grove, Ill.: InterVarsity, 1993), esp. 67–88, "Church as First Family."

58. The phrase comes from the title of Elaine Graham's book of 1995, *Making the Difference*. Suggestive at the liturgical level is Natalie Knödel, "Reconsidering an Obsolete Rite: The Churching of Women and Feminist Liturgical Theology," *Feminist Theology* 14 (1997): 106–125.

59. Midgley, "Natural Sex Differences," 39.

60. See on this, Rowan Williams's "The Body's Grace," in *Theology and Sexuality: Classic and Contemporary Readings*, ed. Eugene F. Rogers Jr. (Oxford: Blackwell, 2002), 309–321.

12

Propriety and Trespass
The Drama of Eating

Ellen F. Davis

I eat my history day by day.
   —Wendell Berry,
    "History"[1]

Eating in Place

Something Darwin has taught us all—even those, like me, who have read only a little of his work—is the extent to which all life forms cohere in a dynamic unity. Each species, *Homo sapiens* included, survives "as one organic miracle linked with others."[2] Evolution means that the unity has historical and genetic dimensions. I see no essential conflict between that and biblical faith, but my focus now is on another, related aspect of Darwin's argument. More important for its bearing on both Genesis and the quality of life on the planet in human time is his demonstration that there is also a *current, functional* unity among life forms. A species survives only when it fits well into the flow of life in its particular place on earth or in the water. There are no exceptions to the great law of propriety. "Propriety" is not Darwin's word, but it expresses the fact on which he insists, namely, that the fit between the life form and the place is exacting, and the place has priority. Over time, species adapt to fit the limits of their place precisely, and if the demands of the species exceed those limits over any significant period of time, then they die. Adaptation to locale is *the* way of life on planet earth.

The fit between life form and place means, at base, that each species finds enough to eat and, further, that it provides food for other species, through relationships of dependency and competition, predation and nurture. In other words, life forms are functionally linked together in the tangle of relations we call food chains; life in each place and on the planet altogether depends on their integrity. Understanding what constitutes that integrity in each place is the work of ecology, the modern science which is, I dare say, Darwin's most important, if indirect, legacy to us.[3] "Food chain," however, is not a very evocative descriptor for the workings of the biotic web. A more satisfying explication of that concept comes from Aldo Leopold, who is sometimes identified as the father of modern ecological thinking, in his justly famous essay "The Land Ethic." Thus, Leopold describes the constellation of events summarized by the one word "land": "Land... is not merely soil; it is a fountain of energy flowing through a circuit of soils, plants, and animals. Food chains are the living channels which conduct energy upward; death and decay return it to the soil.... The circuit is not closed, but it is a sustained circuit, like a slowly augmented revolving fund of life."[4]

Leopold's insight is that land is not an inert *thing*; it is a community, pulsing with energy that is constantly exchanged among its countless inhabitants. Leopold knew the Bible, and I wonder if he was conscious of echoing the beautiful image of the psalmist: "*Kî 'immᵉkha mᵉqôr ḥayyîm* [For with You (God) is a fountain of life; in your light, we see light]" (Ps. 36:10). The poet of Psalm 36 had evidently reflected long on an account of creation very like what we have in the first chapters of Genesis. In this essay, I will consider how Genesis represents biological integrity—or conversely, the loss of biological integrity—with the attention it gives to food and the immediate source of food, the fertile soil. "Land," "soil," "food," "eat"—these are all common words in the early chapters of Genesis, although it is easy for contemporary readers to miss that, since those who go to church and synagogue are generally given the impression that food, especially food production, is not a genuinely theological topic. The biblical writers, however, knew something that most of us have forgotten: the theological significance of agriculture. And if that concept sounds odd to us, that likely testifies to the oddity of our own culture and its dangerous irreverence about eating. For thousands of years, agriculture has been the most widespread form of cultural activity, and it has always (until recently) been imbued with religious significance. To this day, agriculture remains far and away our largest industry and the heaviest consumer of water and energy (in the form of oil). In sum, as evolutionary biologist and Kansas farmer Wes Jackson observes, "It is in agriculture... that human culture and the creation totally interpenetrate."[5]

That statement would not have caused the biblical writers to blink an eye. Living in a culture where most people (85 percent or more)[6] were farmers, they took it as a matter of course that human work approaches God's work most regularly through agriculture. This is one reason that the Bible has so much to say about land use, particularly about farming, as a part of our religious obligation and witness. But in order to understand just what the Bible may have to say to us in this matter, it is necessary to speak briefly about the way we raise our food in industrial societies. Our food production system departs so radically from all that "farming" has traditionally meant that it is more accurately labeled "agribusiness."

One of the most pronounced features of a fully industrialized culture is its willingness (indeed, need) to leave its members in nearly total ignorance about the sources of their food and the other essential stuff of life. We are ignorant because we are not involved in producing our own food; less than 1 percent of the U.S. population is engaged in full-time farming; we have more prisoners than full-time farmers. Globally, the crucial decisions about how we eat are overwhelmingly in the hands of a few multinational conglomerates that control a system that is increasingly integrated, from seed to supermarket. Industrial food production is the most consequential industry the world has ever known. Sixty years of petrochemical "inputs" have increased food production to an unprecedented degree, enabling the world population to grow by 4.5 billion. But at the same time, industrial practices have caused damage on an unprecedented scale: erosion, the drastic reduction of the seed base, the draining of rivers and aquifers, the chemical poisoning of soil and water supplies, the release of deadly floods of effluents and greenhouse gases. Returns on chemical farming are now decreasing; it is evident that we have purchased short-term abundance at the cost of the health of the whole "land community." Our disease is evident everywhere: in the widespread impoverishment of rural communities; in the high rates of rural violence and farmer suicides worldwide; in the short, sick lives of industrially confined animals and the collapse of wild populations—including, most dangerously perhaps, bees and other pollinators;[7] in the trauma injuries and abbreviated lives of people working in both field and factory.[8]

"Catastrophic agriculture,"[9] as we now practice it, will end in the foreseeable future. (That is the good news, sort of.) The oil that makes it possible to eat this way will give out. Half the topsoil in North America's Great Plains is gone; 38 percent of the arable soils worldwide are in crisis. The question is, what will be left for the coming generations to work with, when the dominance of industrial agriculture ends? The urgency of that question has generated the now quite large body of contemporary agrarian literature. For the first time in history, the philosophy of agrarianism has been fully articulated, with a body of *belles lettres* to back it up. Some of that literature, especially the essays, fiction, and poetry of Wendell Berry, ranks with the best writing ever produced on the North American continent. The modern agrarians are diverse in interests and backgrounds: they include farmers and city dwellers, biologists, economists, professors of philosophy, literature, and ecology; even a few theologians. What they all share is a world view that holds together the health of "land" (in the broad sense) and culture. They are concerned about the integrity of biotic communities, their food and energy flows, and equally about human communities, their economic, political, and spiritual well-being. My own work now is focused on reading the Bible with agrarian eyes—and thus recovering a way of thinking that was native to nearly all of the writers of the Old Testament (at least), but which I acquire only by listening to those who live with the land more closely and thoughtfully than I do. So, in the rest of this essay, I shall consider how the first chapters of Genesis express the agrarian concern that the health of the land and human community should both continue in perpetuity.

Genesis 1: Propriety

For ecologically concerned contemporary readers, the first chapter of Genesis is generally viewed as something to get past—at least, the last few verses of it are. The obvious objection is to the commandment to humans to "subdue the earth." Biblical scholar Norman Habel maintains that some editor has taken a sensitive representation of the creation of the earth and its nonhuman creatures, and then tacked onto it a radically anthropocentric story that reduces the earth "to a force or thing that must be subjugated."[10] However, since the whole section covering the seven days of creation (Gen. 1:1–2:4a) is widely acknowledged by virtually all other scholars to be a tightly unified composition, it makes more sense to see if that charge to the human can be reconciled with the larger earth-sensitive story in which it appears.

One hundred years ago, the great German biblical scholar Hermann Gunkel taught us that identifying the genre of a piece is a crucial first step in its interpretation. It is widely acknowledged that the initial creation account (for simplicity, "Genesis 1") comes from the so-called priestly tradition, and so it may be best read as a piece of liturgical poetry,[11] a genre designation that implies several characteristics:

1. Liturgical poetry is theological writing, but not in the mode of abstract doctrine. Every liturgy seeks to open up a deepened perception of

God's presence in and to the world, a perception that translates fairly directly into experience. This poem is giving us a God's-eye view of creation, with particular attention to how humans fit in that design. We are the only creatures who can think about our proper place, the only ones who can recognize when we fall short of it. So this is a poem that instructs us in "propriety," in conforming our behavior to the limits of and hopeful possibilities for the world as God has made it.

2. A liturgical poem is carefully structured, designed for the ear, and so literary devices such as rhythm, repetition, and verbal framing are important. When an established rhythm is broken, that is important.

3. Each word of a good poem is carefully chosen. (This being the first chapter of the Bible, we may assume high quality.) If a word seems awkward or ill chosen, that is noteworthy.

To illustrate these characteristics, I focus here on just two points of the poem, where it seems to be trying to arrest our attention, in one instance by an awkward break in rhythm, in the other by an offensive word choice. As it turns out, in both cases that part of the poem has something to do with eating.

The creation account begins with the elegantly terse diction of divine summons and execution: "Let there be light.... And there was light." There are no descriptive details at all until the middle of the third day. Yet as soon as the dry land appears, descriptors pour forth in profusion:

> And God said:
> "Let the earth sprout-out sprouts [*tadshe' ha'aretz deshe'*],
> plants seeding seed [*mazrî' zera'*],
> fruit trees making fruit, each of its own kind—
> with their seed in them—on the earth,"
> and it was so.
> And the earth brought forth sprouts,
> plants seeding seed each of its own kind,
> and trees making fruit with its seed in it, each of its own kind.
>   (vv. 11–12)

At this point, the poetic lines suddenly become burdened, or overburdened, by seeds and sprouts. Since the poet is capable of good style, then one should ask, why? In a poem about propriety, the answer likely has something to do with the place that humans occupy in the created order, as an Israelite might have understood it. And any Israelite had good reason to be interested in seed, because the most important botanical fact about the land Israel occupied was its remarkable abundance of plant diversity. In terms of genetic heritage, this is one of the nutritional centers of the whole earth, both for human beings and for animals. Its liminal location—contiguous, or nearly so, with three continents—gives that small corridor of land a natural gene flow with few parallels worldwide. Botanical fact led to cultural development; 10–12,000 years ago, the first permanent human settlements appeared in the uplands and foothills bordering the Fertile Crescent, where hunter/gatherers built stone houses and storage facilities for wild grains like emmer wheat, einkorn wheat, and barley, as well as leguminous grains, such as lentils, peas, chickpeas, vetch.[12] Eventually, wild harvests were succeeded by domesticated ones, the first farmed crops.[13] Note that the rare enabling condition for the emergence of agriculture in the Fertile Crescent was not rich soil; it was readily harvestable seed. For the most unusual feature of the native plant distribution was the prevalence of cereals and legumes with nonshattering seed heads—in contrast to the majority of plants, whose seed scatters as soon as the heads reach maturity. Seed-retaining, life-sustaining grains—this is the phenomenon the poet captures with that apparently pleonastic phrase "plants seeding seed...with their seed in them." Genesis 1 celebrates the familiar yet inexhaustible mystery of fruitfulness as the Israelites experienced it.

That understanding may help us to deal with the second, more awkward moment in this first chapter, the assertion of human dominion in verse 28:

> And God blessed them and God said to them:
> "Be fruitful and multiply and fill the earth and conquer it
>   [vᵉkhivshuha],
> and exercise mastery among [radah b-] the fish of the sea and among
>   the birds of the skies
> and among all living things creeping on the earth."

Four aspects of this verse are important for our understanding of the human place in creation. First, an observation about what is missing: we are never told that the divine command is fulfilled. Normally, there is some indication that God's intention has been fulfilled: "Let there be light, and there was light" (1:3). "Let there be a firmament....And it was so" (1:6, 7). But in this case, fulfillment of the divine command remains in the future, out ahead of where the creation story ends. So we are in a position to render some critical judgment on ourselves as we read the charge given "in the beginning." Are we exercising the mastery that God intends?

Second, concerning the command pᵉrû urᵉvû, "Be fruitful and multiply," the most important thing is that God has uttered it before. On the fifth day of creation, one day before the humans come on stage, God blessed all the "animate creatures" (nefesh ḥayah, Gen. 1:20, 21) of sky and sea and charged them, "Be fruitful and multiply and fill the waters of the seas, and let the birds multiply on earth." So when, on the following day, the land creatures are formed and the human is likewise blessed and charged to multiply, we must assume that the second iteration of the commandment is conditioned by the first. Legitimate human fruitfulness cannot be secured to the detriment of life forms that are equally blessed by God. This limiting principle enables us to render accurate judgment on ourselves in the twenty-first century. For we live in our planet's sixth age of massive species extinction, with humans now functioning as "a geophysical force."[14] Reports of widespread bird extinctions and the threatened collapse of fish populations around the world seem to point to the inversion of the blessing of the creatures of the fifth day of creation.[15]

Third, note that I render the Hebrew phrase *radah b-* not as (conventionally) "exercise dominion *over*" but as "exercise mastery *among*." The latter translation conforms to the normal meaning of the Hebrew preposition *b-*, but the more important point here is that humans are blessed and charged to exercise mastery with respect to the very same creatures of sea and sky who have just received their own blessing and charge to multiply. Therefore, the human vocation cannot be fulfilled through activity that cancels the life potential of the nonhuman species.[16]

A fourth point concerns the one word here that seems designed not just to prompt reflection but rather to stop us dead in our tracks: "fill the earth [*v^ekh-ivshuha*], and *conquer* it." "Conquer the land, earth"—the Hebrew word *'eretz* means both, and the phrase appears elsewhere in the Bible with reference to the conquest of the promised land of Canaan. That echo must be deliberate; the two divine commands are parallel: to the humans, "Conquer the earth ['*eretz*]"; to the Israelites, "Conquer the land ['*eretz*]." God's intention in each case is that humans should represent God's benevolent sovereignty. It is relevant to a consideration of eating that the priestly tradition of the conquest of Canaan celebrates the God-given fruitfulness of the land, epitomized by the giant grape cluster that Moses' scouts brought back from their reconnaissance mission .[17] Just as Israel's faithfulness is meant to perpetuate the fruitfulness of Canaan, the human exercise of mastery among the creatures is meant to guarantee that there will be food for all. Accordingly, immediately following the charge to the human, the poet of Genesis 1 returns to the theme of seeds one more time:

> And God said:
> "Look, I give you every plant seeding seed that is on the face of all
>   the earth,
> and every tree that has on it tree-fruit seeding seed;

for you it [all] shall be, for eating.
And to every living thing of the earth
...every kind of green herbage for eating. (vv. 29–30b)

Perpetual fruitfulness is one possible outcome of the "conquest" of either Canaan or the earth itself—but equally, failure is possible. Genesis 1 was likely composed in the period of the Babylonian exile, and so the reminder of the conquest of Canaan is at the same time a reminder of Israel's failure in the land and a warning that the human project on earth could likewise fail. We in the twenty-first century are the first to face the real historical possibility that the fruitfulness of the land may fail altogether, because of our failure to exercise our "mastery" with propriety.[18]

I suggest, then, that the proper exercise of mastery among the creatures has centrally to do with the human role in maintaining the integrity of the food chains, even enhancing their long-term productivity, as indigenous farmers may once have done on the North American continent.[19] As we have seen, that kind of mastery is very far from our present exercise of domination over the planet, which has already degraded some 38 percent of all arable soils[20] and now poses an equal threat to the ocean's ability to sustain life. As we shall see, the second chapter of Genesis substantiates this view and gives a more detailed understanding of the difficulties and promise that such an exercise of mastery entails.

Genesis 2 and 3: Vocation and Trespass

At the beginning of the history of the world that Norman Wirzba aptly calls "the drama of soil,"[21] the Yahwistic writer famously recounts: "YHWH God formed *ha'adam* [the human being] from *ha'adamah* [the fertile soil], human from humus," and with the (literal) inspiration of divine breath, the human became "an animate being [*nefesh ḥayah*]" (Gen. 2:7). That genealogy, *'adam* from *'adamah*, is the starting point for seeing the biological integration of all life. Within a few verses, we hear that "God caused to grow from *ha'adamah* every desirable tree" (2:9) and formed from the same substance every other "animate being" on earth and in the sky (2:18). Thus, the writer sketches a picture of the whole land community, while holding the focus on the complex relationship between *'adam* and *'adamah*.

That relationship is not just genealogical but also vocational: "And YHWH God took the human being and set them in the garden of Eden to..." (Gen. 2:15)—to do what? *L^eovdah ul^eshomrah*, the Hebrew says, and one standard translation is "to till it and tend it." But that is misleading, because neither Hebrew verb is an agricultural term, and both have an ambiguity that is lost in translation. *'Avad* means "work," in the broad sense of the English word: occasionally to work a substance, specifically soil (e.g., Gen. 2:5, 3:23, 4:2), but in the overwhelmingly majority of its uses, the verb means to work *for* someone, to serve a master. So perhaps there is a question implied and left open, namely, "Who is in charge here?" *'Adam* works *'adamah*; we exercise some degree of control over the soil. At the same time, we are controlled by it, limited to what it is able or willing to give (Gen. 3:18, 4:12). Cain (who is a farmer) is condemned for his violence through the soil's bloody "mouth" (Gen. 4:10–11); it withholds from him its strength. Again, the whole question of who has priority—*'adam* or *'adamah*?—is called radically into question.

The second verb, *shamar*, is at least as ambiguous, because it has a broader semantic range. A basic meaning is to "watch over, protect": "Am I my brother's *shomer*?" (Gen. 4:9). But it frequently translates as "observe," with a variety of nuances: to observe natural phenomena (Jer. 7:7), to observe good behavior with the goal of imitating it (Ps. 37:37), to acquire wisdom by observation of the workings of the world (Ps. 107:43; Isa. 42:20), even to observe guidelines, specifically divine commandments or the dictates of justice (Hos. 12:7; Isa. 56:1). So, the human is charged to "protect" the garden but at the same time to "observe" it, to learn from it and respect the limits it sets, to "consult the genius of the place in all"—a phrase of Alexander Pope's[22] that farmer and evolutionary biologist Wes Jackson takes as the motto of his work at the Land Institute in Salina, Kansas.

The Natural Systems Agriculture being developed at the Land Institute is one direct and hopeful application of the charge to the first human(s) in Genesis 2, for it proceeds from three questions:

> What was here?
> What will nature require of us here?
> What will nature help us to do here?[23]

All of those questions acknowledge that observing the land is the first step in working it responsibly. They point to the Darwinian principle of local adaptation: what was *here*? Further, they bespeak a concern for propriety: working respectfully *with* nature, what must or might we do here? Each place has its own answers to yield.[24] Guided by those questions, the scientists and farmers (the same people) at the Land Institute are developing a revolutionary mode of agriculture based on "perennial polyculture"; they are growing edible grains in a way that mimics the natural growth of the North American prairie.

The questions that Jackson poses reflect the complex truth underlying the ambiguous verbs of Genesis: because there is power on both sides of the relationship between 'adam and 'adamah, and potential for lasting benefit or harm, the relationship must be one of mutual service. And when we neglect that essential human vocation, the bond is not broken or even attenuated, even if we are oblivious of it. But the bond is twisted, and the relationship becomes one of mutual suffering and death.

Against this background, it can hardly be coincidence that the first trespass of the limits of the created order is an eating violation. At the moment when the woman makes her fateful decision, the narrative slows down, and (uncharacteristically for biblical storytelling) we are positioned behind her eyes to see precisely how she reasons: "And the woman saw that the tree was good for eating and that it was appealing to the eyes, and the tree was desirable for 'enlightenment,' and she took some of its fruit and ate" (3:6). The woman "saw that the tree was good"; the near-echo of God's seeing what was good in the first days of the world underscores the fact that her perception of the desirable is taking her away from God's intention for creation. God made every tree *except* this one "good for eating" (2:9), and only in the woman's mind does mere consumption yield enlightenment; in fact, the only thing the humans learn from their experience is that they are naked. Based on what we have found in chapter 2, it seems likely that God meant the humans to gain insight into the workings of the world gradually—literally, "by steps"—that is, through walks with God "in the breezy time of day" (Gen. 3:8), through patient observation, "working and watching" the garden (2:15). Instead, "she took some of its fruit, and she ate." She took without thought of tending and, further, without gratitude or memory. This is the first time that a creature appears as the subject of the verb *lakakh* "take";[25] she took, forgetful or ignorant of the simple agrarian understanding that there is

> ...nothing taken
> That was not first a gift.[26]

In this trespass, immediate desire is the standard for action vis-à-vis God and the other creatures of God. Environmental philosopher J. Baird Callicott proposes that here "knowledge of good and evil" denotes the power "to *determine* what is right and what is wrong *in relation to self*."[27] Once the humans have "consumed" that knowledge, they regard themselves as "an axiological point of reference...an intrinsically valuable hub to which other creatures and the creation as a whole may be referred for appraisal"[28]—and, I would add, for appropriation. It is not hard to see why the humans' adoption of that new standard would create a rupture in their relationship with God, who is incredulous

at their obtuseness: "From the tree that I commanded you not to eat from
it...you ate??!" (3:11). Fair enough that the humans have to leave Eden, but why
should the soil suffer a curse (3:17) as a result of the human violation? In order
to see that, one has to adopt an agrarian perspective and standard for human
behavior.

I once studied this passage with a group of young farmers and plant biologists at Wes Jackson's Land Institute. I told them that my mostly urban divinity
students—at that time, I was teaching in New Haven, Connecticut—found the
cursing of the soil troublesome and arbitrary: "This must be a classic instance
of the grumpy God of the Old Testament." When I asked the Land Institute
interns what they thought, they gave a different answer, without a second's
hesitation: "When humans are not in touch with God, the soil will be the first
to suffer." Note, these people were not theologians, nor in most cases were
they conventionally religious. Yet they easily intuited and further, accepted the
biblical view that there is an unbreakable three-way connection among people,
God, and land, a connection so tight that, when the first humans eat against
the rules, disturbance in the divine-human relationship is evidenced in the
landscape:

> Thorns and thistles it will sprout for you, and you shall eat the grass of
>   the field. By the sweat of your face you shall eat bread,
> until you return to the soil, for from it you were taken. (3:18–19a)

Thorns and thistles are signs of eroded and desiccated soil. The biblical
poet is writing in a few lines a short but accurate history of land transformation and degradation in the uplands of the ancient Near East: tree cover (Eden
seems to be an arboreal garden)[29] is cleared for cultivation and grazing; too
often, the bared sloping ground is further denuded by overgrazing and incau-
tious cultivation; as a result, more marginal land must be cleared and mined
for its fertility.[30] Humans and land together have "fallen" into the world the
Israelites knew. Living in a fragile landscape that was already damaged, they
could eat from it, generation to generation, only through unrelenting labor and
wise practices of land care.

The first three chapters of Genesis are sufficient to make clear that the
biblical writers understand that the drama of human eating is fraught with
tension, trouble, and potential tragedy. Yet trouble is not the last word in the
primeval history's account of agriculture. Looking ahead, Noah marks a new
beginning, when after the Flood, "he began [as] 'ish ha'adamah [a man of the
fertile soil]" (Gen. 9:20). We tend to remember only Noah's care for the animals, but from the perspective of the biblical story, Noah exemplifies member-
ship in the whole land community, soil and animals together. His name means

"rest," and in this context, rest would seem to mean long-term stability for both the earth and human communities.[31] Such stability is the mark of agriculture that acts like an ecosystem, observing the propriety of each and every place, of work on the land that stems from patient observation and therefore creates a place for what Wendell Berry calls

> ...the blest
> Sabbath of [God's] unresting love
> which lights all things and gives rest.[32]

NOTES

1. Wendell Berry, *Collected Poems* (San Francisco, Calif.: North Point, 1985).

2. E. O. Wilson, "The Bottleneck," *Scientific American* 286, no. 2 (February 2002): 91; the article is excerpted from his book *The Future of Life* (New York: Knopf, 2002).

3. The term "ecology" was introduced into scientific discourse by field naturalist Ernst Haeckel in his 1866 *Generelle Morphologie der Organismen*, one of a number of books Haeckel wrote on the significance of Darwin's work. See Robert C. Stauffer, "Haeckel, Darwin, and Ecology," *Quarterly Review of Biology* 32, no. 2 (1957): 138–144.

4. Aldo Leopold, "The Land Ethic," in his *A Sand County Almanac* (New York: Ballantine, 1966), 253.

5. Wes Jackson, *Becoming Native to This Place* (Lexington: University Press of Kentucky, 1994), 22.

6. Edward Campbell, *The Oxford History of the Biblical World*, ed. Michael Coogan (New York: Oxford University Press, 1998).

7. Janet Abramovitz, "Putting a Value on Nature's 'Free' Services," *World-Watch* 11, no. 1 (1998): 10–19. On drastic losses among bees, ranging from 30 to 70 percent or more, see Alexei Barrionuevo, "Honeybees Vanish, Leaving Crops and Keepers in Peril," *New York Times* (27 February 2007; http://www.nytimes.com/2007/02/27/business/27bees.html).

8. The average life expectancy of Latino farmworkers in the United States is about one-third less than for the general population: forty-nine years, compared to seventy-three to seventy-nine. Gary Holthaus, *From the Farm to the Table: What All Americans Need to Know about Agriculture* (Lexington: University Press of Kentucky, 2006), 140.

9. Richard Manning, *Against the Grain: How Agriculture Has Hijacked Civilization* (New York: North Point, 2004).

10. Norman Habel, "Geophany: The Earth Story in Genesis 1," in *The Earth Story in Genesis*, ed. Norman Habel and Shirley Wurst (Sheffield, England: Sheffield Academic Press; Cleveland, Ohio: Pilgrim, 2000), 47.

11. I follow Walter Brueggemann in classifying it as a liturgical poem (*Genesis* [Atlanta, Ga.: John Knox, 1982], 30).

12. See Daniel Hillel, *Out of the Earth: Civilization and the Life of the Soil* (New York: Free Press, 1991), 72.

13. Oded Borowski notes: "The domestication of cereals...took place sometime before 7000 B.C.E. in the Near East" (*Agriculture in Iron Age Israel* [Winona Lake, Ind.: Eisenbrauns, 1987], 87).

14. E. O. Wilson observes, "*Homo sapiens* has become a geophysical force, the first species in the history of the planet to attain that dubious distinction" ("The Bottleneck," 84).

15. In 1997, a team of terrestrial ecologists from Stanford University reported that extinction rates for plant and animal species are "now on the order of 100 to 1000 times those before humanity's dominance of Earth.... [A]s many as one-quarter of Earth's bird species have been driven to extinction by human activities over the past two millennia" (Peter Vitousek and Harold A. Mooney, "Human Domination of Earth's Ecosystems," *Science* 277 [25 July 1997]: 498).

16. The linguistic argument is not in itself conclusive, since the whole phrase *radah b-* does in some instances denote a harsh rule "over" others (Lev. 26:27; cf. Lev. 25:43, 46; Neh. 9:28).

17. Num. 13:23.

18. For the full argument, see Ellen F. Davis, *Scripture, Culture, and Agriculture: An Agrarian Reading of the Bible* (Cambridge: Cambridge University Press, 2009).

19. J. Baird Callicott suggests that the abundance of plant and animal life found in the Americas by the first European invaders and settlers was not purely "natural" but instead reflected the land management practices of the native inhabitants. See "Genesis and John Muir," in *Covenant for a New Creation*, ed. Carol S. Robb and Carl J. Casebolt (Maryknoll, N.Y.: Orbis, 1991), 133–134.

20. Wes Jackson, "Right Livelihood Award Acceptance Remarks," Stockholm, 8 December 2000 (http://www.rightlivelihood.org/jackson_speech.html).

21. Norman Wirzba, *The Paradise of God: Renewing Religion in an Ecological Age* (New York: Oxford University Press, 2003), 28–34.

22. Alexander Pope, "Epistle to Richard Boyle, Earl of Burlington," v. 57 (*The Works of Alexander Pope* [London: John Murray, 1881], vol. 3: 176).

23. Wes Jackson most fully set forth the case for Natural Systems Agriculture in his *New Roots for Agriculture* (Lincoln, Neb. and London: University of Nebraska Press, 1980); for a more recent short summary of the guiding questions, see also *Land Report* (Winter 1994): 3.

24. On local adaptation as "the inescapable governing principle of agriculture" (in contrast to industrial agriculture's "governing principle of uniformity"), see the correspondence between Wendell Berry and Wes Jackson, "Letters from a Humble Radical," in Jason Peters, *Wendell Berry: Life and Work* (Lexington: University of Kentucky Press, 2007), 170.

25. Notably, the same three phrases—*ra'ah* (saw), *kî tov* (how good), and *lakakh* (take)—occur together in another account of trespass in the primeval history, when "the divine sons saw the human daughters, how good they were, and took for themselves wives" (Gen. 6:2).

26. Wendell Berry, "Sabbath 1998, VI," in his *Given* (Washington, D.C.: Shoemaker & Hoard, 2005), 61.

27. Callicott, "Genesis and John Muir," 123.

28. Callicott, "Genesis and John Muir," 123–124.

29. Callicott speaks of Eden as "an agroforest permaculture" ("Genesis and John Muir," 118).

30. On the stages of land degradation in Israel and its environs, see Daniel Hillel, *The Natural History of the Bible* (New York: Columbia University Press, 2006), 22–23.

31. When his father, Lamekh, names Noah, he says, "This one will give us rest from our efforts and from our hands' trouble from the soil that YHWH cursed" (Gen. 5:29).

32. Berry, "Sabbaths 2002, X," in *Given*, 117.

13

The Plausibility of Creationism
A Sociological Comment

Mathew Guest

If the system of flood geology can be established
on a sound scientific basis, and be effectively
promoted and publicized, then the entire
evolutionary cosmology, at least in its present
neo-Darwinian form, will collapse. This, in turn,
would mean that every anti-Christian system and
movement (communism, racism, humanism,
libertinism, behaviorism, and all the rest)
would be deprived of their pseudo-intellectual
foundation.
            —Henry M. Morris, *Scientific Creationism*[1]

By the mid-1970s, the "scientific creationism" popularized by figures
like Henry Morris was well established in the United States. The
conviction behind vitriolic statements like the one cited above, that
the truth of the Genesis Flood account could be proven using the
conventional methods of the natural sciences, was no longer merely
the stuff of fundamentalist apologetics, but was part of an applied
and well-resourced scientific agenda. Morris was a trained civil engi-
neer, known during his student days as a gifted mathematician as
well as a zealous evangelical who later gained a Ph.D. in hydraulics
and geology. He used his scientific knowledge to support his "young
earth" creationist beliefs, defending the need for Bible-believing
Christians to address the false claims of evolution on scientific

grounds. Thus, while his famous volume *The Genesis Flood* (cowritten by John Whitcomb and published in 1961) was premised on the inerrancy and infallibility of the scriptures, the claims found within Genesis were supported and elaborated using established scientific laws and geological evidence. In this way, the work of Whitcomb and Morris represented an extension of a trend among the pioneers of fundamentalist Christianity who were writing around the turn of the twentieth century. Their reactionary interpretations of Genesis were not premodern as such, but reflected the modernist assumptions of the age, so that theological refutations of evolution presented the Genesis account as a series of factual, propositional statements, issuing straightforward and unmediated truth, available for all to see. Later, apologists for the creationist perspective would attempt to treat Genesis as a scientific document, extending its factual status into applications in geology, paleontology, archaeology, and the biological sciences. As a reliable guide to life and its origins, Genesis acquired the additional status of textbook, research guide, and historical record. In this sense, the so-called fundamentalist resurgence did not represent a yearning for premodern Christendom, but a thoroughly modern attempt to defend the integrity of the boundaries of biblical Christianity. Creationism emerged as a major dimension to this ongoing maneuver among the champions of conservative Christianity.

But what was at stake in the efforts of figures like Henry Morris was not just the reliability or otherwise of Darwinian evolution as a means of explaining the origins of life. As the citation above vividly demonstrates, evolution had become associated with all that was wrong with Western modernity: materialism, the debasement of humankind, selfishness and ruthless rivalry, the devaluation of life as a gift from God, a rejection of the absolute authority of scripture in all things, plus the usual bêtes noires of the American Right, such as liberalism and communism. The creationist cause had acquired a strong cultural significance in seeking to defend not just biblical authority, but a way of life, a social order, and a complex set of ideological interests. In this respect, the modern appropriation of Genesis has become a matter not just of biblical hermeneutics, but of cultural identity.

Much of the existing scholarship on the evolution-creationism conflict has been historical and theological, charting the contours of the developing debate or commenting on the merits of emerging perspectives. What follows is a sociological discussion; my concern is not with the validity of creationism, but with how creationist ideas function within the social contexts in which they are affirmed, debated, and challenged. Axiomatic to a sociological approach is the assumption that changes in belief may be explained with reference to changes in the social structures of society and not simply with reference to the ideas and behavior of individuals. Hence, Peter Berger's claim that the religious crises of modernity are not due to "any mysterious metamorphoses of consciousness" but can "be explained in terms of empirically available developments in the social structures and the social psychology of modern societies."[2] My concern in this chapter is to explore how the popularity of creationist ideas within contemporary Western cultures may be explained in a similar way. A more specific focus, to use sociological language, is the apparent plausibility of creationism, i.e., how and why the claims associated with creationism are viewed as plausible by those who affirm them.

The Genesis of Creationism

The history of Christian fundamentalism has been characterized by several dramatic controversies which are often said to have played a greater part in shaping the course of this movement than more steady flows of cultural and religious change. Insofar as fundamentalism is an essentially reactionary movement, perhaps this is a fair assessment. These controversies certainly continue to influence the contours of fundamentalist identity in that particular issues remain bones of contention and foci for perennial conflicts with modern culture. The evolution-creationism debate is a prime—perhaps *the* prime—case in point. It represents one of the most enduring points of difference between conservative Christianity and the rest of Western society, and hence generates potent identity markers. This is especially the case in the contemporary United States, in which debates over the respective legitimacy of evolution and creationism continue to inflame the "culture wars" that divide conservatives from liberals, more so since 1960, claims evangelical historian Mark Noll, than any other issue except abortion.[3]

Noll is one of the many contemporary evangelical thinkers who lament the fact that the creationism issue has maintained a position of such importance throughout the twentieth and into the twenty-first century, chiefly because it has contributed to the disengagement of evangelicals from mainstream scholarship to the detriment of theology. Noll points out that the young earth creationism that has become so popular since the 1960s was not characteristic of conservative Protestant thought at the end of the nineteenth or the beginning of the twentieth century. Key conservative figures like James Orr and B. B. Warfield—both of whom wrote for the famous pamphlets published as *The Fundamentals* (1910–1915) and hence were influential within the emerging fundamentalist movement—accepted evolution as the means by which God created the earth. Historian of creationism Ronald Numbers argues that early fundamentalism in the United States viewed higher criticism—which treated scripture as a set of historical documents rather than as the inspired word of God—as a greater threat to Christianity than evolution. The volumes of *The Fundamentals*, which repeatedly touched on the subject of evolution, offered a variety of perspectives on it. As Numbers comments, "Fundamentalists may not have liked evolution, but at this time few, if any, saw the necessity or desirability of launching a crusade to eradicate it from the schools and churches of America."[4]

To be sure, the roots of creationism lie in nineteenth-century millenarianism, especially as maintained by the Plymouth Brethren, who discerned an entire chronology of salvation history in the biblical texts, from terrestrial origins in Genesis, to predictions of the end times in the book of Revelation. Such ideas filtered into broader debates about the nature of biblical truth, and biblical literalism gradually gained popularity in large part because of its support among scholars at Princeton Theological Seminary. However, Darwinian evolutionary theory did not become a major target of fundamentalist hostility until the 1920s. Then, controversy and social drama appeared to overtake steady processes of change, and the so-called Scopes Monkey Trial is frequently cited as the public spectacle that did the most to crystallize the fundamentalist cause. The event took place in Dayton, Tennessee, in 1925, when local schoolteacher John Scopes was tried for teaching biology using a textbook—George William Hunter's *A Civic Biology*—that included a positive account of evolutionary theory. The case has become infamous, symbolizing a deeper conflict between academia and popular wisdom, between freedom of inquiry and the Bible, and marking battle lines that remain visible in U.S. public debate almost a century later. What is often overlooked in popular and scholarly accounts is that the Scopes trial was not a spontaneous expression of insidious cultural tensions but was a stage-managed public event, orchestrated by advocates of the two opposing sides. Recently passed state law had banned the teaching of evolution in Tennessee schools. The American Civil Liberties Union set up the Dayton trial as a test case aimed at challenging this law as unconstitutional and advertised for volunteer teachers to stand in the dock (assuring them that they would not lose their jobs). The ACLU cause focused on freedom of speech and academic freedom, which it claimed were threatened by the new legislation. Meanwhile, the World's Christian Fundamentals Association was in nearby Memphis, debating why Tennessee taxpayers should permit evolution and modernism to be freely taught at schools when the church-state separation outlawed the reading of the scriptures in the classroom. Hence, the pro-Bible faction set themselves up against John Scopes, the willing volunteer teacher, whose case was put by Clarence Darrow, the chief attorney for the defense, whose own inclination was to reject Christianity while affirming materialistic evolution.

The Scopes spectacle and the ripples it caused across the United States have been expertly charted in Edward J. Larson's book *Trial and Error*, which corrects popular wisdom in recounting the history of the evolution-creationism debate as complex and multifaceted, driven by multiple agendas and convoluted interests (for example, the trial coincided with efforts by local leaders who were keen to put Dayton on the map, hence the momentum behind the publicity).⁵ The outcome of the trial is well known: Scopes was convicted, but the decision was soon overturned on a technicality. The defense cried foul play as, without a conviction, they could not appeal and hence continue in their very public attempt to prove that the law was unconstitutional (thus leaving an open door for other states to pass similar antievolution measures). However, the most significant result was the effective discrediting of the antievolution movement, which was ridiculed as backward, ignorant, and uneducated by the media, an image made popular in the fictionalized dramatization of the trial, *Inherit the Wind*, produced in theaters from 1955 and released as a Hollywood movie starring Spencer Tracy in 1960.

What followed was, according to historian George Marsden, a "dark age" for conservative evangelical scholarship as fundamentalists withdrew from public life and, seeking to protect their members from the influence of evolutionary ideas, established organizations over which they could exert strict control. New denominations, church fellowships, and Bible institutes emerged as separatism became the fundamentalist norm. This coincided with what has come to be known as the Great Reversal. Newly pessimistic about the human condition following the horrors of the First World War and highly skeptical of theology tinged with leftist principles following the Russian Revolution of 1917, evangelicals turned away from social reform and instead focused on personal piety and evangelism, portraying the wider culture in increasingly negative terms. Modern science was taken to be representative of this culture, and Marsden associates this period with the genuine polarization of pro-science and pro-Bible camps.⁶ Whereas conservative Protestants had previously allowed some room for argument about the precise status of evolution, the events surrounding the Scopes trial had forced a turn inward, introducing a period of fundamentalist separatism.

A newfound public confidence emerged several decades later, with figures like Ellen G. White and George McCready Price, both Seventh-day Adventists who advanced creation accounts with the deluge center stage, and later, Whitcomb and Morris's *The Genesis Flood*, which put Price's points more persuasively, not least on account of Morris's scientific expertise. The subsequent popularity of creationism is partly, so Mark Noll argues, due to the massive investment in scientific education by the U.S. government in the wake of the U.S.S.R.'s launch of the space shuttle Sputnik in 1957, which generated the production and dissemination of biology textbooks that described the cosmos in evolutionary terms. This was perceived locally as federal interference, and the rise of creationist sentiments was one expression of popular protest.[7] Following the consequent textbook controversies of the 1960s and 1970s, creationism began to be taken seriously by the wider public, including scientists and educators.[8] Some of these professionals attempted to reconceive creationism on scientific rather than theological grounds in order to lend it more credibility among the wider population and as a potential means of getting creationist ideas taught in public schools.[9] This trend has come to be known under the umbrella term of "creation science," with various efforts to challenge evolution on scientific grounds supported by organizations like the Creation Research Society (est. 1963) and the Institute for Creation Research (est. 1970). Later, intelligent design would emerge as a new set of arguments but with the same aim of discrediting evolution as an unreliable or, at least, insufficient explanation of the origins of life.[10]

Ronald Numbers has pointed out that creationism—rather than persisting as a fixed set of ideas—actually *evolved* throughout the twentieth century, taking on different emphases in response to changing cultural challenges and developments among its advocates within conservative Christianity. An early openness and breadth of perspectives gave way to a polarization of positions after the 1920s, with a fresh engagement with science emerging in the 1960s. However, this engagement has not engendered a straightforward accommodation of creationist arguments to the norms of secular modernity. If anything, in the latter decades of the twentieth century and the beginning of the twenty-first, creationists have become more radical in setting up clear boundaries between the Christian world view they represent and that represented by "the world" as they see it.[11]

This trend is reflected in the available survey data. In 1991, a Gallup poll revealed that 47 percent of U.S. citizens, including 25 percent of college graduates, believed that "God created man pretty much in his present form at one time within the last 10,000 years." In 2005, the same organization, this time using slightly different wording, found that 53 percent of Americans agreed with the statement "God created human beings in their present form exactly the way the Bible describes it." The 6 percentage point increase is more striking because the revised wording arguably suggests a more uncompromising, dogmatically biblical position than the original, which at least allows for some margin of error.[12] While the evidence is not conclusive, what evidence there is suggests that creationist beliefs have experienced a steadily increasing level of assent within the United States since the mid-1960s.[13]

A similar pattern is exposed by an examination of levels of skepticism about evolution. In an international survey of over thirty European countries plus the United States and Japan, researchers Miller, Scott, and Okamoto asked a sample of adults whether they believed in the statement "Human beings, as we know them, developed from earlier species of animals." They found that, in 2005, U.S. adults were less likely to accept the concept of evolution than adults in all but one of the nations surveyed. Moreover, drawing from longitudinal data, they found that, over the previous twenty years, the percentage of U.S. adults accepting the idea of evolution had dropped from 45 to 40 percent, with those unsure about evolution increasing from 7 percent in 1985 to 21 percent in 2005. Levels of acceptance of evolution in France, Iceland, Sweden, and Denmark were higher than 80 percent, with 78 percent for Japan and a figure in the mid-70s for the United Kingdom.[14]

The uptake of creationist ideas in the United Kingdom has always been more muted, in part because the fundamentalist controversies were resolved earlier and were less public and less intense, and the very different educational and political institutions of Britain tend to foment popular protest to a lesser degree than their U.S. equivalents. Evidence for creationism's limited appeal can be found in available survey data. By way of illustration, in a survey published in 2005, of over 7,000 Church of England clergy and laity, Francis et al. asked questions about belief in evolution and six-day creation, working with the two statements "God made the world in six days and rested on the seventh" and "I believe that all living things evolved." The survey revealed that 17 percent of the laity and 10 percent of clergy agreed with the first, creationist-style statement, while 67 percent of the laity and 74 percent of clergy believed in evolution.[15] Hence, creationism remains the preference of only a small minority, and church leaders actually appear to be less dogmatic than their congregations on this issue. And yet, in the twenty-first century, creationism has emerged in public controversies in the British context, as sympathetic agencies have sought to reintroduce ideas of creationism or intelligent design into the school classroom. Most concern has been expressed with respect to newly established city academies, which are secondary schools partly funded by private sector benefactors, who thereby achieve some control over the content of the curriculum, pupil recruitment, and staffing.[16] While this has led to some public outcry, the notion that creationism has achieved significant momentum as an alternative explanatory schema among schoolchildren and churchgoers commands only limited evidential backing.

Plausibility Structures and Cognitive Bargaining

One of the dominant strands in the contemporary sociology of religion is the "god of the gaps" hypothesis: within modernity, religion acquires a social function only insofar as this function is not otherwise fulfilled by nonreligious agencies. It is pushed to the margins, concerned mainly with personal, emotional, or private concerns, or else caters to existential needs precipitated by cultural crises, which are therefore atypical or pathological, and emerging religious movements rarely directly challenge dominant cultural norms and values.[17] Such is the nature of secularization in the West, as we witness religious movements bending to fit the increasingly diminishing spaces that society allows them to occupy.[18]

The rise of creationism represents a rather different phenomenon, one that does not so easily fit into this pattern. In many forms, it directly undermines mainstream science, challenging the notion that religious groups have conceded the job of explaining the natural world to the secular sciences. In doing this, creationist sympathizers occupy a new social space in which their evangelical Christianity may extend its cultural influence, thus working against the structural differentiation that many sociologists have argued is quintessential to the modern condition.[19] Religion is not bound within shrinking pockets of significance but is breaking out of them. Most strikingly, perhaps, creationism and its associated belief claims appear to be radically incongruent with the modernized consciousness many have argued is dominant within Western cultures, and yet creationism is growing in popularity, especially in the United States. In other words, one has to account sociologically for the means whereby creationism is maintained as a plausible set of belief claims within a social context largely hostile to such claims.

In reflecting on this question, it is instructive to turn to the classic work of Peter Berger, who originally coined the term "plausibility structures" in his work on the sociology of religion during the 1960s. While the assumptions behind his arguments are complex, his central claim can be formulated with relative simplicity and may be summarized here in a quotation from his seminal work *The Sacred Canopy*, published in Britain as *The Social Reality of Religion*: "Any particular religious world will present itself to consciousness as reality only to the extent that its appropriate plausibility structure is kept in existence."[20] For Berger, a plausibility structure may take a variety of potential forms, whether a relatively durable institution or a more loosely organized network of discursive exchange. He is not arguing that social structural phenomena have causal priority over ideas, nor vice versa. Rather, his claim is simply that there needs to be some kind of affinity between the two for a body of beliefs and values to remain plausible.[21] Hence, Berger's secularization argument, that religion has declined in social significance because the plausibility structures that once supported it have become fragmented or weakened.

Berger's later work on religion is concerned with the options available to religious groups which face the secularizing influence of the modern world. How might they preserve their belief systems once they have become a "cognitive minority"? One option, Berger argues, is cognitive retrenchment, i.e., a denial of the validity of the values of secular modernity and a reaffirmation of the whole of a traditional belief system as it stands.[22] In a defensive form, it requires a withdrawal from society and the creation and maintenance of a closed religious subculture, preserved from the wider society by separation. This is the option most readily cited by Berger, who speaks of the task of maintaining "cognitive deviance" in terms of the construction of "firm plausibility structures."[23] In *A Rumour of Angels*, Berger is more specific still, arguing that conservative religious groups are best equipped to resist the deleterious influences of modern culture by existing as countercommunities that foster homogeneity, solidarity among members, and a clearly defined set of boundaries that set them apart from the outside world.[24] Historically, this strategy has been relatively popular among Christian fundamentalists, who have often sought refuge from the modern world by withdrawing into separatist or sectarian communities, either through radical separation from society—as with the Exclusive Brethren—or by selectively controlling the extent to which their members are exposed to external influences, as occurred during the Great Reversal when fundamentalists in the United States withdrew into their own institutions. A striking example of this trend may be found in the Jehovah's Witnesses who, out of fear of evolution and other "heresies," have discouraged their children from attending school beyond that required by law, quite aside from requesting their absence from religious education and collective acts of worship. While this might be judged to be an effective means of sustaining deviant ideas like those associated with creationism, this strategy has arguably been disabling to the creationist cause. As Ronald Numbers notes, in the U.S. context, educational separatism has meant that the Witnesses produce few scientists or educated individuals capable of engaging with the technical aspects of the creationism debate in a sophisticated manner.[25] Withdrawal denies the group the cultural capital with which it may defend and advance its cause in the wider arena, an endeavor that has preoccupied and, arguably, vitalized creationist sympathizers at least since the passionate debates in the southern U.S. states during the early decades of the twentieth century.

There is also cause to question whether, in the contemporary context, the sectarian form of religion described by Berger is sustainable at all. Given the cultural conditions of late modernity—mass communication and the Internet, increasingly integrated economic markets, the ubiquity of the tele-visual media, increased geographical and social mobility within and between Western nations—social isolationism appears more and more an unachievable aspiration. Even if achieved, it is difficult to imagine how it could be sustained over generations. Support for this view is found in Nancy Ammerman's ethnographic study of fundamentalist Christians within the Southern Baptist Convention during the 1980s. Ammerman finds that creationism is a particularly difficult aspect of the fundamentalist world view to sustain and for new or young believers to fully accept, given the prominence of evolutionary ideas in the wider world and in school curricula. She suggests that full acceptance may depend on a strong commitment to the other aspects of the fundamentalist world view:

> To accept on faith that all the scientific evidence is erroneous requires a strong commitment to the other ideas of Fundamentalism. If the issue of evolution arises too early in the process of integration into the fellowship, it can destroy the plausibility of the rest of the world view. In the outside world, discarding evolution is seen as ridiculous. Only when a convert is firmly on the inside do the arguments against evolution make sense. In the early weeks and months, new members may have to put that issue aside, concentrating instead on the ideas and life changes they find acceptable....As converts devote more and more time and energy to religious activities and adopt Fundamentalists as their primary reference group, even ideas that are difficult to apprehend become plausible.[26]

The sociological concept of defensive cognitive retrenchment has only limited value in accounting for how the plausibility of creationist ideas has been sustained during the modern period. Ammerman's study, among others, suggests that creationist ideas have been taken on gradually and have not been impervious to change and development at the popular, as well as intellectual, level. The relationship of creationism to the cultural context in which it is expressed and affirmed is not rigid and uncompromising, in spite of the rhetorical claims of its advocates and detractors, but has been complex and subtle, one of cognitive bargaining rather than cognitive retrenchment.

If the development of creationism reflects a process of cognitive bargaining, then it is not a process that is unprecedented. Berger cites the example of liberal Protestantism during the nineteenth century, which engaged in a "bargaining process with secular thought" after secular intellectuals, rather than other theologians, had become the "arbiters of cognitive acceptability."[27] The development of creationist thought represents merely another strand in Protestant Christianity's struggle with the modern age, although here, what is up for negotiation is not the virgin birth or Jesus' miracles, but the validity of the Genesis account of the origin of the world. This historical comparison must also be qualified insofar as the liberal Protestants were engaging with a culture that they felt embodied values worthy of praise—not least, Enlightenment rationality and human progress—whereas modern-day creationists have consistently viewed Western culture in thoroughly negative terms. Both cases do reflect, however, some accommodation to the cognitive norms of secular modernity. The emergence of creation science and of intelligent design are prime examples of how the norms and language of mainstream scientific endeavor have been adopted—or at least ostensibly imitated—as a means of garnering credibility for otherwise rather maverick theories. Whether these examples represent a genuine accommodation of the creationist camp to the culture it purportedly opposes, or are better interpreted as a creative negotiation of public discourse, which leaves the underlying convictions relatively intact, is a moot point.

Order and Meaning

One aspect of the popular affirmation of creationism for which there is significant evidence relates to the need for a sense of cosmic order congruent with a fundamentalist perspective on truth. This lies at the heart of Nancy Ammerman's empirical study of fundamentalist beliefs, which concerns itself with how fundamentalist Christians preserve a clear framework for dealing with the world and their place in it and that renders clearly their religious obligations. Because creationism instills a greater sense of orderliness (in contrast with evolutionary theory, which is associated with random chance) and because it is viewed as biblical, it is well suited for this purpose. Ammerman makes this point in her discussion of how Southern Baptists interpret Romans 8:28: "And we know that in all things God works for the good of those who love him, and who have been called according to his purpose":

> The members of Southside take that verse to mean that God has a purpose for everything and that because they are Christians they will be able to discover and live by God's orderly plan. Just as they are sure that the universe did not originate by chance evolution, so

they are also sure that nothing in today's world happens by chance either. Believers can know that God causes everything as surely as they know that day follows night and that for everything there is a season.[28]

Hence, creationism embodies the popular Christian affirmation that there is an order and purpose to the world and to human existence and that this order is ordained by God and revealed in the scriptures. Creationism also functions as an effective fundamentalist identity marker precisely because it is understood over and against evolution, which carries connotations of chance, disorder, and a faith in science—the world—over the Bible.[29] The fact that this quest for order and certainty in an otherwise uncertain world arguably gained momentum in the late twentieth and early twenty-first centuries evokes descriptions of the postmodern character of contemporary Western culture.[30] The projection of a Bible-based chronology onto human history may then be interpreted sociologically as a response to cultural instability, providing a framework of meaning that has clear temporal, as well as theological, boundaries. Perhaps it is unsurprising, therefore, that creationism can often be found alongside apocalypticism as an ideological priority among world-renouncing elements of the Christian community.

In another of the few detailed studies of creationist belief, this time set in the UK context, the role of creationism in instilling a sense of ontological order is illuminated further. Leslie Francis explored how creationist ideas are viewed by young people. In his survey of 34,000 thirteen- to fifteen-year-olds in England and Wales, he found that 20 percent agreed or strongly agreed with the creationist belief that "God made the world in six days and rested on the seventh."[31] Cross-tabulation with responses to other questions revealed some interesting patterns, including a positive correlation between belief in creationism and belief in a series of other rather unconventional ideas, including astrology, the devil, contacting the spirits of the dead, and ghosts. Jeff Astley addresses these patterns in the data and argues for associating these beliefs with credulity, i.e., those who believe in creationism are also ready to believe in a wide range of unconventional ideas.[32] Perhaps underlying this is a propensity among some to find plausibility in things countercultural, or at least counter to a model of culture they have learned is to be opposed. The world-denying logic of conservative forms of evangelicalism—often structured around strict dichotomies—lends credence to this underlying pattern, although we might be surprised to find beliefs in horoscopes and ghosts openly endorsed within their churches. An alternative explanation might be that those willing to profess belief in creationism are skeptical of the rational scientific world view, and their commitment to things like astrology and black magic reflects this skepticism and a concomitant belief in things preternatural. Here, creationism belongs to the same family of beliefs as horoscopes because it expresses a skepticism toward the view that life can satisfactorily be dealt with by reference to purely rational or scientific arguments. According to this argument, creationism might be adopted as part of a complex wider constellation of convictions and interests which represents an alternative world view (or set of world views) from that associated with hard, traditional science, which is sometimes viewed as a threat to religion and even, among some, as undermining a holistic understanding of selfhood. Eileen Barker advances a similar argument, suggesting that a cultural climate receptive to creationist claims was fostered during the 1960s following a sense of disillusionment with mainstream science. Viewed as cold, overly rational, and mechanistic, science failed to resonate with newfound cultural values like spontaneity, humanitarianism, and a sense of higher truth beyond the material.[33] In this sense, creationism may have gained credence on the basis of the same set of cultural values as some practices associated with the New Age movement, even though their usual contexts of expression are likely to emphasize their differences.

The above argument rests on a set of assumptions about the grounds of plausibility that breaks somewhat with Berger's work, or at least interprets his arguments more broadly than is usual. Here, plausibility structures may not necessarily inhere in identifiable social frameworks—for example, schools, churches, or relatively coherent patterns of shared discourse among like-minded peers—but may emerge more disparately, from more deeply embedded cultural norms that may exist on a subconscious or prereflexive level. These structures may become manifest in institutional forms, but they need not entirely depend upon them and, because of their deep embeddedness, are difficult to challenge effectively. Such an understanding of plausibility structures underpins historian George Marsden's astute comments on the development of Christian fundamentalism on both sides of the Atlantic. Marsden charts how the revivalist and millenarian traditions of the early nineteenth century were highly influential among evangelicals in the United States and in England, and yet they gave way to very different patterns of development in subsequent decades. Most strikingly, the vitriolic and public attacks on evolution which characterized the U.S. movement from the 1920s onward sustained only limited sympathy among conservative Christians in the United Kingdom. Marsden appeals to a variety of factors in attempting to explain the transatlantic difference, including the geographical peculiarities that render regional cross-fertilization of ideas far slower in the U.S. context, although he has to qualify his argument on account of the fact that the principal centers of the fundamentalist movement were initially urban and northern—not least, Princeton Seminary—rather than rural and relatively isolated.[34] Much more persuasive is Marsden's invocation of culturally established traditions of meaning and legitimacy, which are often rooted in complex expressions of political and religious thought that have subsequently been subsumed into the governing norms of social life. For example, he cites a predisposition among the nineteenth-century English for gradualist ideas, ideas which had shaped the intellectual climate for some time and which meant that the English were more naturally receptive to Darwin's theories (and to higher criticism of scripture, which also rested on an assumption of historical contingency) than were the North Americans. By contrast, the newness of the United States demanded a written and rationally defined constitution, which became enshrined in the nation's self-understanding. Revivalism in the United States was heavily shaped by the Calvinist tradition, with its predilection for "formulated statements of religious truth," which were invoked as a yardstick of Christian legitimacy, with little or no room for error or ambiguity.[35] The dominant philosophical framework underpinning theological debates and educational processes remained the commonsense realism of the Scottish Enlightenment, which was based on the assumption that knowledge may be acquired by the individual through direct, unmediated observation of the world. Filtered into popular theological understandings of human experience and the divine therein, this left little room for interpretation or development; as knowledge was plain and evident, so too was the truth of the Bible, unchangeable and timeless in the form it was received. This complex of factors fostered a culture of understanding based around clearly formulated, unchanging truths. Within this context, the gradualist, developmental emphases of Darwinism were not only theologically offensive; they were intellectually and culturally incongruent.

Creationism as Engaged Orthodoxy

An alternative way of viewing creationism is through the notion of engaged orthodoxy, which was formulated by sociologist Christian Smith in his research into contemporary evangelicalism. On the basis of his extensive empirical studies of evangelical Christianity across the United States, Smith has argued for a positive correlation between evangelical vitality and cultural engagement. This orientation he refers to as "engaged orthodoxy," drawing illustrations from the so-called new evangelicals of the 1940s, like Carl F. H. Henry, Charles Fuller, and Billy Graham. These influential figures remained "fully committed to maintaining and promoting confidently traditional, orthodox

Protestant theology and belief, while at the same time becoming confidently and proactively engaged in the intellectual, cultural, social, and political life of the nation."[36]

For Smith, a key to the evangelical response to modernity is the impulse to draw clear symbolic boundaries, thus distinguishing believers from relevant "outgroups," including secular culture and other religious traditions. However, this does not lead in the direction of sectarianism. While Berger and James Davison Hunter in his work[37] tend to paint religion as a relatively passive force, fending off the forces of modernity from a defensive position, Smith highlights the drives internal to evangelicalism which foster an orientation characterized by *active engagement* with the world. Moreover, this active engagement appears to include a capacity for a strategic renegotiation of collective identity in light of the changing sociocultural environments that evangelicals confront. In other words, evangelicals *do* accommodate their position in response to cultural change, but part of this process of accommodation involves a revitalization of evangelical identity, not least by focusing on new sources of opposition. Smith contrasts the anticommunism and anti-Catholicism of previous generations with the opposition to moral relativism and homosexual rights in more recent decades. An adjustment is evident, but a strong sense of evangelical identity boundaries remains firmly intact. Moreover, the pluralism characteristic of late modern culture offers evangelicals a favorable environment in which to thrive because it "creates a situation in which evangelicals can perpetually maintain but can never resolve their struggle with the non-evangelical world."[38] It is this struggle, which previous commentators have often interpreted as an index of weakness, that Smith argues actually generates vitality, reinforcing evangelicalism's boundaries while at the same time creating opportunities for engagement with a wider culture in need of redemption.[39]

Smith's analysis is focused explicitly on evangelical Christianity, his arguments only applying to fundamentalism to a limited degree, in part because of a tendency among fundamentalists to withdraw from, rather than engage with, the wider cultural context. Given the association of creationist belief with fundamentalist Christianity, rather than with evangelicalism as such, we might legitimately ask whether Smith's arguments really apply in this case. Indeed, according to other studies, creationism commands only limited assent among self-described evangelicals, even in the United States.[40] And yet creationism as we have presented it above is not bound by any particular Christian group, nor is it inextricably entwined with a coherent world view. Its history suggests a tendency toward dynamic redeployment among resourceful Christians whose cause has been enlivened through their energetic attempts to campaign for a greater public status of creationism in political, educational, and civic contexts.

It has momentum within the context of power struggles which have a far wider reference than Christian belief and, as such, circulates as religious and cultural capital beyond the immediate scope of individual or corporate advocacy. Consequently, I would argue that we stand to learn more about the social significance of creationism by studying its deployment as a means of cultural engagement rather than as a propositional tenet to which individuals may or may not subscribe.

Conclusion

In order to illustrate the positive potential of an analysis of creationism from this perspective, I would like to offer three points by way of conclusion, all of which look backward to what we know about this phenomenon, while pointing forward to likely future trajectories. First, the cultural engagement embodied in Smith's model emphasizes the combative character of evangelicalism, the sense of struggle with the world. This is in perfect congruence with the history of creationism, which has been a channel for the affirmation of a strict truth-world dichotomy—undeniably essential to the plausibility of the conservative Protestant perspective—while not, for the most part, withdrawing into strict sectarianism. This is in part due to the fact that, from the very beginnings of fundamentalist controversy, creationism was a matter of public education and hence drew the interest of entire communities. It is not incidental that the issue has arisen in the presumably post-Christian United Kingdom within educational debates about proper approaches to biology. Indeed, the late twentieth- and twenty-first-century prominence of passionate atheists in the public arena, like Richard Dawkins, Polly Toynbee, and Christopher Hitchens, will probably ensure that such matters are, for the time being, kept on the national agenda.[41] It is conflict and disagreement, rather than consensus, that feeds the creationist controversy.

Second, the logic of cultural engagement requires a certain lack of resolution, a sense that discussion is in progress, that debate is ongoing. Again, this has characterized the development of creationism insofar as it has remained a highly contentious issue, perhaps inevitably within a modern context. But this tension is also sustained by an epistemological trend at the heart of contemporary conservative Protestantism: that truth is both plain and encoded. The *Plain Truth* is the title of a well-known magazine that advocates creationist ideas, and the notion conveyed in its title echoes the commonsense realism that so radically shaped the U.S. evangelical tradition. The truth is there for all who will see. Insofar as this is the case, the mediatory functions of church, leaders, and tradition are bypassed, and this voluntarist tradition is now well established across the Western evangelical movement. However, the conditions of late modernity have radicalized it, as the forces of globalization and the mass media have empowered individuals to seek out truth through consumer products they purchase and appropriate according to their own tastes. The interactive possibilities of the Internet offer individuals the opportunity to also be the producers of this culture, and the Web is now awash with home pages promoting new conspiracy theories, hidden messages in ancient texts, and insidious connections between unsavory power brokers. The popularity of Dan Brown's *The Da Vinci Code* and the *Left Behind* series has heightened this sense that "the truth is out there," if only people would see. While creationists might not naturally turn to *The X-Files* for answers, they are still exposed to this media-driven ethos, and the market provides them with products that will not offend their Christian sensibilities. This devolved truth seeking represents a paradox at the heart of contemporary evangelicalism, born out of a dogmatic notion of truth, which is in part pursued within a deregulated religious marketplace. Only by placing cultural engagement at the forefront of our analysis can we hope to unravel the possible future trajectories through which this paradox may evolve.

Third, cultural engagement is a useful perspective because it taps into the nature of creationism as a thoroughly discursive form of Christian expression. As driven by combative debate, legal dispute, and educational conflict, it is not surprising that creationism appears to us historically as a strand of fundamentalist affirmation characterized by complex and impassioned rhetoric. And yet this trend runs deeper, into the theological affinities of the early movement. Ronald Numbers notes that, during the 1960s, theologians in the Wesleyan/Holiness tradition tended to remain faithful to the gap and day/age readings of Genesis 1, rather than switch allegiance to the increasingly novel Genesis Flood geology associated with authors like Whitcomb and Morris, in contrast with many Baptists, Adventists, and Lutherans, who expressed more sympathy with the new ideas.[42] Why this should be is uncertain, although the established theological tensions between Pentecostals and Reformed Protestants may have been a contributing factor, with a continuing distrust between the two parties lending neither any strong inclination to adopt the other's peculiar identity markers. Pentecostals appear predisposed, because of their experiential, conversionist focus, to prioritize evangelism and celebration over the discursive engagement with science and worldly questions which so attracts those conservative Protestants preoccupied with matters of doctrine. This synergy appears so strong that one might venture to suggest that the future of the creationist cause may in part depend on whether a Reformed, conservative evangelicalism maintains a dominant place among theologians, church leaders, the active laity, and the more nebulous grassroots forces at the popular level in virtual and off-line reality. That this tradition appears in the ascendancy within the UK context[43] raises interesting questions about the future of creationism and its capacity as a cultural force within a society typically suspicious of conservative religion.

NOTES

1. Henry M. Morris, ed., *Scientific Creationism* (San Diego, Calif.: Creation-Life, 1974), 252.

2. Peter Berger, *The Social Reality of Religion* (London: Faber & Faber, 1969), 155.

3. Mark A. Noll, *The Scandal of the Evangelical Mind* (Grand Rapids, Mich.: Eerdmans, 1994), 192.

4. Ronald L. Numbers, *The Creationists: From Scientific Creationism to Intelligent Design*, 2nd ed. (Cambridge, Mass.: Harvard University Press, 2006), 53.

5. Edward J. Larson, *Trial and Error: The American Controversy over Creation and Evolution*, updated ed. (New York: Oxford University Press, 1985).

6. George Marsden, *Understanding Fundamentalism and Evangelicalism* (Grand Rapids, Mich.: Eerdmans, 1991), 148–149.

7. Noll, *Scandal of the Evangelical Mind*, 193.

8. Numbers, *The Creationists*, 351.

9. Numbers, *The Creationists*, 273–275.

10. See Steve Olson, "Evolution and Creationism: Shapes of a Wedge," *Science 7*, vol. 304, no. 5672 (May 2004): 825–826.

11. Numbers, *The Creationists*, 370.

12. Cited in Numbers, *The Creationists*, 1, 6.

13. Numbers, *The Creationists*, 330–331.

14. Jon D. Miller, Eugene C. Scott, and Shinji Okomato, "Public Acceptance of Evolution," *Science* 313, no. 5788 (August 2006): 765–766.

15. Leslie Francis, Mandy Robbins, and Jeff Astley, *Fragmented Faith: Exposing the Fault-Lines of the Church of England* (Milton Keynes: Paternoster, 2005), 153.

16. Joachim Allgaier and Richard Holliman, "The Emergence of the Controversy around the Theory of Evolution and Creationism in UK Newspaper Reports," *Curriculum Journal* 17, no. 3 (2006): 263–279. Media coverage of the controversy has largely focused on the schools in northeast England supported by prominent evangelical businessman Sir Peter Vardy.

17. See Steve Bruce, *God Is Dead: Secularization in the West* (Oxford: Blackwell, 2002), 30–37.

18. One is reminded of Peter Berger's comment that religious consumers living within a secularized society will "prefer religious products that can be made consonant with secularized consciousness over those that cannot." Berger, *Social Reality of Religion*, 145.

19. For example, see James Davison Hunter, *American Evangelicalism: Conservative Religion and the Quandary of Modernity* (New Brunswick, N.J.: Rutgers University Press, 1983).

20. Berger, *Social Reality of Religion*, 149.

21. Berger, *Social Reality of Religion*, 154.

22. Given the concerns of the current chapter, it is worth noting that so-called deviant science—from intelligent design to acupuncture—may be sustained by means of the same social mechanism. See R. G. A. Dolby, "Reflections on Deviant Science," in *On the Margins of Science: The Social Construction of Rejected Knowledge*, ed. Roy Wallis (Keele: University of Keele, 1979), 27–28.

23. Berger, *Social Reality of Religion*, 163.

24. Peter Berger, *A Rumour of Angels: Modern Society and the Rediscovery of the Supernatural* (London: Penguin, 1969), 32.

25. Numbers, *The Creationists*, 348.

26. Nancy T. Ammerman, *Bible Believers: Fundamentalists in the Modern World* (New Brunswick, N.J.: Rutgers University Press, 1987), 165.

27. Berger, *Social Reality of Religion*, 159, 158.

28. Ammerman, *Bible Believers*, 41.

29. Within this context, creationism functions in a similar way to uncompromising opposition to homosexuality, i.e., as an expression of Christian legitimacy: it marks Christians as different from "the world" and, by the standards of their own tradition, as reliably biblical.

30. For example, see Zigmunt Bauman, "Postmodern Religion?" in *Religion, Modernity and Postmodernity*, ed. Paul Heelas (Oxford: Blackwell, 1998), 55–78.

31. Leslie Francis, *The Values Debate: A Voice from the Pupils* (London: Woburn, 2001).

32. Jeff Astley, "The Science and Religion Interface within Young People's Attitudes and Beliefs," in *Religion, Education and Adolescence: International Empirical Perspectives*, ed. Leslie Francis, Mandy Robbins, and Jeff Astley (Cardiff: University of Wales Press, 2005), 39–54.

33. Eileen Barker, "In the Beginning: The Battle of Creationist Science against Evolutionism," in Wallis, *On the Margins of Science*, 182–184.

34. George Marsden, "Fundamentalism as an American Phenomenon: A Comparison with English Evangelicalism," *Church History* 46, no. 2 (June 1977): 224–225.

35. Marsden, "Fundamentalism," 227.

36. Christian Smith, *American Evangelicalism: Embattled and Thriving* (Chicago: University of Chicago Press, 1998), 10.

37. For example, see James Davison Hunter, *Evangelicalism: The Coming Generation* (Chicago: University of Chicago Press, 1987).

38. Smith, *American Evangelicalism*, 150.

39. Smith, *American Evangelicalism*, 89.

40. James M. Penning and Corwin E. Smidt, *Evangelicalism: The Next Generation* (Grand Rapids, Mich.: Baker Academic, 2002), 124.

41. Tina Beattie, *The New Atheists: The Twilight of Reason and the War on Religion* (London: Darton, Longman and Todd, 2007).

42. Numbers, *The Creationists*, 337, 345.

43. See Mathew Guest, *Evangelical Identity and Contemporary Culture: A Congregational Study in Innovation* (Milton Keynes: Paternoster, 2007), 212–217.

Index of Modern Authors

Subject Index